Stephen Colbert
and Philosophy

Popular Culture and Philosophy®
Series Editor: George A. Reisch

Popular Culture and Philosophy®

Stephen Colbert and Philosophy

I Am Philosophy (And So Can You!)

Edited by
AARON ALLEN SCHILLER

OPEN COURT
Chicago and La Salle, Illinois

Volume 41 in the series, Popular Culture and Philosophy®, edited by George A. Reisch

To order books from Open Court, call toll-free 1-800-815-2280, or visit our website at www.opencourtbooks.com.

Open Court Publishing Company is a division of Carus Publishing Company.

Library of Congress Cataloging-in-Publication Data

Stephen Colbert and philosophy : I am philosophy (and so can you!) / edited by Aaron Allen Schiller.
    p. cm.—(Popular culture and philosophy ; v. 41)
    Includes bibliographical references and index.
    ISBN 978-0-8126-9661-5 (trade paper : alk. paper)
    1. Colbert, Stephen, 1964—Criticism and interpretation. I. Schiller, Aaron Allen, 1974
    PN2287.C5695S35 2009
    791.4502'8092—dc22
    [B]

2008039722

This book is dedicated to the Colbert Nation

Contents

Acknowledgments

First and foremost, a big thank you to all the contributors. Your hard work and dedication made this book possible. And your love for the material made it fun and interesting. It was truly a pleasure to work with each and every one of you!

Thanks to my editorial assistant, Dan Rosenberg, whose help is visible on every page.

Thanks to the folks at Open Court—especially George A. Reisch, David Ramsay Steele, and Cindy Pineo—for their advice, support, and the chance.

Thanks to the folks at the many wonderful Colbert fan sites, in particular *No Fact Zone*, for their detailed episode guide, *Colbert University*, for their interesting character studies, and *Colbert Nation*, for their lively forums.

Thanks to my colleagues, friends, and family for their guidance, support, and encouragement. In particular: John Jacobson, Nina Brewer-Davis, Jeff Schiller, Debbie Schiller, and Larry Schiller.

A special thanks to my adoring (and adored) wife, Denise Helene Brauer Schiller, for always being right beside me.

And a big, American-sized thanks to Dr. Stephen T. Colbert, D.F.A. On behalf of myself and the contributors, we hope you'll consider this the Number One Philosophy Book on all things Colbert.

Philosophy for Heroes

AARON ALLEN SCHILLER

Ask Stephen. He'll tell you: Stephen Colbert is a bone fide American cultural institution. He's been named one of *Time*'s 100 Most Influential People for the past three years in a row (2006–2008). He's coined words that capture the spirit of the times such as "truthiness" and "wikiality." He ran for President in 2008. He's received Emmy Awards, Peabody Awards, an honorary Doctorate, a key to the city of Columbia, South Carolina. He even has his own Ben and Jerry's ice cream flavor: *Stephen Colbert's Americone Dream*. Not bad for a man with a suspiciously French-sounding name and funny right ear.

From his bully pulpit behind his C-shaped desk, faux-pundit and right-wing-blowhard Stephen Colbert fights four nights a week for the American way. He doesn't just report the news to us—he *feels* the news *at* us. He opines on the issues of the day in the WØRD segment, talks to politicians in Better Know a District, tells us what we should fear in The ThreatDown, speaks directly to his own in Colbert Platinum, and nails guests nightly against the backdrop of his own portrait. Yet despite it all, though Colbert may *speak* the language of truthiness, his fans see through it to the penetrating truth.

And speaking of fans, Stephen Colbert has a rabid following: The Colbert Nation. Like an army of holy warriors ready to take up arms at a moment's notice, members of The Nation—otherwise known as the "Heroes"—faithfully answer Colbert's calls to action. Whether it's to complete one of Colbert's Green Screen Challenges, or to make things a bit more "truthy" on some Wikipedia entry, the dedication that the Nation shows their fearless leader would make any dictator jealous.

But Colbert isn't just a pop culture phenomenon. Philosophers love him, too. This isn't just because philosophers, like all academics, are a bunch of left-wing elitists. (I'm looking at you, Noam Chomsky.) It's because Colbert regularly plays around with concepts that are near and dear to the philosopher's heart, concepts such as Truth and Reality. In fact, let me hazard a prediction here and say that from this day forth no philosophical tract on the nature of Truth will be complete without some consideration to the concept of Truthiness. And who cares about Reality now that we have Wikiality?

Not only that, but for a philosopher, who so prides him or herself on clear, logical thinking, trying to follow Colbert's reasoning can be a bit like watching a train wreck. But a beautiful train wreck. Colbert tortures logic like Mozart writes symphonies: with seemingly effortless grace and charm. I guess what I'm saying is that Colbert is the Mozart of bad arguments.

Now just as you don't need to be a musician to appreciate Mozart, you don't need to be a philosopher to appreciate Stephen Colbert, as the sheer size of Colbert's fan base will attest. If you too find grace and charm in Colbert's tortured logic, or if the concepts of truthiness or wikiality get under your skin but you're not quite sure why, this book was written for you.

The WØRD: First Principles of Colbertian Philosophy

1

Colbert, Truthiness, and Thinking from the Gut

DAVID KYLE JOHNSON

> Every night on my show, the *Colbert Report,* I speak straight from the gut. . . . I give people the truth, unfiltered by rational argument.
>
> —Stephen Colbert, White House Correspondents' Association Dinner, April 29th, 2006

As we all know (and love), during the opening moments of his first show, Colbert coined the word "Truthiness." In doing so, he captured his entire intellectual philosophy. Something is truthy for me if that thing *feels true* to me. Someone who is satisfied believing something based on its truthiness *thinks with his gut.* This is what Colbert does. And, according to Colbert, he is not alone. George W. Bush is a *gut-thinker.* As Colbert said on his first show:

> If you think about Harriet Miers, of course her nomination is absurd. But the president didn't say he "thought" about his selection. He said this: "I know her heart." Notice how he said nothing about her brain? He didn't have to. He *feels* the truth about Harriet Miers. And what about Iraq? If you think about it, maybe there are a few missing pieces to the rationale for war. But doesn't taking Saddam out feel like the right thing—right here, right here in the gut?[1]

Colbert identifies Bush as a gut-thinker, but he owes his own combative personality and extreme opinions to the gut-thinking conservative pundit class, to cable TV news hosts like Bill O'Reilly and Sean Hannity, and the countless AM radio talk show hosts who

---

[1] Episode 1001, originally aired October 17th, 2005.

keep the Republican's Evangelical base fired up. Of course, we all know that Colbert doesn't mean it. Although he is Catholic, he's not the kind of Republican Catholic conservative he portrays. He doesn't really agree with everything Papa Bear Bill O'Reilly and people like him say. He's making fun of them by doing what they often do—*thinking from the gut*—and drawing attention to it by explicitly acknowledging that he is doing it. All this is done in an effort to expose the absurdity of such thinking. (Did I just take the fun out of it?) And we all sit back and laugh because *thinking from the gut* is obviously absurd.

Or so we think . . .

The thing is, the absurdity isn't obvious. If it were, there would be fewer people doing it. We all know people—conservative, liberal, religious, atheist, whatever (you can think of one right now)—who do this! In fact, we know a lot of them![2] They issue their positions, without argument, and when you prove their position to be false (with argument and facts), even lacking a defense they will simply say, "Well, that is just how you see it. I have a right to my opinion and we'll just have to agree to disagree."[3] What?!? No! It's not just how I see it—it's how it is! You don't have a right to an opinion you can't defend. And we don't have to agree to disagree—if you were intellectually honest, you'd agree that you're wrong!

I'm not suggesting that all issues are black and white and that when people do not agree with you, you should intellectually beat them down until they acquiesce. That would be just as bad as *thinking from the gut*. All critical, open-minded thinkers consider objections, weigh evidence, and revise their beliefs when they are proven wrong. The smartest person doesn't think he's right about everything; the smartest person admits how much he doesn't know.

That's what the smartest people I know do. Even Socrates (469–399 B.C.E.), the father of Western philosophy, did this. He actually suggested that he had no knowledge at all. According to the *Apology*, the Oracle at Delphi said Socrates was the wisest. Socrates set out to prove the Oracle wrong by finding someone who knew more than he did—which shouldn't have been hard given that he claimed to know *nothing*. He questioned the politicians, generals, teachers, and other persons who claimed to have

---

[2] Are you reading this in a bookstore? Look up. There's one now!

[3] 'Agree to disagree' is probably the worst phrase ever coined in the English language.

knowledge, only to discover that *they* knew nothing. It then dawned on him what the Oracle meant. He was the wisest because he admitted his own ignorance—something everyone else refused to do.

So what am I suggesting? Think about your friend who thinks that JFK must have been shot by someone on the grassy knoll, simply because the direction JFK's head moved after the gun shot. ("Back, and to the left. Back, and to the left." He watched the movie *JFK* one too many times.) You've explained to him that bullets do not always force the object they hit in the direction of the bullet's trajectory. If the bullet causes projectiles to be expelled from the side opposite the bullet's impact (that is, if the opposite end of the object explodes), like JFK's head did, the force of the explosion will actually push the object *toward* the point of entry. Maybe you even show this person the episode of Penn and Teller's *Bullshit*,[4] where they debunk this evidence by shooting a melon the size and weight of a human head, showing how it reacts just like JFK's head did—it falls toward the point of entry as the opposite side explodes. So the movement of JFK's head actually *confirms* that Oswald was the only shooter. But your friend says, "Nope. There was a shooter on the grassy knoll; I don't care what you say. That's my truth; I have a right to my opinion."

This is the person Colbert mocks; this is the person Colbert pretends to be—the person who exaggerates what their evidence can support, can't respond to criticism yet hides his ignorance behind a "right to opinion" under the mantra that his opinion is "true for him"—all so he doesn't have to give up what he wants to believe. Colbert is more concerned with people who do this in the political arena—it's a little harder to detect there—but what he is saying is that these people are just as dumb (sorry, *"intellectually challenged"*) as your conspiracy theory friend. Colbert just doesn't come right out and say it. He takes the long way around showing the error of their ways by imitating them.

Well, I won't be doing that. I am going straight for the jugular. I will *argue* that they are dum . . . dang it, sorry . . . grossly mistaken. Maybe it seems like I am beating up a straw man—*thinking from the gut* is so obviously stupid; and it is! And if it didn't happen ALL THE TIME, I wouldn't bother. But it does. That is why

---

[4] Episode 29, "Conspiracy Theories."

Colbert mocks it; that is why I will refute it. And perhaps, the next time you run into your friend, you can make him read this chapter so he can realize that he shouldn't think from the gut.

My Truth

[My book is] not just some collection of reasoned arguments supported by facts. That is the coward's way out. This book is Truth. *My Truth.*

—Stephen Colbert, from the introduction to *I Am America (And So Can You!)*

There are a couple of ways that Colbert *thinks from the gut.* Sometimes he's a relativist. There are many kinds of relativism, but the form Colbert seems to espouse in the above quote is called "individual relativism." All forms of relativism suggest that there is no truth in a universal sense; truth is relative. Individual relativism suggests that truth is relative to individuals. Truth can be "mine." But what does that mean?

Well, first, we have to understand what "truth" is. A table can't be true, although it might be sturdy. The action of walking can't be true, although it could be straight. A person can't be true, although she can be truthful. In philosophy, truth is a property had only by propositions or beliefs. "Magic is Colbert's all time favorite science" (*I Am America*, p. 200) is something that can be true. (It could also be false.) And a proposition or belief is true if it accurately corresponds to the way the world is.[5] (If it doesn't, it's false.) "Rosie O'Donnell is a blazing liberal." That's true because it accurately describes the world. Philosophers call the part of the world that makes a proposition true its "truthmaker." Rosie O'Donnell and her political beliefs are the truthmaker for the proposition "Rosie O'Donnell is a blazing liberal."

Next, we have to understand what it is for a truth to be relative. Some truths actually are relative. "You should drive on the right side of the road." There is no *piece of the world* that makes this statement universally true (true "everywhere"). What side of the road you should drive on is dependent upon the tradition or laws of the place you are in. That proposition is true in America, but false in England; its truth is relative to culture. An example of some-

---

[5] When philosophers say "the way the world is" they mean "the way the universe is." They're talking about everything that exists.

thing that is relative to an individual is taste in comedy. You think Jane Fonda fondling Colbert during an interview about her new movie *Georgia Rule* is funny.[6] Your friend doesn't get it. The truth of "Jane Fonda fondling Colbert is funny" is relative to the individual. It depends on what you thought. It's kind of like having a favorite band. It's not like there is a universal truth about "Metallica is the best band ever." It's a matter of preference. Something similar can be said about the false dichotomy Colbert presented Barney Frank: "President Bush: Great president, or the greatest president?"[7]

The individual relativist suggests that *all truths* are like this. In the same way that the truth of propositions about comic value and music preference are relative to individuals, the truth of propositions about politics, morality and religion are relative to individuals too. There's no universal truth; there is just what you think. "You should drive on the right side of the road" can be true for Americans but not for the British; "Abortion is wrong" can be true for one person, but not for another. One who thinks that there is universal truth is wrong. If your gut tells you something's true, it's true for you.

But the absurdity of individual relativism becomes quite obvious upon even superficial examination. If the truth of all propositions is relative, then no proposition is universally true. But a proposition is universally true if it matches up to the way the world is. It follows that, if relativism is true, no proposition matches up to the way the world is. And if that's the case, the world must not be *any way at all*. If the world cannot be accurately described by any proposition, the world must have *no content*—it must contain nothing. And that's ridiculous!

Maybe that was a bit too philosophical. Let me break it down. If individual relativism is true, then if your friend wants to say that "Abraham Lincoln *was not* assassinated" is true because that is what his gut says, according to the individual relativist, that is fine—that's his truth. And he's just as right as you are when you say that Lincoln *was* assassinated.[8] Since there is no universal truth, no one's right and no one's wrong. So it can't even be universally true that "you are reading this book right now" or that "you exist." If someone believes that you don't exist, they are not wrong . . . that

---

[6] Episode 3063, originally aired May 9th, 2007.

[7] Episode 1008, originally aired October 27th, 2005.

[8] Why am I obsessed with presidential assassinations?

you don't exist is *true for that person*.

But the problems don't stop there. It can't even be universally true that there are no universal truths. And that means that the individual relativist must admit that his own view is not universally true—it's just true for him. But isn't that what he tried to establish—that his view of "no universal truth" is universally true?

Hopefully, the absurdity of these consequences digs into your skull with the same ferocity of Stephen Jr.'s talons ripping into a Canadian salmon. If someone's gut tells them that you exist, that is not "true for them." That's not true for anyone. You exist and no person believing that you don't can make you *not exist*. In addition, the relativist contradicts himself when he says there is no universal truth. "Really? There is NO universal truth? Is that universally true?"

Actually, it probably seems like there are more individual relativists than there actually are. People often equate the phrase "X is true for me" with "I believe that X is true." When they say "X is true for me but not for you" they don't really mean "the world *is* a different way for you than it is for me." They mean "The world seems a different way to me than it does to you—we believe different things." And that's fine; very rarely do two people see things exactly the same way. But we don't think they are both right; perhaps they are both wrong, but at best only one is right.

Moral Relativism

We live in a democracy, which means that we should treat every theory equally.

—Stephen Colbert, *I Am America (And So Can You!)*

I am being a little unfair. Obviously truths about physical states of affairs—your sitting in a chair, your existence, Lincoln's assassination—can't be relative to individuals. So there are some universal truths. But some individual relativists don't think that all truth is relative, just specific kinds. For instance, aren't moral and political truths relative to individuals? Can't "abortion is wrong" be true for one person, but not for another? Can't "America should return to family values" be true for Hannity but not for Colmes?

These sound more promising, but individual moral relativism is quickly pushed into absurdities too. A person's action can only be morally condemned if that person was in the moral wrong. But if there is no universal moral truth, one can't be in the moral wrong.

If moral truth is relative to individuals, then Hitler wasn't *wrong* for trying to exterminate the Jews. "The Jews should be exterminated" was true for him. We can't morally condemn female genital mutilation (a.k.a. female circumcision). That it should be practiced is true for those who believe it should be done. We can't blame Colbert for not springing for a new typewriter—one with a working lowercase "p"—for his executive assistant Thomas Bindlestaff. That Thomas should be forced to reverse his paper and type an upside down lowercase "d" every time he needs the letter "p" is true for Colbert (*I Am America*, p. 168). But that's not right. Hitler, female genital mutilators, and Colbert (in this case) are acting wrongly!

In addition, if we are individual moral relativists, we can't ever say that someone has made moral progress. If those who see female genital mutilation as justified finally see the light and abolish the practice, we can't say they are acting morally better than they were. Before, "Female genital mutilation is morally acceptable" was true for them; so they weren't doing anything wrong. Now, "Female genital mutilation isn't morally acceptable" is true for them; so they still aren't doing anything wrong. Since, in both cases, they were not acting wrongly, they have not made any moral progress (they have not gone from acting wrongly to acting properly). But again, that doesn't seem correct. If female genital mutilators stop the practice, they have made a moral improvement! They have gone from wrong to right!

The truth is, individual moral relativism is often motivated by issues where the truth is hard to find. And it's true, there are such issues. We may never all agree on the morality of abortion, euthanasia or whether the no-goodniks no-godniks are right (*I Am America*, p. 61). But the fact that the truth is hard—even impossible—to find does not mean that the truth is not there. That something can exist, even when you can't see it, is something that we should have all learned around the time we started walking.

So what have we learned so far? As I tell my students: "If you ever use the phrase 'it is true for me' in class or in a paper, I will fail you. You are either mistaking this phrase for 'I believe it,' or you are espousing the clearly false doctrine of individual relativism. Either way, I am warranted in making your repeat the course." I am sure you can find a way to translate this into a useful threat to use on your friend.

Moving on.

Justifying from the Gut

. . . like our Founding Fathers, I hold my Truths to be self-evident, which is why I did absolutely no research. I didn't need to. The only research I needed was a long hard look in the mirror.

—Stephen Colbert, from the introduction to *I Am America (And So Can You!)*

[They] cannot be mistaken in what they feel. [This is how] they support themselves and are sure reason hath nothing to do with what they see and feel in themselves: what they have a sensible experience of admits no doubt, needs no probation. . . . It is its own proof and can have no other.

—John Locke, *An Essay Concerning Human Understanding*

Another way Colbert thinks from the gut is by being an *intuitionist*. Intuitionists are like relativists. Their intuitive reaction to something is all the evidence they need. But unlike the relativists, they believe in universal truth. Their gut gives them the Truth, and anyone who disagrees with them, and thus their gut, must be wrong.

Don't confuse this with philosophers who refer to their own intuition in the course of an argument. Philosophers will, sometimes, point out that a certain position, when taken to its logical conclusion, conflicts with intuition. In doing so, they are not thinking *from the gut*. They are merely pointing out that accepting a certain position will force one to abandon a commonly accepted belief. In addition, sometimes philosophers will construct arguments to defend intuitions they have. But in these cases, the intuition is the beginning of inquiry, not the end. They will reject their intuition if proven wrong. The intuitionist, on the other hand, *ends* his inquiry with his intuition. "My gut tells me it's true so I don't need an argument; my gut is all the evidence I need."[9]

Locke (1632–1704) called these kinds of thinkers merely *"enthusiastic."* It is such thinkers he's talking about in the above passage when he says: "This is the way of talking of these men: they are sure because they are sure, and their persuasions are right only because they are strong in them."[10] He is actually concerned

---

[9] For more on the difference between the philosopher's use of "intuition" and truthiness, see Chapter 9 in this volume.

[10] *An Essay Concerning Human Understanding* (Dutton, 1978), p. 291

about people who profess something with certainly simply based on the feeling that they have received it, via revelation, from God. But his criticism of them applies to those who justify their beliefs with their gut too. They're stuck in a circle. *"It is a revelation, because they firmly believe it;* and *they believe it, because it is a revelation"* (p. 292). We might say: "They believe it is true because their gut says it, and their gut says it because it is true." But a belief can't be its own justification. So those who justify their belief with their gut (and in turn, their gut with their belief) have no grounds for their position at all.

Locke points out that, if what your gut says really is true, it would stand up to rational inquiry. In fact, if it is true, it should be provable. Even when the prophets of the Old Testament received a revelation (gut feeling) from God, God did not expect them to trust it alone. He gave them signs to verify the revelation's accuracy (for example, a burning bush). Whether or not you buy the stories of the Old Testament the point is, even for prophets, gut feelings are not good evidence on their own. The conclusions towards which they drive you must be tested by rational means. No matter how strongly you feel about something, "Reason must be our last judge in everything."[11] Gut-thinkers are not justified; they simply are enthusiastic.

"That's My Right"

I'm no fan of dictionaries or reference books. They're elitist, constantly telling us what is or isn't true . . . Who's *Britannica* to tell me the Panama Canal was finished in 1914? If I want to say it happened in 1941, *that's my right* . . . we are [a nation] divided by those who think with their head and those who know with their heart.

—Stephen Colbert, *The Colbert Report*[12]

---

[11] p. 295. For those of you who worry that Locke is putting reason above God, Locke goes on to clarify: "I do not mean that we must consult reason and examine whether a proposition revealed from God can be made out by natural principles, and if it cannot, that then we may reject it; but consult it we must and by it examine whether it be a revelation from God or no; and if reason finds it to be revealed from God, reason then declares for it as much as for any other truth, and makes it one of her dictates" (p. 295). Locke was pointing out that reason was needed to make sure the revelation did not come from some other source—like the Devil or yourself.

[12] Episode 1001, originally aired October 17th, 2005.

Your conspiracy-loving friend used his "right to opinion" to protect his gut-based belief. The supposition that everyone has—or should have—a *right* to their belief is widespread indeed. In a legal sense, the supposition is right. In America—God's country—there are no laws restricting freedom of opinion. No one can be thrown in jail for something he believes.[13]

But the legal right to an opinion is not what your friend is refer-ring to when he can't answer the multitude of objections you have raised against his position and just says "Hey, I have a right to my opinion." If he did have the legal right in mind, he would be point-ing out to you that you can't report him to authorities and have him hauled away to jail for continuing to believe in grassy knoll shoot-ers. I highly doubt he thinks you're considering doing so. No, your friend likely means one of two things. Either he thinks he has an *epistemic right* to his opinion or he thinks he has a *moral right* to his opinion. In either case, he is wrong.

Epistemology is the "study of knowledge." A belief is epistemi-cally justified if it's backed up by evidence and argument. A belief is not epistemically justified if it can't be defended against objec-tion. If your friend has an epistemic right to his belief, it's only because his belief is epistemically justified. Given that he has given no argument for his belief, and he has not answered any of your arguments against his belief, his belief is not epistemically justified. So, if he thinks he has an epistemic right to his opinion, he is obvi-ously mistaken.

More likely, he thinks he has a *moral right* to his opinion. But what could this mean? As philosopher Jamie Whyte[14] points out, if your friend has a moral right to his opinion, you must have a cer-tain kind of moral duty to treat his opinion a certain way.[15] That's what moral rights do; they create duties for others. According to Whyte, this duty could amount to three things.

Perhaps your friend's right to his opinion means that you have a duty to agree with his opinion. But that can't be right. If he has a right to his opinion, then you have a right to yours—and you

---

[13] Besides, think how hard that law would be to enforce! But that is not to say we shouldn't try. You know who I'm talking about.

[14] Jamie Whyte, *Crimes Against Logic* (McGraw-Hill, 2004), Chapter 1.

[15] Whether or not moral rights are always coupled with moral duties is a debat-able issue. For an argument that contests this issue, see Joel Feinberg, *Social Philosophy* (Prentice-Hall, 1973), pp. 61–64.

can't both be obligated to agree with each other. Perhaps it means that you are obligated to listen to his opinion. Again, this seems unlikely. If he has that right, everyone does. And that means you are obligated to listen to everyone—O'Reilly on culture wars, Colmes on the Iraq War, delusional Canadian mayors (like Oshawa Ontario's Mayor John Gray) who think that their local hockey team (The Oshawa Generals) could beat a team with a mascot named after Colbert (the Saginaw Spirit's Steagle Colbeagle the Eagle), when clearly they cannot! If nothing else, we just don't have the time to listen to every ill-conceived thing another says. It'd be impossible! And we can't be obligated to do the impossible, can we?

Perhaps you have a duty to let your friend keep his opinion. This seems most likely what he meant. He thinks you're obligated to not change his belief with argument and evidence because *it is his belief.* But your possession of such a duty is hardly obvious. As Whyte points out, I am not obligated to let you continue to believe that no cars are coming if you are about to unknowingly step in front of one. Why? Because you care about knowing whether or not you are about to be hit by a car. "If someone is interested in believing the truth, then she will not take the presentation of contrary evidence and argument as some kind of injury."[16] Only if eliminating your friend's false belief were doing him injury would you have a duty to avoid doing it; and if he cares about having true beliefs, he cannot consider it harm!

But this exposes what is at the heart of your friend's response. He takes your presentation of argument and evidence contrary to his belief as harmful because, in fact, he is not concerned with truth. And it's for this reason that he thinks you have a duty to cease and desist presenting evidence against it. If you don't stop, he will have to give up his belief, and he doesn't want to! He isn't interested in truth; he is interested in believing what makes him intellectually comfortable. He thinks you have a duty not to make him uncomfortable with "new ideas."

Colbert recognizes the discomfort that new ideas can bring.

Let me ask you this: Why were you happier when you were a kid? Because you didn't know anything. The more you know, the sadder

---

[16] *Crimes Against Logic*, p. 9.

you get. *Don't believe me?* By the time you finish reading this chapter, over a hundred dogs and cats in animal shelters around the nation will be euthanized. Bet you wish you could erase that knowledge. But it's too late. You learned a *New Idea*, and it made you sad. . . . Look at the story of Adam and Eve. Their lives were pretty great—until they ate from the Tree of Knowledge. . . . *God's point:* Ignorance isn't just bliss, it's paradise. (*I Am America*, pp. 120, 122)

In his usual mocking way, Colbert is making fun of those who, like your friend, reject knowledge because of the discomfort it brings. But Colbert stops there. He's happy just making fun of them.

But I'm not happy stopping there; I want to press further.

The fact that your friend would be made uncomfortable by your changing his belief hardly gives you a duty to not change his belief. Only if he had a right to be intellectually comfortable would that be the case. But no one possesses a right of intellectual comfort. A right to life? Sure. A right to property? Okay. The right to watch that crazy Jon Stewart? Why not? But a right to intellectual comfort? Come on! If that's a right then, if global climate change is happening, Al Gore violates our rights when he points out the evidence for it. If that's a right then, if we're running out of oil, James Kunstler violates our right when he reminds us that we are.[17] If that's a right, Colbert violates our rights when he points out that, according to a full page ad by Exxon in the *New York Times*, no percentage of the price of gas goes to corporate profits.[18] If that's a right, as Colbert suggests, the media actually was doing us a disservice by reporting on NSA wiretapping and secret prisons in Eastern Europe.

> Those things are secret for a very important reason: they're super-depressing. And if that's your goal, well, misery accomplished. Over the last five years you people were so good—over tax cuts, WMD intelligence, the effect of global warming. We Americans didn't want to know and you had the courtesy not to try to find out. Those were good times—as far as we knew.[19]

If we each possessed a right to intellectual comfort, one would have a moral duty *not* to be an educator. As Colbert points out, nothing is more intellectually uncomfortable than learning new ideas.

---

[17] James Kunstler, *The Long Emergency* (Grove, 2006).

[18] Episode 4063, originally aired May 8th, 2008.

[19] Stephen Colbert, White House Correspondents' Dinner, April 29th, 2006.

So what have we learned now? When your friend won't budge on his JFK conspiracy mumbo-jumbo, no matter how much unanswered argument and evidence you give him—and he keeps saying he has a right to his opinion—you can tell him he doesn't. You're not obligated to agree with, listen to or let him keep his opinion. If anything, you're obligated to convince him otherwise. At the least, if he thinks he has a right to his opinion, he must admit that he has that right only in virtue of the fact that he has no interest in the truth.

The Truth about Politics and Philosophy

If a tree falls in the forest and no one hears it, I hope it lands on a philosophy professor.

—Stephen Colbert, *I Am America (And So Can You!)*

That's how Colbert summarized Introduction to Philosophy. (Ouch! That wounds deeply, Stephen.) Unfortunately, far too many people think philosophers are a bunch of old white guys talking about esoteric crap and "paradoxes" that can't be answered and don't matter in real life. "If anything just comes down to opinion, it's philosophy." And even though politics has more obvious, real world implications, getting to the fact of political matters seems just as impossible. How can you *establish* that individual liberty is more important than national security? How could you verify that church and state should be separate? Doesn't it just come down to opinion? If so—if there is no way to prove who's right—don't we all just have a right to our own opinion? Can't we just *think from the gut* about politics and philosophy?

The answer is "no." For one thing, these conceptions of philosophy and politics are mistaken. The thought that philosophers sit around all day and think about whether God could make a rock bigger than he could lift is a gross mischaracterization. I've never even used that one—well, maybe once while teaching Metaphysics. "Nothing here you can't pick up by eating the wrong mushrooms on a camping trip" (*I Am America*, p. 126)—so says Colbert about Introduction to Metaphysics. Funny? Yes. Mischaracterization? Double Yes.

Philosophy, in Greek, means "love of wisdom." What philosophers do is think about everything. They will break down any problem to its bare bones—its assumptions, its methods, it concepts—analyze them, identify what they imply and raise objections until they solve the problem at hand. Sometimes they do indeed analyze trivial things. "How many angels can dance on the head of a pin?" is said to be a question that concerned Medieval philosophers.[20] But now, most of the questions we consider are about stuff we worry about everyday: ethics, the law, liberty, religion, God, and freewill just to name a few. Part of the purpose of this series of books is to expose the general public to this fact.

Actually, philosophy is the forefather of many disciplines. Hippocrates (460–377 B.C.E.), the father of modern medicine, was a philosopher. He thought a lot about how the human body worked and the ethical obligations of physicians, became convinced that illness wasn't due to evil spirits, wrote the Hippocratic Oath and POOF! . . . modern medicine was born. The ancient Greek philosopher Aristotle (384–322 B.C.E.) was the first to categorize species of animals—like biologists do today. Descartes (1596–1650), who revolutionized philosophy with his *Meditations on First Philosophy*, also revolutionized mathematics with the Cartesian coordinate system. The same is true for the greatest political thinkers: Hobbes (1588–1679), Locke, Rousseau (1712–1778), Mill (1806–1873), Rawls (1921–2002) were all philosophers—philosophers, mind you, who still influence us today. (Locke argued for our natural right to life, liberty and property—sound familiar?) The list goes on. This is why when you get a doctoral degree in almost any discipline, it is called a "Ph.D."—the "Ph" stands for "Philosophy."

The point is, *thinking from the gut* is hardly acceptable in any other discipline; why would it be acceptable in philosophy or politics? Answer: it's not. You have to give arguments in philosophy and politics just like you do everywhere else. The reason people usually assume *thinking from the gut* is acceptable in philosophy and politics is because of intellectual impatience—the answers are hard to find. It's not like science where we can take measurements and make observations to settle disputes. Without a quick way to settle disputes, people get frustrated, throw up their hands, and decide there is no answer—"everyone has a right to their opinion!"

---

[20] Actually this question was never really asked by medieval philosophers—another misconception. That's just the kind of question they are accused of asking too often. But, truth be told, they talked about a lot of important stuff too.

But *there are* answers to philosophical and political questions—it just takes us a while to get there. You may not see some of the questions you are asking now answered in your lifetime, but we are making progress. We've figured out that Plato's metaphysics is bunk and that theocratic dictatorships are a bad idea. So we're closer to the philosophical and political truth than we were yesterday; we will be even closer tomorrow. Taking part in philosophy and politics is taking part in a grand, prolonged effort—an effort to find the truth. And since we're after truth, spouting opinion without argument isn't going to cut it!

But even if the truth eludes us, truthiness is not an acceptable substitute. We may never answer the "morality of abortion" question but there are good arguments on both sides. Those who put forth those arguments, and answer objections, do have an epistemic right to their opinion. But he who makes no arguments, who does not consider objections, but just believes what he wants because he wants to, has no right to his opinion—even if he agrees with one who does. *Thinking from the gut* is never allowable.[21]

This also means, if you continue believing something just because your mom, your church, or your political party told you to, you don't have a right to that opinion either. If you can't defend it, you don't have a right to it. Now, that is not to say that believing something based on someone else's testimony is wrong. Most of the beliefs we have are based on testimony—the testimony of news anchors, teachers, reference books, media—and most often testimony is a reliable source of justified belief. But if you continue to believe something, despite objections and evidence you can't dismiss, just because that thing is what your mom always told you—well, in that case, you don't have a right to that belief. Your mother's testimony can't outweigh the evidence. You're not justified in continuing to hold that belief and no one has a duty to allow you to do so.

---

[21] Actually, this may be a bit too strong. As Malcolm Gladwell points out in *Blink*, when it comes to recognizing danger and "reading people" our gut may be more reliable than reason. (Back Bay Books, 2007). But this doesn't defend the Colbertian gut-thinker, since he gut thinks about politics and philosophy, not danger and body language.

Where Do We Go from Here?

So to have a right to my opinion, I just need to put forth an argument?

—Any Given Student, *Introduction to Philosophy*

Close, but not exactly. It needs to be a good argument.

> Well, there are those who argue that some people are born gay. But this is just silly, because we are made in God's image. So if someone were born gay, that would mean that God is part gay, and he is definitely not. He is one hundred percent hetero. God is all Man. (*I Am America*, p. 112)

This argument can't justify Colbert's position that homosexuals are not born that way; it's not a good argument. It makes grandiose assumptions (we are made in God's image), it misconstrues (or at least limits) the meaning of the term "image," and it assigns a sexual preference to a being with no gender. (I doubt many really think God "the Father" has a reproductive organ.) So Colbert can't claim to have a right to this belief.

But figuring out who does have a right to his opinion, once arguments start flying around, is difficult. You have to find out who is giving good arguments, who isn't, and whether there is a reasonable way to settle the issue. I can't teach that in one chapter. Go take Logic or Critical Thinking. But when you do come across a good argument, don't be afraid to change your mind. We don't need any more gut-thinkers.

2

Formidable Opponent and the Necessity of Moral Doubt

STEVEN GIMBEL

Life imitates art. Sometimes that's a good thing and sometimes it's not. In the case of Stephen Colbert's "Formidable Opponent," it would be a wonderful thing, if only it would happen. But, alas!

In the last decade, we have seen the criminalization of moral doubt. You have "character" in some ethically important way, the line goes, only if you are resolutely and absolutely determined in every possible moral inclination, that is, only if you are so black and white in your internal deliberations that, in Colbert's words, you "believe on Wednesday the same thing you believed on Monday, no matter what happened on Tuesday." Your mind must be closed off to rational arguments from those whose points of view differ from yours in even the most minute fashion if you want to be considered to be serious about your values. Today, nothing worse can be said of you than "He has more flip flops than Jimmy Buffett's closet." Ralph Waldo Emerson famously said that "a foolish consistency is the hobgoblin of little minds," and these days we are condemned as morally damaged if we don't resort to having little minds.

And the result is that we're becoming morally retarded, unable to engage in the real debates that we must have as a functioning democracy. We occupy a place in the world at a time in history where hard questions continually confront us. The only way we can make good decisions is to weigh different approaches. But this is exactly what we don't do when we retreat to our intellectual foxholes, only to lob sound bite grenades at our strawman "enemies."

Indeed, the basic premise of *The Colbert Report* is to lampoon this lack of authentic consideration of different viewpoints in today's punditry. Colbert's character is the essence of the denial of alternate perspectives. "George Bush: great President or the greatest President?" is a flippant way of putting on a bumper sticker the replacement of open-minded, passionate, fair conversation with trite, partisan jingoism. By parodying such narrowness with Colbert's incredible precision, perhaps they can be shamed into changing. If we take creating a better pundit class as a social goal of the *Report*, we're not only shown how bad it is now, but we're also given a glimpse of how good it could be, a look behind the mask in that one small, occasional segment, Formidable Opponent.

For Colbert, the only opponent he could possibly find formidable, of course, is yet another Stephen Colbert. The shtick consists of two different camera angles such that a blue-tie-wearing Colbert debates a red-tie wearing Colbert. For the joke to work, the dueling Stephens must actually lay out strong arguments for both sides of a contemporary political or ethical issue. We therefore get to see someone confronting his own conflicting moral intuitions. We get to see internal wrestling instead of the sort of *faux*-certainty that comes from ideology instead of contemplation. We capture a short glance of authentic ethical deliberation the way it really happens in our own minds. There it is on the screen, the thing we need and the thing they are trying to beat out of us. To save America and the world, more of us need to emulate the dueling Stephen Colbert's in Formidable Opponent.

Moral Doubt

It's the birthright, of every new generation to utter the words, "I remember when *Saturday Night Live* was funny." Of course, I actually do remember when *Saturday Night Live* was funny. "Weekend Update" featured a regular Point-Counterpoint segment with Dan Aykroyd and Jane Curtain which was a spoof of the end of *60 Minutes* back in the pre-Andy Rooney days which concluded each Sunday with dueling commentaries by conservative James J. Kilpatrick and liberal Shana Alexander. In the *Saturday Night Live* version, Aykroyd would invariably begin his conservative response to Curtain's liberal discussion with the famous line "Jane, you ignorant slut." It was funny. It was outrageous. Surely, no one trying to discuss politics would actually say that, especially on television.

Ah, the innocent 1970s with their disco music, bell bottoms, and Studio 54! That simpler time when there was no sense of the impending wave of Ann Coulter, Rush Limbaugh, and Papa Bear O'Reilly. If only our contemporary debate was as civil as the theatre of the absurd from a mere couple of decades before.

But what we have these days is not merely a lack of civility, but a lack of actual debate, even in our forums that supposedly are set aside for it. No one pointed this out better than Jon Stewart in his infamous appearance on *Crossfire* with conservative bowtie boy Tucker Carlson and Clintonista Paul Begala:

> You're doing theater, when you should be doing debate. . . . It's not honest. What you do is not honest. What you do is partisan hackery. . . . You have a responsibility to the public discourse, and you fail miserably. . . . we need what you do. This is such a great opportunity you have here to actually get politicians off of their marketing and strategy. (October 15th, 2004)

Stewart pointed out quite dramatically that what gets substituted for actual discourse is pre-packaged, focus group tested talking points, not open-minded, passionate, good faith discussions of hard issues.

The issues we face seem so hard because they are, in fact, hard. There are no simple solutions to difficult, multi-faceted problems like abortion, protecting ourselves from terrorist attacks, or fixing the educational and health care systems. Pragmatic policy aspects and moral dimensions are inextricably woven through these issues. It's dangerous and disingenuous to offer simple solutions to hard problems. Whenever someone tries to sell you on a simple solution, your best option is to put your hand on your wallet and run like hell.

Why Moral Doubt Is a Good Thing

In facing hard moral questions, there are two reasons why we need to embrace our moral doubt and not see it as an indication of a flaw in our character. The first is that a lack of moral doubt will trap us in our own perspective. It may be true that Stephen Colbert does not see race, that when other people tell him that he's white that he believes them because he shops at Eddie Bauer. And if all of this is true, then when Stephen Colbert is informed of his skin color, his set of beliefs about the world have been enlarged by someone else's perspective in a meaningful way that might be operative in teasing out the subtle differences in the way he and the *Report*'s black Republican correspondent, P.K. Winsome, may view a given issue or event.

Every perspective emphasizes a different aspect that deserves legitimate concern. Liberals will emphasize fairness, equality, and the need to be concerned about the least among us. Fiscal conservatives will highlight the fact that our proposed solutions will affect the larger economy and that bureaucratizing functions often causes us to be less effective at actually realizing the help we intend to lend. Greens will point out how our choices affect the Earth and the way that larger influences, especially corporate interests, have to be understood to look at the problem correctly. Libertarians will stress the need to protect individual freedoms. Supporters of Lyndon Larouche will remind us that the Queen of England is a CIA operative listening to our thoughts through the fillings in our teeth.

This is not to say that no opinions are wrong. Of course, some are. Nor is it to say that some ideas are worse than others. Of course, some are. Some opinions are well reasoned, based on reality, and ready for implementation. Others are ideological, ill-informed, impractical, and plain old stupid. We should prefer the good ones to the bad ones. Just because everyone has a right to his or her opinion doesn't mean that some opinions aren't utterly irrational to hold.

This, then, is the second reason why moral doubt is a good thing. Sometimes even the best of us can get it wrong. One guard against error is competition.

When Stephen Colbert says he trusts the marketplace, this need not only be the financial market, but also the marketplace of ideas. A philosophical movement called the Enlightenment, including figures like John Locke and later John Stuart Mill, championed democratic governance, trials by jury, and free market economics, all because they contended that people are rational and when confronted with a fair competition among the strongest arguments on opposing sides, the truth will almost always win out. Think of it as intellectual survival of the fittest. It's only by challenging our beliefs that we can guarantee that they stand up. Moral doubt allows us to put even our most cherished beliefs on the level playing field to see if they can compete.

In a complicated world, problems are tricky. There's nothing wrong with moral doubt, that sense that we don't know which of two or more competing views is the best one to hold. It means we are authentically trying to figure out what actually is right.

Black and white thinking, the sense that we have all the answers and there is nothing to be learned from anyone who disagrees with us, is the mark of intellectual immaturity. Those who disagree with us may hold insights that we need to integrate into our own view, or if that is not possible, at least acknowledge in maintaining a conflicting standpoint. The problem is not that we argue passionately—passion of this sort is essential—rather, what we need to do is figure out how to talk passionately about hard issues without talking past each other. We need to get to be a culture of Formidable Opponents.

The Source of Moral Doubt

So where does this moral doubt come from? If we deserve a tip of the hat for intellectual maturity instead of a wag of the finger for insufficient moral commitment, what explains the sense of internal tension we experience in the case of hard moral questions? If we are to hold moral doubt to be desirable, we need to understand what it is, where it comes from, and what is opposing it.

A big part involves what we mean by the term "morally right." We have an intuitive sense, but when asked to explain it clearly, we often find it difficult. We know that helping an old lady across the street with her groceries is a morally good thing, and that running off and stealing the groceries on the other side of the street is a bad thing. But why? What makes an action morally good or morally bad?

Those who champion the sort of moral absolutism that shuns moral doubt have a legitimate fear. They're worried that without a simple definition of ethical right and wrong, the whole moral project might dissolve. Unless we have a straightforward, unambiguous ethic, the concern is that all force is removed from ethical prescriptions.

But it turns out that whether an act is morally acceptable or not is a complex question. Actually, it's a series of questions. When we think about ethics there are at least five relevant parts of the ethical situation we consider: who did it, what he did, the effect of having done it, the person to whom it was done, and how it affects those to whom we have special moral obligations. Each one of these is tied to a piece of what we mean by "morally right" and "morally wrong" and provides us with one aspect of the complete moral picture. Thinking from the gut is not necessarily problematic. Rather, the problem is that we turn out to be like cows who have several stomachs—our gut will often be its own formidable opponent.

The Who in Ethics

When we act, it shapes who we are. There are two parts to acting well. First you have to figure out what the right thing to do is and the second is actually doing it. We don't always do what we know we should do. After all, there are doctors who smoke, policemen who steal, and sixth-grade English teachers who dangle their participles in public.

Doing what we know we should is a function of character and the ancient Greek philosopher Aristotle argued that our character is shaped by our actions. We are creatures of habit and when we act in a certain way, we make it more likely that we will act that way again the next time. By doing the right thing over and over, we will automatically do the right thing in the future. Do the wrong thing, and it makes it easier to flub it the next time too. We all have within us the seeds of greatness. There is a potential perfect self that we come closer to actualizing when we act well and that we retard when we act badly. We could all be Alpha Dog of the Week, but we need to train our inner-puppy well by doing the right thing.

A good act, then, is one that makes us more virtuous and a bad act is one that makes us less virtuous. Right and wrong, on this view, are all about you.

The What in Ethics

But we also need to look at the act itself. There's something about lying, cheating, stealing, and bears that seems inherently problematic. When we judge something right or wrong, it's the action we're judging and therefore the action we ought to look at.

To decide which actions are allowable and which ones are morally forbidden we need a set of rules. But where could these rules come from? Further, there are a potentially infinite number of possible actions and therefore potentially an infinite number of rules we would need to know. Since we can't know an infinite number of things, we could never be held morally responsible for anything since you might not have known the requisite rule.

The German philosopher Immanuel Kant solved these problems by coming up with a meta-rule, a multi-rule, a mega-rule, the godfather of rules, the hardest working rule in show business, the categorical imperative. The idea is to strip the situation of all the contextual factors—who did it, why they did it, when they did it, whether the person with whom they did it has appeared in *Girls Gone Wild* videos—and just get it down to the bare act itself and ask whether the rule that act obeys should be a universal law. So, the question is whether "always lie" or "never lie" should be the universal rule, completely ignoring whether that four year old walking down the street with her Mommy would be happier believing that there really is a Santa Claus.

The How Much in Ethics

But our actions change the world. What we do has consequences. Surely, the morally right thing is that which leaves the world a better place. When we talk about right and wrong, we often refer to how people's actions affect others and judge it as morally right if it brought about the best consequences for all involved and morally wrong if it did not. There is something morally important in standing up against the growing robot menace even if you have to be tough and nasty to do it.

This view is called Utilitarianism and was championed by many philosophers, including Jeremy Bentham (1748–1832), whose dead body was treated by the local taxidermist and remains on display to this day at the London School of Economics (making a portrait hanging in the Smithsonian pale by comparison, no?). Bentham argued that if moral statements were to make any real sense, they should refer to something we can measure: experienced pleasure and pain. Other things may be good as means, but pleasure is an end—no one ever asks you what you want all that pleasure for—and we ought to judge actions based upon whether they bring about the greatest balance of pleasure over pain in the world.

We need to do ethical accounting before we act, tallying up the ways in which we affect the situation. We need to rank the costs and benefits, determine which possible action brings about the greatest returns of good to bad, and act accordingly. Think ThreatDown. We take those aspects of contemporary culture that bring with them the greatest dangers and we must act to stop them . . . now!

The Whom in Ethics

Then there is the one on the receiving end. Of course, we need to also consider the person to whom the act was done. Oliver Wendell Holmes said that the right to swing my fist ends at my neighbor's nose. I can think about myself and the act of swinging my fist all I want, but in coming to a decision about how to act ethically I also need to think of my neighbor's nose when deciding what to pick.

The notion of rights has been incredibly powerful in approaching some of the worst examples of injustice over the last hundred years—civil rights, human rights, women's rights, gay rights, animal rights. Thinkers like John Locke and Thomas Hobbes advanced views in which there are two kinds of rights. The first variety are thought to be innate and inalienable—rights you're born with and which cannot be taken away from you. The other type are the result of a social contract that underlies the moral structure of society, forming the basic constitutional rules of behavior by which civilization separates itself from a state of nature. These are rights that come from being a member of the society and as a result are yours to surrender or trade for other rights.

These rights are largely prohibitive, that is, they don't tell you what you have to do, but rather tell others what they cannot do to you. They are little ethical shields that protect your body, your property, and your portrait. When I buy, for example, a copy of *I Am America (And So Can You!)*, it is mine to do with as I choose. I can read it, shred it, lend it to a friend, or wallpaper my den with its pages. It's mine. As long as I'm not violating someone else's rights—say, by trying to shove it up my neighbor's nose—I can do whatever I want, helpful to the world or not.

When we act, then, we need to morally consider the rights of those whom the act affects. To violate these rights makes the action ethically unacceptable.

Special Status in Ethics

So far, we've looked at the person acting, the action itself, the consequences of the action on everyone, and the person to whom the action was done. There is one more group of morally relevant individuals, those with whom we have deep interpersonal relationships. By virtue of these relationships, we come to have special moral obligations.

Think of the relationship between parents and children. This is not a contractual or merely duty-based relationship. We don't act in our children's interests simply because there are rules we are following. Rather, that sort of relationship is based on care. We're concerned about them, their development and well-being. We want what's best for them, both in terms of personal hopes, but also morally. Philosophers like Nel Noddings and Sara Ruddick pointed out that care-based relationships come with certain ethical obligations that we don't have to strangers.

Consider the episodes of the *Report* during the writers' strike. These are people who work together and their relationship could be just a professional one based on punching the clock and getting paid. But one could tell that the *Report* is like a family. When the writers were not there, the content of Colbert's performances reflected a genuine concern for the well-being of those who help keep him funny. His support and concern was evident and it shows a depth of moral character that should be appreciated.

Explaining Moral Doubt

Having several moving parts to our understanding of "morally right" and "morally wrong" is not usually a problem. In the overwhelming number of cases, almost every case we come across in day-to-day life, these parts work in harmony and the ethical machine hums along beautifully. All the senses of right and wrong line up and give us the same answers.

But our hard cases, the ethical problems that seem intractable, are the ones where our different parts work in different directions. The 'what' tells us yes while the 'how' much tells us no. The 'who' says we have to while the 'whom' says we can't. We think of all five of these moral aspects when we try to decide how to act, and when our multi-faceted internal thought process turns on itself, we feel that knot in our stomach and sense that there's a problem.

We may think that our politics answers the question for us, that, say, liberals prefer to consider care and the consequences where conservatives look at rules or rights. Certainly this is the case with some issues. In the case of abortion, for example, many pro-choice arguments are based on the negative consequences of making the procedure legally unavailable while the pro-life positions are generally justified on the basis of "do not kill" type rules or arguments about a fetus's right to life. But just as often, liberals take a rights or duty based approach, say to endangered species, where we have a duty to protect nature and the conservative line is sometimes a utilitarian approach considering the cost to industry and other times a land owners' right line. In the case of flag burning, liberals stress the right to free speech while conservatives make care-based arguments around those who sacrificed for the flag in battle. But when it comes to foreign aid, it's liberals who make the care-based appeals while conservatives make the rights based "it's my money, not the government's" argument.

The small-minded cynic would say that both sides are just picking and choosing which system fits their pre-existing biases. Hint: don't listen to small-minded cynics. Liberals and conservatives here are doing exactly what they should be doing. We do use all of these tools in evaluating right and wrong and in some cases one overrides the others and in other cases not. How do we decide which trumps which others when?

That's where open-minded conversation comes in. That's where we need to turn to Stephen Colbert as our model. This is where we need individually and as a culture to see ourselves as Formidable Opponents. It's only through passionate discourse, allowing ourselves to develop our conflicting intuitions and supporting both sides with the strongest arguments that we begin to honestly open our minds to the possibility of progress.

Most of the time our five components to moral rightness all point in the same direction, but in the hard questions, they do not. They oppose each other and we have to decide which system is the one to obey. Our intuitions will simultaneously be pulled in different directions and it's only through good faith and open-minded conversation that we can hope to come to a rational decision. This means we have to wrestle with ourselves. Take both sides. Argue authentically with yourself. Don't worry about changing your mind. It doesn't show a lack of character to be swayed by a reasonable argument you didn't buy at first. It's a sign of intellectual maturity.

Fear not the flip-flop. We need the moral doubt.

3

Things that Make You Go "What?"

ROBEN TOROSYAN

One thing that's so cool about *The Colbert Report* is that you can learn to think critically simply by watching it. As Colbert said of his audience in his first episode,

> You're not the elites. You're not the country club crowd. I know for a fact that my country club would never let you in. But you get it. And you come from a long line of 'it-getters'. You're the folks who say, 'something's got to be done'. Well, you're doing something right now. You're watching TV.[1]

Yet watching Colbert really can amount to doing something constructive. The show is so fascinating partly because Colbert's character regularly exudes the very *opposite* of seven critical thinking attitudes:

- **inquisitive**
- **open-minded**
- **truthseeking**
- **systematic**
- **analytical**
- **judicious**
- **confident in reasoning**[2]

---

[1] Episode 1001, originally aired October 17th, 2005.
[2] See American Philosophical Association, *Critical Thinking: A Statement of*

According to the American Philosophical Association (APA), these seven action-dispositions define critical thinking. By contrast, Colbert's cocky character shows repeatedly how to fail at living, as Socrates recommended, "an examined life." In fact, Colbert shows it so well that an astute viewer can deduce how to think critically precisely by *not* using the Colbert character's manipulations of language and logic—and by catching such abuses whether committed by others, or by ourselves.

To Avoid Begging the Question, Don't Ask Questions!

Inquisitive:

- ***curious with regard to a wide range of issues***
- ***concern to become and remain well-informed***

Colbert often chafes at being asked to imagine beyond what his experience and intuition present at face value. He gets frustrated with theoretical physicist Lisa Randall, for instance:

> What do you mean—like there are other *dimensions*? Extra? This, obviously, this . . . this makes my brain break. What's that mean? Why would you study this? What purpose does it serve to think about things that we cannot see or touch?[3]

With his indignation, Colbert not only assumes that only sensory data count, but betrays an attitude of utter discomfort with being curious about anything not already obvious. When we get truly curious, by contrast, we move *towards* the things we don't understand, trying to find out more.

But to Colbert, nothing demands more sympathy than a mind forced to become informed. He highlights a caption from pundit

---

Expert Consensus for Purposes of Educational Assessment and Instruction. "The Delphi Report," Committee on Pre-College Philosophy. (ERIC Doc. No. ED 315 423). 1990. The APA also described six cognitive skills, such as interpretation, evaluation and inference. I'll draw freely on the dispositions, attitudes, and skills in italicized sub-headings.

[3] Episode 4022, originally aired February 12th, 2008.

Neil Cavuto's news show that reads, "Students forced to watch *An Inconvenient Truth* or fail," then comments about one complaining student named "Barry":

> At a 'college', Barry was forced to think something that he didn't already think . . . Of course he's bitter: he's enrolled in a class where the professor thinks he knows more about the subject than the students. The last time I checked, that is the definition of elitism. . . . That's why all colleges should be forced to advertise every element of their curriculum—so students are guaranteed that when they leave college they'll be exactly the same as when they went in. *That*, folks, is what I believe college is for. You take these young unformed lumps of clay, *leave* them unformed lumps, then fire them in the kiln of unchallenged thought so they become rigid and never move again.[4]

By describing Barry as forced to think something he didn't already think, Colbert satirizes the assumption that people should never have to confront their preconceptions. Labeling knowledge and learning as "elitism," he avoids the attitude of trying to stay informed.

Being inquisitive demands exactly that we avoid becoming the rigid and unmoving "lumps of clay" Colbert wishes for, and instead that we actively seek out what we don't know. A risk is that openly questioning everything can lead to a wishy-washy relativism, an "anything goes" lack of foundational beliefs. But it doesn't have to. It's possible to both find things out *and* make decisions, to both *commit* to values and keep *probing* and learning more.

To end the segment (and even end inquiry), Colbert comments, "That's how you get well educated like Barry," and shows a clip of Cavuto interviewing the student:

CAVUTO: What was your grade?
BARRY: Umm, my grade was well. (sic)
COLBERT: See? His grade was "well." Now, he make double-plus-think, *despite* unwell-school. Let's just hope our future generations can do the same.[5]

Besides discrediting the source as uneducated, Colbert's parody refers to Orwellian "doublethink." In the novel *Nineteen Eighty-*

---

[4] Episode 3066, originally aired May 15th, 2007.
[5] Episode 3066, originally aired May 15th, 2007.

Four, the government endlessly reiterates the equivalence of concepts with their denials, in slogans like "War Is Peace" and "Freedom Is Slavery." What a school says was taught, Cavuto says was "forced." Colbert lauds the student for his "double-plus-think" in the face of "unwell" schooling because he doesn't want the student to seek actual information about things like global warming. In effect, Colbert the performer uses Colbert the character as a caveat or warning of how we can let ourselves be controlled by other forces if we don't keep up a habit of asking questions and seeking out information.

Giving Everyone the Chance to Agree with You

Open-minded:

- *regard for divergent world views*
- *flexibility in considering alternatives and opinions*
- *willingness to reconsider and revise views where honest reflection suggests that change is warranted*

When one guest disagrees with him, Colbert replies, "It's one thing to express your views. It's another thing for those views to be different than *mine*."[6] Here Colbert brooks no dissent, embodying the very opposite of the "open-minded" disposition. Colbert suggests instead that others may have a right to free speech, but not the right to differ with him.

As to raising a family, Colbert offers his own parenting tips in *I Am America (And So Can You!)*. He admits that while he mistrusts children, "I respect my opponents" (p. 11). Besides the humor of characterizing kids as "opponents," an added irony here is that while Colbert often makes surface statements of respect for others, his character's intention is inevitably to disrespect or show lack of courtesy—to put others in their place as beneath Colbert himself.

This duplicity shows in Tip Number One to parents, to "Set Some Rules." As Colbert writes, "Don't worry if a rule makes sense—the important thing is that it's a rule. Arbitrary rules teach kids discipline: If every rule made sense, they wouldn't be learning respect for authority, they'd be learning logic" (p. 11). One irony

---

[6] Episode 2064, originally aired May 15th, 2006.

here is that Colbert has no confidence in reason or patience with making sense of rules, yet critical thinking requires precisely that people understand the reasoning behind agreements.

Worse yet, Colbert has said, "I believe in free speech as much as the next authoritarian."[7] His chief problem with logic, then, seems to be that it can be used to show how an authority like him may be wrong. Because Colbert *assumes* that an authority is by definition right, logic cannot be right. But by definition authority only involves "the right and power to command" (Webster's), and may be right or wrong, just or unjust.

For Colbert, however, authority matters more than truth or justice. And Colbert values not just his own authority. He defers to pundits, such as Bill O'Reilly, whom he judges authoritative. The mindset implies that logic should submit to authority, rather than promote, as the APA does, "rational autonomy" and "intellectual freedom" from dictation by any authority.

What's more, the authority that often matters most to Colbert is his own. When he titles his book *I Am America (And So Can You!)*, he implies at once that he as an individual encompasses all of America's diversity. But with his subtitle, he suggests that anyone else can claim such authority, just as egotistically as he does. At once, this seems to contradict his belief in himself as ultimate authority— if others can be America, then what does that make him? Colbert might reply, however, that this makes him the one everyone needs most in order to be all that they can be (Army motto intended). In contrast to openness to different perspectives, Colbert suggests you should close your mind as often as possible, except when opening it to the idea that Colbert's mind is the one that matters most.

But Colbert's is an equal opportunity closed mind for he values not only his own opinion. He also values the Bible as an exemplar of truth claims, arguing, "it's the best selling book of all time. . . . The market doesn't lie." This statement illustrates the logical fallacy of the *appeal to popularity*, by assuming that what the majority thinks must be right. The problem? The majority could simply be deluded or misinformed.

In his own book, Colbert further lauds the Bible: "The only good book is the Good Book. Come on, the word 'Good' is right there in the title" (p. 122). First, Colbert uses a cliché but then rep-

---

[7] Episode 3109, originally aired August 21st, 2007.

resents it as the actual title of the work. This lets him avoid facing his bias towards the book, and instead imply again that merely saying something is good makes it good. But not just anyone can say so. To Colbert's character, the ultimate justification for his version of the truth is simply that it is *his* truth.

Therefore, while he's no fan of books, Colbert has a reason for why he wrote one himself: "Well, like a lot of other dictators, there is one man's opinion that I value above all others. Mine." He parodies the tendency to seek only whatever would further validate one's own opinions and preconceptions, rather than be open to other views. By contrast, open-mindedness means welcoming contrary perspectives and trying to become comfortable with difference.

Truthseeking in the No Fact Zone: Helping You Spread the Message of Me

Truthseeking:

- *honesty in facing one's own biases, prejudices, stereotypes, or egocentric tendencies*

- *distinguishing a main idea from subordinate ideas, without bias*

- *judging the logical strength of arguments*

When Colbert rants about a news item in "The WØRD" a directly opposing idea usually appears in a textbox at the right. By subverting his own character's meaning quite directly, the vehicle usually implies that its opposite claim is true.

Before one installment, "Pencils Down," Colbert attacks a Government Accounting Office (GAO) test for exposing weaknesses at our borders and ports—"It's ruining the curve for everyone."[8] Colbert goes on to call such tests "useless":

> **COLBERT:** Now another thing about tests, they disrupt the status quo. When someone fails a test it means they gotta do something. They have to study harder or think of a baby name.
> **BULLET:** Or run as an Independent.

---

[8] Episode 2101, originally aired August 9th, 2006.

COLBERT: Exactly.
BULLET: Yes.

In a departure from his normal behavior, Colbert here acknowledges the bullet, but only to create his own echo chamber, much as media pundits echo back their own opinions rather than explore facts. He continues:

> **COLBERT:** Well folks, I propose a new test. I say we test the testers. So, GAO, now that you've revealed lapses in our national security, you've got to answer the following questions. Question 1: Are you satisfied?
> **BULLET:** Kinda scared, actually.

Ironically, Colbert tries to turn tests back on testers much as the bullet turns the intentions of Colbert back on himself.

> **COLBERT:** Question 2: True or false: Who the Hell do you think you are?
> **BULLET:** True?

Colbert attacks the bullet for speaking the truth. But in addition, this self-reflexive turn illustrates a principle of post-modernity, a period of philosophical fragmentation that arose in the late twentieth century. That principle is that every assertion risks being undermined by its own reasoning, much as the Colbert bullet routinely undermines Colbert the character.

In "deconstruction," the stream of thought associated with the philosopher Jacques Derrida (1930–2004), any attempt at meaning is shot through with "différance." On one hand, we understand words only by seeing how they *differ* with other words. On the other hand, every word always *defers* its meaning, as if pointing away, "Don't look at me for a definition! Look at those other words." (Look a word up in the dictionary, and you get only more words, and more definitions.) So the Colbert bullet at once differs with the naïveté of Colbert the character, but at the same time represents the critical opinion of Colbert the performer.

In a related portrayal of the endless egocentricity of political pundits, Colbert repeatedly tries to railroad interviewees into agreeing with him, regardless of the truth. In the segment "Better Know a District," Colbert, referring to representatives who took illegal

monies from disreputable source Jack Abramoff, says to a congressman, "Let's just go ahead and say you took the money so that
the rest of my questions make sense."[9] Rather than seek the truth,
Colbert forces the answer to fit his presumptions.

Seeing religion as diametrically opposed to science's truth
claims, Colbert comes across a journal article entitled "Is There a
Paleolimnological Explanation for 'Walking on Water' in the Sea of
Galilee?" He is offended by such assertions:

> So once again scientists are telling us what *may* have happened. If
> they had any balls, they'd just say "This is what *did* happen," with or
> without evidence. That's what the Bible does . . .[10]

Here Colbert complains about relying on facts to assert a claim,
preferring to believe what he wishes were the truth, and with certainty rather than probability (which is more accurate), instead of
actually finding it out. Ironically, by doing fairly extensive research
in order to find such an article in a scholarly scientific journal,
Colbert's team actually goes to great lengths to stay informed.

When Colbert's character refuses to look for evidence, let alone
respect the value of checking out doubts, he embodies how good
it would feel not to have to worry about the truth. Such careful
thought bogs Colbert down, leading to his utter disregard for science. Rather than value the scientific method for facing biases,
Colbert terms scientists "fanatical" because they "put their blind
faith in empirical observation" (*I Am America*, p. 191).

Colbert interviews Janna Levin, a novelist who relies on science:

COLBERT: You've written a book, *A Madman Dreams of Turing
Machines*. Now this is science. But it's also a novel.
LEVIN: Yes.
COLBERT: So you admit that most science is fiction.[11]

This all or nothing thinking is technically called the *fallacy of com-
position*. In this fallacy, rather than pursue any interest in informing yourself, you leap from a fact about a single part to an
overgeneralization about the entire whole. Because the science is

---

[9] Episode 2051, originally aired April 20th, 2006.
[10] Episode 2047, originally aired April 17th, 2006.
[11] Episode 2110, originally aired August 24th, 2006.

embedded in a work of fiction, Colbert assumes that all of science must be fiction. The error he makes is to blur the science and fiction within the book and then leap to blur science and fiction outside of the book.

Eventually, however, he actually asks after the truth:

COLBERT: Why is there something, rather than nothing?
LEVIN: We actually don't know.
COLBERT: Hah, I stumped a theoretical physicist. And all it took was the hardest question in the world. I got a bucket full of them.[12]

Rather than seek understanding, Colbert is disdainful that he could make an intellectual admit ignorance—on the assumption that smart people don't say "I don't know." This illustrates the logical fallacy of an *appeal to ignorance*, where you assume that just because something can't be proven false, it must be true, or in this case, just because something can't be proven true, it must be false. But then Colbert admits it's the hardest question in the world, giving himself credit for stumping his guest. Interestingly, however, when he says there's more where that came from, implying he could further stump anyone, he actually reveals that we're all ignorant and that there are many unanswered questions.

In another instance of an all or nothing dismissal, Colbert attempts to "nail" Australian scientist Tim Flannery, author of *The Weather Makers*:

COLBERT: Our president is going to take action on this as soon as all the science is in. That's what he said. Is all the science in, sir? All of it. Simple question: yes or no. Is ALL the science in? ALL of it!
FLANNERY: Certainty is a rare thing in this world. You know, we educate our kids with no certain outcome. We buy certain stocks and bonds without a certain outcome. We live in a world of probabilities. And the scientific probabilities are that we are having a big impact on this climate of ours. So I don't think you can wait for certainty. You'll be dead before you can get it.[13]

---

[12] Episode 2110, originally aired August 24th, 2006.
[13] Episode 2073, originally aired June 13th, 2006.

What Colbert's character misses is the fact of "non-allness," a term in general semantics for the idea that one can never know everything about anything. This fact flies in the face of our intuition that science determines "truth." In reality, scientists only ever determine what is "probable." By contrast, Colbert only thinks it's possible to know everything because it's only to himself that he ever looks for the truth. If instead we think critically, we realize that answers are often neither absolutely certain nor totally unknowable, but exist on a continuum, along shades of gray, from highly unlikely to highly likely.

Systematically Anti-Systematic: He Said, She Said, Enough Said

Systematic:

- *alertness to opportunities for critical thinking*

- *routinely justifying reasoning in terms of standards and contextual factors used*

Interviewing Philip Zimbardo, the psychologist behind the classic Stanford prison experiment and author of *The Lucifer Effect: How Good People Turn Evil*, Colbert quibbles:

> **COLBERT:** How do you know what authority is unjust or not? I mean, you do what people tell you to do who are in power and then you have to *trust* that that's the right thing to do. What else is society based on?
>
> **ZIMBARDO:** It's based on being mindful and doing critical thinking. Because a lot of authority is unjust. A lot of orders are wrong orders.
>
> **COLBERT:** If they were unjust, they wouldn't be authorities.[14]

As usual, Colbert simply assumes his premise is true, rather than arguing to support it. Here, the missing premise is that an authority must by definition be "just," when an authority really only has power. Colbert's abuse of logic is like saying, "I feel the death penalty is wrong. Therefore the death penalty is wrong." The miss-

---

[14] Episode 4021, originally aired February 11th, 2008.

ing premise is "What I feel is wrong is wrong." That's an assumption. There's no evidence or argument that one morality is true for all or that thinking something wrong necessarily makes it wrong.

The irony is that when Colbert speaks, the unsound premise is often not missing but stated, proudly—no matter how unsound. For instance, in an interview with paleontologist Ted Daeschler, Colbert argues for the value of impulse or "the gut" over reason. Daeschler counters with an evolutionary perspective, and actually integrates Colbert's own "gut" emphasis, only to meet Colbert's refusal to reason:

> **DAESCHLER:** When you do learn those facts, it's in your gut. You know evolution happened. But first you have to get it in your head.
>
> **COLBERT:** What you're saying is something actually goes from your head to your gut. Because everything *I* learn goes in my eyes, ears, or mouth straight to my gut. I don't include my head in at all. Because it overthinks it.
>
> **DAESCHLER:** Um, that's your problem.
>
> **COLBERT:** Some say problem, some say superpower. I'm impervious to logic. . . .
>
> **DAESCHLER:** Evolution is a fact of life.
>
> **COLBERT:** But then why do I have to *believe* it?[15]

Rather than be methodical in his thinking, Colbert asserts right off, directly, that he has no respect for such use of logic, portraying himself as an impenetrable warrior rather than a thinking organism. Further, he demonstrates *circular reasoning* or using your assumption to support your assumption. He argues: If my gut feels something, then it must be right. But that's based on the premise that the gut is right because my gut tells me it's right.

If Colbert were to consider evolution thoroughly, he would need to do more than simply re-label his opponent's criticism ("Some say problem, some say superpower") and childishly refuse to reason ("I'm impervious to logic"). Instead he would need to appeal to standards such as—in the case of evolution—the scientific method, which insists that findings be reproducible (whether one agrees or not) and that we eliminate inconsistencies between

---

[15] Episode 2067, originally aired May 18th, 2006.

theory (or what we think) and experiment (or what we observe). What such systematic thinking does is push beyond the impulsivity of "he said, she said" rants to the consistency of disciplined argument or careful observation and analysis.

Hundred Percent Hypo-Analytical: Don't Like It? Label It!

Analytical:

- *prudence in suspending, making, or altering judgments*

- *querying evidence*

- *identifying elements needed to draw reasonable conclusions*

To Colbert, an analytic reaction feels more like an allergic reaction: it violates his whole system. Disagreeing with one guest, Colbert taunts him, "You can say no, but I can say yes, and my word has *three* letters" (February 8th, 2007). Avoiding an analytic look at actual reasoning, Colbert tries to quash the dispute by making up criteria for a good argument on the spot—whoever uses the most letters in a one word reply wins.

Such whimsy constitutes the logical fallacy behind *wishful thinking*: One assumes that wishing something so is enough to make it so. Thus when Colbert dislikes hearing out a counterargument, he simply contradicts it, as if saying the opposite were enough to change the reality.

But the example also illustrates how a *red herring* can be used to reframe attention, distracting one from the argument at hand. The absurdity of Colbert's retort directs attention away from reasoning to instead fixate on something as random as letter-count. Such reliance on random criteria fails to provide reasonable support for conclusions, as analytic thinking requires.

In one aside, Colbert says, "I used to hate guys like me. But then I became a guy like me, and now I like guys like me" (January 15th, 2008). Regardless of whether he contradicts himself, that was then, and this is now. What gives Colbert joy is simply the fact that he *has* his own views, as a-historical, inconsistent, and radically oriented to the present as they may be. While being analytical requires prudence in suspending, making, or altering judgments, Colbert's character instead *delights* in his judgments so much that can even claim to criticize himself ("I used to hate guys like me"), yet avoid taking any distance from his own perspective ("now I like guys like me").

In leaping to this wild conclusion, Colbert not only does whatever it takes to like himself, but he again uses circular reasoning. His premise is that he hates and likes who he feels like, because he hates and likes who he feels like. To avoid being circular, or begging the question, the premise of one's argument can not rely on the premise itself. He would need a reason for his hating or liking. But in Colbert's world of fallacious logic, one needs no reasons.

To illustrate, in one edition of "The WØRD" entitled "Casualty of War," Colbert rants:

> The one thing we cannot do is leave because then Iraq will explode in more chaos. But we will leave if Americans keep *hearing* about these casualties. So, saying there are *no* casualties is the only way to prevent greater casualties. Therefore Nation, it's not a lie to say fewer Iraqis were killed than were actually killed, because by doing so we're stopping more Iraqis from being killed in the future. Every lie we tell now will become truth then but only if we have the courage not to tell the truth now.[16]

Here Colbert commits the logical fallacy of an *appeal to consequences*. In this error, one assumes that if something leads to a good consequence, then it must be true, even if it's not really true. Colbert argues that by labeling casualties non-existent, we prevent the U.S. from leaving Iraq, and thus avoid chaos. Therefore such a label must be true. But regardless of how we may feel about a consequence like chaos in Iraq, it's still a lie to say there were no casualties if there were.

Colbert also uses this labeling ploy in committing a *reductio ad absurdum*, where one's reasoning ends with a statement that's clearly false. Colbert concludes absurdly that the lie we tell now is a truth, simply because some good things *might* follow—when a lie is still a lie, regardless of what we call it.

In one interview, author Ron Suskind critiques then-Vice President Dick Cheney's "One Percent Doctrine":

---

[16] Episode 2156, originally aired December 12th, 2006.

SUSKIND: If there's a one percent chance that WMDs have been given to terrorists, [Cheney] says to folks inside the White House, we need to treat it as a certainty. Not in our analysis, but in our response. It's not about evidence. It *frees* us from the *evidentiary* burdens that, well, have been guiding us for a long time.

COLBERT: No offense to the V.P., but isn't that soft on terror? One percent? Shouldn't it be a zero percent doctrine? I mean even if there's *no* chance that someone's a threat to the United States, and they just look at us funny, shouldn't we just [punching his palm] tag 'em? . . . The problem with evidence is that it doesn't always support your opinion. . . . That's what the Vice President was protecting us from. . . . If we waited, we wouldn't have invaded: That's true because it rhymes.[17]

By taking the one percent reasoning to the extreme and implying zero percent is sufficient grounds, Colbert shows how fallacious it is to turn so blind an eye to the weight and burden of evidence, as an analytic mind should. Rather than even attempt to lay out any elements needed for a reasonable conclusion, Colbert again uses random criteria: Suddenly the ability to rhyme makes something more true than evidence or argument ever could.

Laying irony on irony, Colbert himself made news when U.S. congressmen kept appearing on his show, only to have embarrassing clips of themselves appear on regular news shows. In response, Colbert explained:

I'll *tell* the *Today Show* and *Good Morning America* why congressmen want to come on my show. Because this show *is* the news. Not only is this show "*the* news," evidently it *is* news. It's gotta be news, because you morning shows are the news, and you're doing reports on it. So I guess congressmen come on my show in the hopes that you'll use their appearance on my show on *your* show.[18]

First, Colbert illustrates the trouble with looking only to authorities like the news media to tell you what's valuable or newsworthy. If all you seek is someone else's validation, then you reinforce shows that focus exclusively on giving you that validation.

---

[17] Episode 2087, originally aired July 13th, 2006.
[18] Episode 2093, originally aired July 25th, 2006.

Being analytical would require not just taking statements from authorities at face value, but also asking tough questions of them. Colbert then goes on to say those shows might be right:

> **COLBERT:** I could be asking the wrong questions. I asked U.S. congressmen Lynn Westmoreland, who proposed requiring the display of the Ten Commandments in the House and Senate chambers, if he could name the Ten Commandments. What I should have asked him was this—
>
> **NEWSCLIP:** Is it possible that tanning is *addictive*?
>
> **NEWSCLIP:** How long does it take you to grow that thing?
>
> **NEWSCLIP:** Do you really need to wait a half hour after you eat to go swimming?
>
> **COLBERT:** Mea culpa.[19]

With his mock resignation, Colbert suggests that he's been bested at asking dumb questions by the regular news shows, whose questions actually make his absurd ones look almost reasonable. The escalation moves further and further away from breaking down arguments, as the typical news shows assume viewers want only questions that ask nothing, and thus demand nothing of your mind. The final irony comes with Colbert's admitting "Mea culpa" (Latin for "my fault")—reminding the viewer of how pundits rarely if ever alter their judgments, let alone admit fault.

Anti-Judicious: Giving You the Chance to See Why You're Wrong

Judicious:

- *understanding of the opinions of other people*

- *fair-mindedness in appraising reasoning*

- *meta-cognitive self-regulation, or self-conscious monitoring and correcting of one's reasoning*

When a guest wants to retire the penny (Colbert's rejoinder: "Then what am I supposed to use for tipping?"), Colbert banters with him,

---

[19] Episode 2093, originally aired July 25th, 2006.

"I'll tell you why. You wanna know why? You tell me why and then I'll tell you why you're wrong." Then Colbert smirks and adds under his breath, "I think I should say that at the beginning of *every* interview" (April 9th, 2008). He begins by pretending to seek a fair-minded exchange, inviting the guest to express his opinion. But then Colbert reveals his deeper interest in asserting his own position rather than actually discussing more than one position with any fairness.

A related revelation came when interviewing former presidential candidate George McGovern:

> **McGovern:** If you will concede that idealists can also be realists, . . .
>
> **Colbert:** I will not concede anything. You're on the wrong show.[20]

By not even implying but instead boldly admitting he does not make concessions or attempt to acknowledge the views of others, Colbert asserts his desire to avoid appraising his own reasoning. This directly contradicts the habit of being judicious, which asks us to first try and understand opposing views, and even be able to summarize them ourselves, before we disagree with them.

In an edition of "Formidable Opponent," Colbert takes on his own alter-ego, portrayed from an opposing camera angle—one Colbert wears a blue tie and tries to convince the other, wearing a red tie, that U.S. troops should remain in Iraq:

> **Colbert (blue):** Building a stable democracy takes time. Let's say you're baking a cake. You like cake, right?
>
> **Colbert (red):** Who doesn't?
>
> **Colbert (blue):** Terrorists. They hate it. Because in this case, the cake represents democracy.
>
> **Colbert (red):** Mmm, sounds delicious.
>
> **Colbert (blue):** And you have to wait for the cake of a democratic Middle East to rise. If you pull it out of the oven too soon, the cake will fall.
>
> **Colbert (red):** Yeah but what if the cake is exploding, and we're caught in a violent sectarian struggle between the flour and the eggs?[21]

---

[20] Episode 4032, originally aired March 10th, 2008.

[21] Episode 2113, originally aired September 13th, 2006.

As often occurs in the segment, one Colbert (here in red tie) argues sincerely against Colbert's usual pundit character, here weighing the tradeoffs involved in extending U.S. military power in a war that may be worsening security.

> **Colbert (blue):** Hey, a bakery is no place for the squeamish. We placed our soldiers in that oven and we have to keep them there 'til the cake is done.
> **Colbert (red):** But if you leave the cake in too long, it'll dry out.
> **Colbert (blue):** Well, if it's too dry, we'll just wash it down with milk.
> **Colbert (red):** Wait, what does the milk represent?
> **Colbert (blue):** Ahh [shrugging shoulders], oil?
> **Colbert (red):** Well, we must not bake a cake over oil. No blood for milk!
> **Colbert (blue):** What?
> **Colbert (red):** I'm sorry, I've lost the metaphor.

At one surface level, the exchange shows how one risks incoherence in any communication if one sticks solely to speaking in metaphors for too long.

Further, though, when questioned about unforeseen consequences of the war, Colbert refuses to weigh the risk of ruining the very reasons we went to war. Rather than correct his own reasoning, Colbert avoids answering the question. To do so, he simply makes up something to suit his metaphor (milk/oil), as if to say that weighing tradeoffs matters less than sounding good.

The exchange then takes a surreal turn:

> **Colbert (red):** Um, you know, we should probably wrap this up. You sir, are a . . .
> **Colbert (blue):** So you admit defeat?
> **Colbert (red):** No, I'm just getting us out of this.
> **Colbert (blue):** Well, the minute you leave I'm gonna claim I won.
> **Colbert (red):** It's not a tie if I'm the only one left. You should, ah, cut and run along.
> **Colbert (red):** Make me. [*a gun is raised at red-tied Colbert's face*] Two can play at that game. [*raising his own gun at the other's face*] Get out!

COLBERT (BLUE): [*gun in face*] I will see you in Hell! [*wrapping his mouth around the gun barrel*] Go ahead.[22]

Portraying such violent potential, the exchange acts as if to symbolize the way that an argument will always return to one's preconceptions if one never seeks to correct or modify them. However, arguments can risk deadly consequences when people identify with positions personally. All the more reason to be judicious and try to consider counterpoints fairly before leaping to action.

Under-Confidence in Reason: Once It's Easier Said, then It's Done

Confident in reasoning:

- *trust in the processes of reasoned inquiry*
- *self-confidence in one's own abilities to reason as opposed to blindly relying on authority*

Colbert often cuts off an interviewee, "Clearly you're uncomfortable with the subject, let's move on." While the guest might simply disagree, Colbert has no confidence in reasoned exchanged but only in manipulating discourse. He also relies on authorities blindly, as when he argues, "Isn't the Bush administration's leadership a lot like religion? You just have *faith* that they're gonna do the right thing. . . . There's a *reason* why God put him in office."[23]

In another edition of Formidable Opponent, Colbert opines on the controversial issue of embryonic stem cell research. Wearing his red tie he says, "An issue this explosive should only be handled by history's greatest moral philosophers. A Maimonides, a Socrates, a Thomas Aquinas . . .," then the Colbert in blue tie cuts in, "A Stephen Colbert. *This* is Formidable Opponent."[24] Placing himself in the canon of ancient and medieval philosophers, Colbert portrays how pundits display over-exuberant confidence, not in reason but in their own authority.

---

[22] Episode 2113, originally aired September 13th, 2006.
[23] Episode 2087, originally aired July 13th, 2006.
[24] Episode 2093, originally aired July 25th, 2006.

Thinking critically, by contrast, requires that you develop confidence not in your *self* as an authority but in the self's capacity for *reason*, the possibility that one *can* think issues through without simply resorting to an authority. By contrast, when Colbert gets frustrated by disagreements among authorities and by the nuances of the stem cell debate itself, he retreats:

> COLBERT (RED): Wait, wait. ...This is so complicated.
>
> COLBERT (BLUE): Hey, buddy, it comes down to one simple question. Which is more important to you—a potential cure, or a potential life?
>
> COLBERT (RED): Oh, well if you put it that way, it seems . . . *much* more complicated! God bless it, help me out here!
>
> COLBERT (BLUE): Okay, let me complicate it some more. Human cloning could be *part* of stem cell research. You don't want clones do you?[25]

Blue-tied Colbert assumes that if there's one possible abuse of science, then science should be scrapped. This is tempting precisely because at times it can feel so overwhelming to tackle complex arguments. Arguments beget counterarguments, which beget responses to those counterarguments, and so on. But it's exactly this patience with complexity that you need to develop in order to understand important issues. Shooting from the hip works sometimes. But with life's big decisions, if often helps to hold two or more contrary views in mind at the same time. Mindfulness means noticing the discomfort such internal or external conversations can cause. But instead of retreating, you wait it out and see what you can learn from the experience.

When blue-tied Colbert says "Let's say you're dying," red-tied Colbert replies "Oh no! What's wrong with me?" With his credulous alarm, Colbert shows that fearing complexity makes one gullible. Having *no* faith in reason risks that one avoids questioning authorities, and instead assumes the problem must lie with oneself. Such vulnerability leaves one easily duped. The opposing blue-tied Colbert then responds, "I don't know. But I'm glad I don't have it!" This disdainful disregard betrays the hypocrisy behind appearing to care for life (the potential in a cell), but not actually caring about real people

---

[25] Episode 2093, originally aired July 25th, 2006.

(an actual human who is dying). Such inconsistency arises from a belief that reason should be used to serve one's own purposes.

Blue-tied Colbert even fakes an attempt to reason both sides of the argument. At first arguing against stem cell research, he shifts to the tradeoffs of *not* doing such research:

> COLBERT (BLUE): But, you've gotta stay alive. Who'll provide for your family—Brenda and the fifteen kids?
>
> COLBERT (RED): Oh, little Mary and Stephens one through fourteen.
>
> COLBERT (BLUE): And buddy you didn't save one red cent, nor do you have life insurance.
>
> COLBERT (RED): That gypsy told me I was immortal!
>
> COLBERT (BLUE): No, you're thinking of Dracula.
>
> COLBERT (RED): Well, I guess I'd better do it. Shoot me up.
>
> COLBERT (BLUE): Done [dusting off his hands], you're cured.
>
> COLBERT (RED): Yay![26]

In a visual and acoustic move typical of the brilliance of Formidable Opponent, red-tied Colbert raises his hand in joy, then blue-tied Colbert, mouth still open, aims his raised hand down to point at the other in accusation—his mouth moving from "Yay" to "Iiiironically, one of the embryos used to fix you would have grown up to be a doctor who discovered a cure that didn't need to destroy embryos." Cleverly, the visual and acoustic medium captures and embodies *physically* the very mindset Colbert's character appears to contradict *intellectually*. The episode displays indirectly how to reason through contrary "takes"—in the sense of both a framing that takes an argument in one direction and a visual take, shot from a particular camera angle.

With a circular return, the exchange closes with red-tied Colbert lamenting, "God, I hate having ethics," and blue-tied Colbert replying, "Well, maybe someday science will discover a cure for it." So impatient is Colbert with the complexity of reasoning that he concludes debating ethics is itself akin to a sickness, for which he seeks relief.

Throughout the show, Colbert demonstrates how, ironically, we create greater pain for ourselves in the long run if we avoid the

---

[26] Episode 2093, originally aired July 25th, 2006.

milder pain of critical thinking in the short run. To live comfortably with the challenges of complexity is a task neither easily said nor done. Yet it's what we need in order to manage the demands of life realistically and thoughtfully.[27]

[27] For their detailed commentary, encouragement, and laughter, I want to thank my friends Chris Worsley of Montréal and Leslie Ortquist-Ahrens of Otterbein College. And for his support of my research agenda in teaching and learning, my deepest thanks go to my supervisor, colleague and friend Larry Miners of Fairfield University.

4
Philosophy at Play

RACHAEL SOTOS

Alfred North Whitehead (1861–1947) said that the history of philosophy is a series of footnotes to Plato. And now we may add Stephen Colbert to the long list of Plato-footnoters.

This isn't because Stephen Colbert—either the character or the man—has written treatises explicating Plato's theory of the immortal forms (the Ideas), but rather because Colbert's TV show *performs* philosophy four nights a week. The *Colbert Report* doesn't merely entertain, but by engaging our intellectual and emotional faculties in fun, it *plays* with us in a spirit that Plato and his primary character, Socrates, would recognize and approve.

Not only did Plato theorize the immortal ideas, write philosophical dialogues, and sketch the numerous puzzles which have kept professional thinkers occupied for millennia; *he was also a great proponent of play*. Indeed Plato considered a *playful* attitude an essential feature of the philosophical quest for truth, and playful activities essential to the human capacity to be free in any truly worthwhile sense. To take one of many examples, in Plato's dialogue, *The Laws*, he invites his readers to conceive of life itself as a kind of play and, "to imagine that each of us living creatures is a puppet made by the gods, possibly as a mere plaything, or possibly with some more serious purpose" (*Laws*, line 644d).

But perhaps the claim that we're *playthings* of higher powers appears contrary to human freedom and responsibility? The puppet metaphor isn't intended to wish away responsibility, but rather, by revealing the "cords or strings by which we are worked," the philosopher teaches us how to be free. Plato invites us to imagine that within each "puppet" there are competing counselors and con-

51

flicting expectations; individuals are variously pulled toward "pleasure" and away from "pain;" diversely directed by "hope" and
"courage," but also by "fear." Some of the strings are "hard and brittle," but some are "soft," such as the "golden" cord pulling us
toward what is truly lawful and just (the common good). By learning to dance in harmony with the latter golden cord we exercise
our own judgment in a manner which is "gentle and free from violence" (lines 644–645a). In short, we learn how to be truly free.

It's in such a *playful* Platonic spirit that *The Colbert Report* performs philosophy: by engaging our preconceptions of what is to be
hoped for and feared, the just and the true, virtue and sin, it reveals
the extent to which we are determined and the conditions in which
we might best thrive and grow. Stephen Colbert, the quintessential
plaything of higher (and often lower) powers, entertains us and
simultaneously teaches us to be free.

Play and Seriousness

Few philosophers blur the line between play and seriousness like
Plato. In his writings on both politics and ethics, Aristotle (384–322
B.C.), Plato's own student, stands with "seriousness" against "mere
play." In contrast to Plato's divine playthings, Aristotle offers the
model of "the serious man," the "*spoudaios*." Translators often mis-
takenly render the term with "the good man," but this does not capture Aristotle's emphasis, the authority conveyed in the Greek verb
spoudadzo: to be busy, serious, earnest, grave. As Eric Voegelin, an
acute philosophical commentator, remarks: "It would perhaps be
better to speak of the serious, or weighty man; or, in order to
oppose him to the 'young man' who is unfit for ethical debate, one
might call the *spoudaios* the mature man, or the man who has
attained full human stature."[1]

Aristotle details the perfect specimen of seriousness in his
account of the "magnanimous" or "great-souled man," "the *mega-
lopsychos*." Such a serious, weighty man is one who "walks slowly
and speaks in a deep voice."[2] Such a "perfect," "mature" man certainly need not imagine himself a puppet, for he is one conveyed
by his own weight; he is *serious*, with all the dignified virtues the

---

[1] Eric Voegelin, *Order and History III: Plato and Aristotle* (Louisiana State
University Press, 1957), p. 300.

[2] *Nicomachean Ethics*, 1124b20.

Romans will later name "*gravitas.*" Above all, "the serious man" does not question which "cords" might be compelling him externally or internally; rather, he himself is "the measure" of all virtue. According to Aristotle, not only may "the serious man" *immediately* trust his own likes and dislikes as inherently virtuous, but we should deem his preferences as inherently excellent and take them as the "canon and measure" of our own conduct.[3]

Viewers of *The Colbert Report* instantly see a critique of Aristotle's "serious man." Colbert claims, after all, to be *himself* the "canon and measure" of all virtue: *I Am America, (And So Can You!)*. Colbert's audience thus has a preliminary conception of Plato and Aristotle's very different approaches, specifically as Aristotle's quest for seriousness reflects a less radical conception of philosophy. Whereas Plato is typically intent *to critique* pompous claims of seriousness and omniscient perfection (whether made by politicians or sophist-philosopher types), Aristotle is typically intent *to legitimate* authority.

Stephen Colbert's satire of the "character-driven" news has much in common with the parodies of the sophists found in Plato, particularly in the early Socratic dialogues, which are always critical of claims to authority. In the dialogue *Protagoras*, the famed sophist who claims to know and teach all virtue, appears as a "serious man" among a party of obsequious disciples, men "enchanted" by his weighty pontificating, holding forth with a "voice like Orpheus."[4] Likewise in the same dialogue, the words of the sophist Prodicus are not intelligible, but "owing to the depth of his voice the room was filled with a booming sound."[5] So viewers of *The Report* witness Colbert without a hair out of place, bearing all the external marks of seriousness, "walking tall and speaking in a deep tone of voice." Colbert no less than Protagoras, Prodicus and Aristotle, claims to himself be "the canon and measure," offering to all his "Tip of the Hat, Wag of the Finger."

Politics, Play, and the End of Life

Aristotle's veneration of "the serious man" hearkens back to the authority claimed by politicians and sophists in the *polis,* the clas-

---

[3] *Nicomachean Ethics*, 1113a29–35.

[4] *Protagoras* 315a.

[5] *Protagoras* 315e–316a.

sical Greek city-state. His arguments are echoed by numerous philosophical voices throughout later history, but in many respects the traditional Aristotelian prejudices against play go against the institutions and traditions of ancient Greek culture. The Greeks not only gave us philosophy and democracy, but the Olympics and the dramatic contests which produced comedy and tragedy. Some have suggested that, "the whole of life was play for the Greeks!"[6]

To appreciate the political significance of play and playfulness among the ancient Greeks (as well as the connection between play and the origin of western philosophy), we should keep in mind that the Greek word for education, "*paideia,*" is rooted in the words for child and play: "*pais*" and "*paidia.*" Along these lines we might also think of the Greek philosopher Heraclitus (around 535–475 B.C.), who, more than a century before Aristotle, considered playfulness to be essential to the nature of reality itself: "time [eternity, history or an individual lifetime] is a child at play; that child is the legitimate authority in the world."[7] Given such reverence for play and playfulness, it's not surprising that Heraclitus is also believed to have said, "A man is most himself when he achieves the seriousness of a child at play."

For Aristotle however, there is no possibility of confusing authority and playfulness or play with the "leisure," "*skhole,*" of "the serious man." The serious, mature man engages in pleasurable leisured activities such as philosophizing, but these are *not* children's activities, for "a thing that is an end does not belong to anything that is imperfect."[8] Play, Aristotle explains, is not "the end of life," but merely necessary for rest and relaxation: "for a man who is at work needs rest and rest is the object of play." Play is a kind of "medicine," "a relaxation of the soul."[9] Moreover, as Aristotle conceives play as "relaxation," he insists that play *is not essentially connected to learning.* Play is not even the object of learning for the young: "we do not learn through playing, for learning is with

---

[6] Johan Huizinga, *Homo Ludens: A Study of the Play Element in Culture* (Beacon Press, 1955), p.30.

[7] DK B52.

[8] *Politics*, 1339a.

[9] *Politics*, 1337b35. In the words of the political theorist Hannah Arendt, thinking in an Aristotelian spirit, "Entertainment, like labor and sleep, is irrevocably part of the biological life process." Hannah Arendt, "The Crisis in Culture," in *Between Past and Future* (Penguin, 1961), p. 205.

pain."[10] According to Aristotle's own logic, if intellectual pursuits were tied to play, "play would necessarily be the end of life."

But in several significant ways *The Report* proves the greater wisdom of Heraclitus and Plato over Aristotle, and by so performing philosophy, gives us a better indication of "the end of life." When we watch *The Report* our entertainment transcends play as relaxing medicinal rest; we are swept up in the intensity of a play in which we feel most alive and, as Heraclitus says, are "most ourselves."

Athletes, sports-fans, game-players and spectators of all sorts have great fun and experience delightful intensity, but few play activities compare with the vital suspension of disbelief Colbert inspires. For Aristotle and his ilk to disparage play as a biological need, such as sleep or rest, is certainly to underestimate the work of the imagination ignited in dreams and childhood play. Adults no less than children need to stretch their imaginations in play. We in the "Colbert Nation" conveyed to "the Eagle's Nest" four nights a week do not merely rest, but rather exercise our "fun muscles." Our best and most engaging playmate, Stephen Colbert, is our trainer and coach. He gives us an invaluable workout: the reminiscence of childhood spontaneity and creativity.

If we have any doubts about the significance of this exercise in fun, and whether play gives us an indication of the "end of life," we might consider that while play is present in all higher animals (yes of course, cats and dogs and even fish, play), play is likely at the root of all human achievement. In the words of the philosopher Kurt Riezler:

> Man's playing is his greatest victory over his dependence and finiteness, his servitude to things. Not only can he conquer his environment and force conditions to comply with his needs and demands far beyond the power of any other animal. He can also play, i.e. detach himself from things and their demands and replace the world of given conditions with a playworld of his own mood, set himself rules and goals and thus defy the world of blind necessities, meaningless things, and stupid demands. Religious rites, festivities, social codes, language, music, art—even science—all contain at least an element of play. You can almost say that culture is play.[11]

---

[10] *Politics*, 1339a.
[11] Kurt Riezler, "Play and Seriousness," *Journal of Philosophy* 38:19 (1941), p. 513.

There's another, specifically political sense in which *The Report* proves Heraclitus's and Plato's wisdom. We're not only amused by Colbert, we feel as if we *know him*, even as we are aware that *the man* Stephen Colbert—the father and Sunday-school teacher—is far from the character Stephen, the simple-minded apple-pie fascist who delights us. And it's because we feel that we *know* Stephen in his playful persona that the absurdist bits such as "Better Know a District," "Better Know a Lobby," and "Better Know a Governor," are relevant to our political culture. The key to the coveted "Colbert Bump" is in the performance (for better or worse) a politician is able to muster in the presence of our favorite divine puppet. Only if one can withstand Colbert's ridiculous questioning, ideally with grace and aplomb, can he or she have a claim to seriousness, *gravitas*.

Not everyone would view Colbert's revelation of character through absurdist play so generously. For Aristotle and others who disparage "mere play," it's very difficult to conceive play in politically relevant terms because, they say, there's a fundamental difference between genuinely edifying artworks and "mere entertainment." At an extreme of the opposition between so-called "high" and "low" culture, we have the entertainment provided by the Roman Emperors in order to appease and distract a disenfranchised Roman populace: "bread and circuses," *"panis et circenses."* Politically speaking, such entertainment, like fresh bread, satisfies the base needs of "hungry people," but it does not educate or empower an informed citizenry. Rather, such "mere entertainment" is precisely intended to distract them from engaging in the necessary, serious business of politics.[12]

But the *Report* does not merely divert. Rather, by transporting "the Nation" to a realm where claims of seriousness can be interrogated, it serves essential political functions. It might seem sheer nonsense that we play at worrying about "People Destroying America," or that we learn on a weekly basis about "The Number One Threat Facing America: BEARS!" But in a corporate-media-saturated political culture where the politics of fear are manipulated both by politicians and those intent to raise ratings alike, these bits are revelatory. Colbert teaches us freedom by disclosing the sources of manipulation, reminding us of the fact that we are being

---

[12] The coinage "bread and circuses" originates with the Roman satirist Juvenal. See Arendt, "The Crisis in Culture," p. 206.

played but need not be. To follow the metaphor of the Platonic puppet, we might say that by continually parodying seriousness, Colbert loosens some of the hard, brittle cords so that we may better dance with the golden thread pulling toward virtue.

Sin, Play, and the "Synagogues of Satan"

Unlike Heraclitus and Plato, Aristotle didn't think highly of play, deeming it primarily for rest and relaxation. In later centuries, Aristotle's preference for "the serious" was taken up by Christian theologians, Catholic and Protestant alike. At the gloomy extreme are thinkers generally hostile to play (a.k.a. pagan festivity). In the much cited words of the early Christian John of Chrysostom: "It is not God, but the devil, who is the author of fun."[13]

More gently, in the late Middle Ages Thomas Aquinas (1225–1274) found a wholesome dimension in the pervasive play of the medieval period (when somewhere near a third of the days of the year were reserved for festival). In his monumental *Summa Theologica*, the "angelic doctor" judiciously determines that, while we would not want to confuse serious virtue with play, because play facilitates "friendly human interaction", "*eutrapelia,*" there is sin in "a lack of play."[14] Aquinas here follows Aristotle's slight qualification of the "serious man" (for one must have a few friends for pleasure). Nevertheless, Aquinas assures the reader that faith takes the path of seriousness and that play is directed toward rest and relaxation.

Three centuries later, in *The Praise of Folly*, the Renaissance hero Erasmus (1466–1536) takes Aquinas's tentative affirmation of play to another level, essentially inverting the traditional hierarchy of seriousness over mere play. Striking a pose remarkably similar to Colbert's "well-intentioned, poorly informed, high-status idiot,"[15] Erasmus, the quintessential court jester speaking truth to power

---

[13] Cited in Thomas Aquinas, *Summa Theologica Second and Revised Edition,*. Second Part of the Second Part; Question 168, Article 2, "Can There Be a Virtue about Playful Actions?", online edition: www.newadvent.org/summa/3168.htm, accessed on September 22nd, 2008.

[14] *Summa Theologica*, Question 168, Article 4, "The Sin Existing in a Lack of Play."

[15] This is Colbert's self-description in his interview with Deborah Soloman, "Funny about the News," (*New York Times Magazine*, September 25th, 2005).

(both secular and ecclesiastical), speaks in the voice of the goddess Folly (Silliness, Stupidity, Foolishness). Herself an illegitimate "play-child," raised by Drunkenness and Ignorance, companion of Self-love, Laziness, Pleasure, Flattery, Madness, and Forgetfulness, Folly disparages book-learning and ignores traditional Christian worry about sin. Like the fool Stephen Colbert, who deems himself a divine gift, Folly boastfully sings her own praises: "The nature of all things is such, that the more of Folly they have, the more they conduce to Humane Life, which if it were not pleasant, would not be worth living!"[16]

Inverting the traditional opposition between seriousness and play, Erasmus offers critique, but also thoughts about virtue—even the virtues of faith and piety. From the standpoint of the ridiculousness of human behavior, history appears in a bright, often harsh light. In the pose of the unreasoning fool, Folly artfully indicts the Catholic Church and its officials for dogma, superstition, hypocrisy, and corruption. She is no less scathing when it comes to the greed, belligerence, and incompetence of kings, princes, courtiers, and merchants. What readers of Erasmus and viewers of Colbert must keep in mind, however, is that there is a substantive analysis of virtue as well as a negative critique. Erasmus not only concurs with Aquinas's claim that play and fun are necessary to "friendly human intercourse," he finds a harmony between a simpler, purer form of Christianity and the wisdom of the fool. God, we may trust, is on the side of play, for Jesus, "ever abhors and condemns those wise men, as such they put confidence in their own wisdom." Indeed, *Christ saves as he plays*:

> And yet Christ himself, that he might better relieve this Folly, being the wisdom of the Father, yet in some manner became a fool, when taking upon him the nature of man, he was found in shape as a man; as in like manner he was made Sin, that he might heal sinners (p. 174)

If we're to understand how it is that Colbert performs philosophy and simultaneously teaches us to be free, it's helpful to place his foolish persona in the scenery of the particular religiosity and authoritarianism of American political culture. Doing so will help us keep in mind the extent to which we have a *need* for play.

---

[16] *Praise of Folly*, p. 35.

Recall the first grim colonists in New England. Men of the Protestant Reformation, the Pilgrims were intent to revolutionize the world. Inspired as Luther originally was by Erasmus's radical critique of Church institutions, they were however deeply suspicious of the *playfulness* of the Renaissance. For those worried about sinful propensities and intent to build "a City on a Hill," the idea that we might think of ourselves as "playthings" of the divine was anathema: much safer that spontaneity and idiosyncratic proclivities be channeled into "God's plan," better that punishment for sin be meted out according to the letter of the Bible.

Trusting Aristotle's seriousness more than Erasmus's reanimation of the Platonic puppet, the Puritans allowed for certain, regulated "Sober Mirth" necessary to recuperate from hard work, but remained deeply skeptical of playfulness itself.[17] Theaters were banned as dens of depravity, "Synagogues of Satan," the sites of all forms of depravity: idleness, effeminacy, adultery, gluttony, "temptation to whoredom and adultery," "inducements to sodomy."[18] As a Philadelphia minister explained as late as 1840, because human nature is "depraved," it must not be the subject of theatrical presentation, which would inevitably make it "attractive" (pp. 346–47). Sinners might be allowed "Sober Mirth," but certainly no mocking of the divine, ridicule of legitimate authority, or subversive pagan festivity!

The Colbert Report makes a timely intervention in the contemporary "culture wars" on the side of the Renaissance and play, on the side of "the Synagogues of Satan." Of course, in many respects we Americans are distantly removed from the original gloomy inhabitants of the Northern parts. And yet the original Puritan founding continues to haunt American culture, leading not a few observers to suggest that Americans suffer from a kind of play deficit.

As Daniels puts it,

Many people, particularly foreigners, feel that Americans do not know how to play properly. According to this view the seeming hedonism of Americans camouflages their true inability to relax. Coexisting with

---

[17] Bruce C. Daniels, *Puritans at Play: Leisure and Recreation in Colonial New England* (St. Martin's Press, 1995).

[18] Edmund S. Morgan "Puritan Hostility to the Theater," *Proceedings of the American Philosophical Society* 110:5 (1966), p. 342.

the American values of freedom of expression and behavior are deeper
feelings that bespeak a repressive, censorious morality. . . . Americans
work too hard at play, a sure sign that they are not too good at it. They
take their leisure and their recreation just as they take their role in the
world—too seriously. (*Puritans at Play*, p. xi)

Not only do we work ourselves to death relative to our European
counterparts, but we are the most fundamentalist of modern indus-
trialized nations. Our ideal of an embracing unity (*E Pluribus
Unum*, "One out of Many") is continually punctuated by spasms of
hypocritical moralism and racial intolerance. Americans are free,
but many feel that "others" threaten the necessary, hierarchical
order of "God's plan," be they women, workers, minorities, homosexuals, hippies and all the others who are, as Colbert would put
it, "hurting America."

Colbert never fails to offer a caricature of a narrow-minded
American suffering from a Puritanical hangover (or some such
equivalent fundamentalist Catholic ailment), appearing always as
the emblem of ultra-orthodox, unthinking obedience. At the famed
2006 White House Correspondents' Association Dinner Colbert was
characteristically intolerant; he welcomed guests of various faiths—
Hindu, Jewish, Muslim, generously affirming "infinite paths to
accepting Jesus Christ as your personal savior.[19] A Catholic of the
Counter-Reformation rather than the Renaissance, the character
Stephen Colbert is ever firm in his faith in dogma for its own sake,
proclaiming his preference for Ratzinger before he became Pope
Benedict XVI, when he was still "John Paul's rotweiller."[20]

What is most remarkable is not simply that Colbert affirms law
and order over flexibility, play and independent thought. Rather it's
the zeal with which he *plays* at the contemporary culture wars, the
absolute delight he takes opposing "The War on Christmas," "The
War on Easter," and all other things threatened by "Big Secularism"
(*I Am America*, p. 62). Or to be more precise: because Colbert
plays so well at the puritan/fundamentalist vice of "hating sin more
than loving the good," *he proves the importance of play to political
culture.*

---

[19] The text of Colbert's speech is conveniently located at the end of *I Am
America*, pp. 218–227.

[20] Episode 2148, originally aired November 28th, 2006. The WØRD of the night
was "Ecu-Menace."

Because Colbert is *playing* rather than actually fighting, the humanity underlying both sides of conflict is affirmed. In a sense (surely lost on Bill O'Reilly), Colbert's character is the best friend the blustering pundits on Fox News could have; he reveals their folly, but in a way that is not hateful. Colbert appears a "well-intentioned . . . idiot," but surely not one deserving of hellfire. Even as he spews *faux* ill-will, we in the "Nation" love Colbert and are thus humanized. In playing we overcome our sinful lack of friendliness and learn to love the good more than we hate sin.

In this sense the *Report* proves Erasmus's radical claim that there's virtue in play itself. We might even say that Colbert "saves" in a manner similar to that of Erasmus's Christ. Neither literally "takes away" our sin, but rather, by playing at sin, the character Colbert embodies a fallen nature and helps us to identify our own shortcomings. Playing at sin he demonstrates the all too human preference for one's own self and the all too common confusion of one's own particularity with wider universality and/or the common good.

When Colbert's character undertakes a beneficent project of eugenics, boldly promoting the sale of his own "man-seed," it is so ridiculous it is impossible to hate him. When he claims "not to see race" and simultaneously boasts about his one "black friend," the "Nation" pauses to mark the unwarranted self-congratulations offered to a country many of whose citizens are incapable of empathizing with or even perceiving a reality impacting millions.[21] Perhaps the example which best captures the psychological, political, and philosophical implications of Colbert's characteristic embodiment of the sin of self-related myopia occurred on February 1st, 2007, when Colbert worried out loud that he might be attracted to Ellen DeGeneres's dancing at the Oscars.[22] He inspired the "Nation" to investigate and report on Wikiality, the online "truthiness" encyclopedia, regarding the "scientific phenomenon" of the "The Ellen DeGeneres Parodox": "the confused state arising when a heterosexual man (with repressed homosexual tendencies) feels attracted to a lesbian, but only when she dances"[23] With a brilliant riff on Heisenberg's Uncertainty Principle, the Wikiality

---

[21] For more on race in the *Report*, see Chapter 14 in this volume.

[22] Episode 3016, originally aired February 1st, 2007.

[23] Wikiality.com: The Truthiness Encyclopedia. (http://www.wikiality.com/) Retrieved on June 11th, 2008.

entry characteristically engages the subjectivity of truth in a manner that speaks to the dangers of fundamentalist prejudice. As observation itself necessary alters our perception of phenomena, it is difficult to make precise calculation of one's location on the "gaydar spectrum" ("delusions of gaydeur" or "ubergay"?). This is certainly true and a politically relevant and psychologically astute intervention into the culture wars in the spirit of Erasmus's humanism. It reminds us that we need not give our freedom up to a fixed system or dogmatic moralistic ideology. We can respect truth and virtue by maintaining a playful relation to reality. From the Platonic perspective of this chapter, we might see Colbert's wistful attraction for dancing Ellen DeGeneres as the charming confession of a puppet wishing to cut the strings of Aristotelian seriousness, wishing to dance with virtue, but playfully resisting the gentle pull of the "golden cord."[1]

---

[24] I would like to thank my closest family, Charles Bancroft, Penelope Blum, and Randall Moore, who each, from their very unique but wise perspectives, shared my questions and helped to shape my thoughts on play in 2008.

5

No Need for the Wordinistas at Webster's

JASON SOUTHWORTH

The character played by Stephen Colbert on the *Colbert Report*, also known as Stephen Colbert, often says things that are confusing. I'm referring not to negative things the character says about Democrats, which are often confusing because they're false, nor am I referring to positions he holds which seem to be evidence that he is not rational (like his denial of there being such a thing as truth). Rather, the confusion to which I'm referring is even more fundamental. At times, Colbert uses words or combinations of words that are hard to understand. Sometimes this confusion stems from his having just coined a new word, such as "super-stantial" or "wordanista." Sometimes the confusion stems from the obvious literal falsehood of his claims, or an inappropriate grammatical structure, like in the case of "I am America (and So Can You!)" And yet, in spite of this surface confusion, we can still come to understand what Colbert means when he makes one of these utterances.

The Meaningness of Terms

When doing philosophy, it's always important to get clear on our terms before we start throwing them around. While it might seem strange, the first term that we need to define is *meaning*. In our everyday talk, *meaning* is often confused with something philosophers of language call *reference*. Words refer to things, and we call those things 'referents'. The referent of a word is the thing in the world which a word picks out. For instance, *The Colbert Report* refers to the television show that Stephen Colbert hosts.

Often, the referent of a word depends on the situation in which the word is used. So, in an ordinary sentence like "I left the book on the table," referents for "I," "book," and "table" will depend on who said that they left a book on the table and exactly which book and table they are talking about. When we give the meaning of something, however, we give a detailed description of what that thing is. So, what I *mean* when I use the word "table" is "a piece of furniture with a large flat surface held up by one or more supports." When I use this word in a sentence like "that table has a broken leg," the *referent* is the specific table that I am indicating with the "that," but the *meaning* of this sentence is something like, "there is a specific piece of furniture that has a large flat surface that is held up by at least one support, and one of those supports is not functioning properly."

The concept of meaning is often complicated further by making a distinction between literal and non-literal meaning. The literal meaning of what someone says is simply the ordinary meaning of the sentence. The way Colbert might put this is that the literal meaning of a word or sentence is the meaning that the wordinistas at Webster's want you to believe. The meaning I gave above for "that table has a broken leg" is the literal meaning. Non-literal meaning, as you might have guessed, is when the meaning of a sentence is something other than the literal meaning. Non-literal meanings come in various types. Hyperbole and metaphor are two common types of sentences that have non-literal meanings. If Mrs. Colbert says to Stephen, "you are the cream in my coffee," what she has said is literally false. But there is a separate metaphorical meaning which probably is true. She's saying that Stephen goes well with her, or complements her nicely.

Senseness and Nonsenseness

Before I explain how it is that we come to understand what Colbert means when he makes his confusing utterances, I will say something to those who don't believe that these utterances mean anything at all. The way this objection would be phrased is that the reason we're confused about the sentence "I am America (and So Can You!)," is because, while it looks like an English sentence, its ungrammatical form makes it no better than a series of unrelated words strung together ("He banana place or," for example)—in other words, nonsense. The same will hold for newly coined words. We are confused about what "trustigious" means because it doesn't mean anything, since it isn't actually a word.

The answer to this objection can be found in a modified version of an argument made by Bertrand Russell (1872–1970), one of the most influential philosophers of the twentieth century. In *The Philosophy of Logical Atomism*,[1] Russell argues that names are actually abbreviated definite descriptions. What this means is that names have certain meanings, and these meanings are descriptions of the individual to whom the name refers. In support of this view, Russell gives an argument that has come to be known as the "spot check test."[2]

The way that the spot check test works is that when someone utters a sentence with a person's name in it, like, "Stephen Colbert is a very deep thinker," we can sensibly ask the question "Who is it that you're talking about?" and the response we will get will be a description of the individual that sets him apart from all other people. So, in the case of Stephen Colbert, the type of answer we might get is, "The guy who used to play a character in *Strangers with Candy* and who's now the host of *The Colbert Report*."

Our argument against the people who think Colbert's confusing words and sentences are nonsense or meaningless will take a similar form to the spot check test. Given one of these words or sentences, it seems that we can sensibly ask a question similar to Russell's "Who are you talking about?" The question would be, "What do you mean by that?" or, to a third party, "What does he mean by that?" These questions also seem to be easily answerable. If asked, "What does he mean by 'I am America (and So Can You!)'?" most people will not deny that there is meaning—they will attempt to give a paraphrase of the sentence. One such paraphrase might be, "I represent the values of America, and it is the case that you can represent these values also." If something can be paraphrased, then it must have a meaning. Thus we can safely set aside the objection that these sentences and words are meaningless. We may now set to the task of figuring out how it is we are able to arrange these paraphrases.

---

[1] This work was originally published as articles in 1918 and 1924, and as a book in 1972. I'm using the Open Court edition of 1985.

[2] William Lycan is the first person to refer to the test as the "spot check test," and he does so in *Philosophy of Language: a Contemporary Introduction*. The most recent edition of the book was published in 2008, and anyone interested in philosophy of language should own a copy.

Paul Grice's Implicature

I have made some claims about what Colbert might have meant by his sentence "I am America (and So Can You!)" To do this, I had to do some reasoning about what Colbert must have meant by the utterance, since literally it is false. The process of reasoning that I was using is a process that the philosopher Paul Grice (1913–1988) spent much of his career attempting to make clear. Grice made a distinction between *what is said* and *what is implied*. According to this distinction, what is said is the literal meaning of the sentence, and what is implied is some thing other than the literal meaning that the speaker intends for you to understand. Grice argued that, in linguistic exchanges, we adhere to, or at least we ought to adhere to, what he called the cooperation principle. The cooperation principle is actually a shorthand term for eight maxims he identified for the successful transference of information. These maxims are:

1. **Make your contribution to a conversation as informative as is required (for the current purposes of the exchange).**

2. **Do not make your contribution more informative than is required.**

3. **Do not say what you believe to be false.**

4. **Do not say that for which you lack adequate evidence.**

5. **Be relevant.**

6. **Avoid ambiguity.**

7. **Be brief.**

8. **Be orderly.**[3]

Grice argues that all we need to determine what's implied by an utterance are these maxims and an understanding of the context in which the utterance is made. Grice says very little about what features make up a context, but other more contemporary philoso-

---

[3] These maxims are regularly employed by Grice, but made their first appearance in his "Logic and Conversation" (1975) which has often been reprinted. The copy I am using can be found in *Studies in the Way of Words* published in 1989 by Harvard University Press.

phers, myself included, have spent quite a bit of time trying to spell this out. Rather than spend a lot of time going over the debate about what does and does not count as an element of context, I will identify some non-controversial elements.

The features that make up context that everyone agrees on are: the conversation in which the sentence takes place, the setting in which the conversation takes place, and any information that the individuals involved share from past experiences or culture.[4]

Think back to when Colbert was just a correspondent for *The Daily Show,* and he was giving updates from the campaign trail (with a still photo of a campaign rally on the green screen behind him). The context of this conversation would have been that it was taking place on *The Daily Show,* that Colbert and Jon Stewart had had previous conversations about the fake news, that Colbert was "at a political rally," whatever had already been said in the conversation, and all the background information that an average viewer might be expected to know.

With these maxims and an understanding of context in hand, we can now make sense of utterances that at first pass seem to make no sense. Before we take a look at some of Stephen Colbert's utterances, let's consider a much simpler example. Imagine that I speak the sentence, "There's the door," to a person in my home, let's call her Ruth. I say it because I want Ruth to leave. She has just told me that she will not be able to pay me back the fifty dollars she owes me and I am upset. After I make the utterance, Ruth will reason in something like the following way:

> The door? That has nothing to do with the fifty bucks I owe him. Well, since he made the utterance within the context of this conversation, it has to be relevant in some way, and this has to be in a way that the speaker knows I can figure out, otherwise he wouldn't have said it. So, why would he point out the door? Well that is where I came into the house, and that is where I will leave when we are done. Oh, I see, he wants me to leave the house.

Notice how important context is in drawing this conclusion. For one thing, Ruth has to recognize that doors are used to leave

---

[4] Two good books that will help you get a handle on linguistic context are *Contextualism in Philosophy: Knowledge, Meaning and Truth,* by Gerhard Preyer, (Oxford University Press, 2005), and *Vagueness in Context* by Stewart Shapiro (Oxford University Press, 2008).

houses in order to draw the inference that I currently want her to leave mine.

Grice does not claim that we have all the thoughts I just mentioned above in real time. These are just the logical steps that lead to a correct conclusion about the meaning implied by the conversation—its implicature. If Ruth actually had each of those independent thoughts as I laid them out above, it would take an uncomfortably long time for her to come to the correct conclusion. Instead, as we have reasoned in similar ways in the past and since childhood, our minds are able to make the inferences required quickly and easily. This is also why we're often able to give a paraphrase to an utterance (like I did above) quickly and easily, but if asked to explain how we arrived at it, we'd have to work at it a bit.

Colbert Examplality

Now we can consider some of Colbert's utterances. Let's start with a fairly simple one. In the first episode of *The Colbert Report*, our faithful anchor said the following:

> That's where the truth comes from, ladies and gentlemen—the gut. Do you know you have more nerve endings in your gut than you have in your head? Look it up. Now, somebody is going to say, "I did look that up and it's wrong." Well, Mister, that's because you looked it up in a book. Next time try looking it up in your gut. I did and my gut tells me that's how our nervous system works.[5]

When we hear Colbert make this statement, as with the example of "There's the door," we know what he means. But how? Using Grice's process, we know that he can't literally mean that we look things up in our gut, because that is obviously false, and as a result violates Maxim 3. (Do not say what you believe to be false). So what does he mean? Well, he's talking about how we come to hold certain things as true. One way some people hold that something is true (although this is not a way endorsed by many philosophers) is through an intuitive feeling or belief that it is true, and it is a feature of our culture that this is often expressed as a feeling in one's gut. So, we are able to conclude that what Colbert means is that the way he identifies something as true is based on whether or not he

---

[5] Episode 1001, originally aired October 17th, 2005.

feels that it is true in this physical, almost visceral way. For those that have some history with Colbert, we also know that Colbert thinks his feelings about reality are of are more importance than any facts that could be brought up (he often makes disparaging comments about the "factinistas," another new Colbert word).

We are now at the point where we can explain how we come to understand what the sentence, "What is it with you wordinistas telling me what is and what isn't a word?" means. What's interesting about this sentence is that it introduces an original Colbert word. The sentence itself provides some context for figuring out what a wordinista is. From the context, it is clear that one thing a wordinista does is tell people what is and is not a word. This isn't enough to capture the whole meaning of the term, however. The "What is with it with you" prior to the term also implies that the word is meant to have a negative connotation, as "what is it with you" normally precedes a negative term.

We're not done, however. The "inista" part of the word should make most people immediately think of the word "Sandinista." Some people are no doubt thinking: What does this word have to do with the Clash? But everyone else will recall that the Sandinistas are a radical Marxist political party from Nicaragua. So, it seems "wordinista" is also intended to suggest a radical disposition. Putting these things together, a "wordinista" is a person who is radical about correcting others about their misuse of words and their use of non-established words.

Let's move on to an example I used earlier, "I am America (and So Can You!)" There are reasons why Colbert could not actually mean this sentence literally. First, he is not literally the country, and second the "can" makes the sentence ungrammatical. With an example this complicated, it will help to deal with these problems separately. The first seems pretty straightforward. "I am America," if taken literally, violates Maxim 3 (Do not say what you believe to be false) because it is false. So, we should reason that he is implying something true. The context in which this sentence appears is as the title of Colbert's book about various social issues that play an important role in American politics (homosexuality and families, for instance). Given that, the title must also be relevant, in order to conform to Maxim 6 (avoid ambiguity). The most obvious way that this part of the utterance can be relevant and true would be if it is a metaphor. What this metaphor means is something like I said above, that Stephen Colbert exemplifies American values.

The second part of this sentence now seems to be less of a problem. If what "I am America," means is this, then the "(and So Can You!)" would follow grammatically in the paraphrased sentence "I represent the values of America and so can you."

Implicature and Humorosity

Violating the Maxims often helps to explain why some utterances are funny. When Colbert had Representative John Yarmuth on the *Report* for an interview, Colbert opened by saying: "Tonight's subject: Throwing kittens in a woodchipper. I'm against it, I think it's wrong. John, tear me a new one."[6]

This violates Maxims 4 (Do not say that which you lack adequate evidence for) and 5 (Be relevant). Saying "John, tear me a new one," implies that Representative Yarmuth is in support of throwing kittens in a woodchipper, something for which there is no evidence. Additionally, the comment isn't relevent. The forum in which it is given is an interview with a politician on a political show, so unless the Representative has a public position on killing kittens, or this issue is topical (neither of which were the case), it's the wrong place for the comment.

Original Wordality

There are other new words that have appeared in the *Colbert Report* for which it's even more difficult to determine meanings. These are the words that appear next to Colbert at the start of the show. It's more difficult to determine meanings for these words because they are removed from both a sentence and a conversation, and thus contain very little context. All we have to go on in determining what they mean is that the words refer in some way either to Colbert or the *Colbert Report,* and any features of the shared history that we have with Stephen Colbert to which the component parts or roots of the words allude. As you will recall, we used these cultural connections when we figured out what "wordanista" meant, but now that will be all we have to go on (as we don't have a full sentence from which to piece together meaning). Some examples of these words are "Lincolnish," "superstantial," "megamerican," "grippy," and "freem."

---

[6] Episode 3032, originally aired March 8th, 2007.

Of these examples I have just given, "Lincolnish" seems to wear its meaning most clearly on its sleeve. While "Lincoln" is not an uncommon last name, there is only one Lincoln who is well known in the culture in which this term appears—the sixteenth President of the United States, Abraham Lincoln. The second part of this term, "ish," is common in English, the language used by Colbert when he's not making up new words. I say that it is his language when he's not making up new words, because it isn't clear that the new words are English. Certainly the new words are not in the lexicon yet, even though some or all of them may be integrated into the English language in the future.

As you, the reader of this article, know (because reading this article requires that you be fairly competent at understanding English), when "ish" is added to a noun, the new, composite word is used to refer to something other than an instance of the original noun which is similar to that noun in relevant ways. A common example is "sheepish." We say someone is sheepish when that person is a bit ashamed of what they are saying or doing, because we know in our gut that sheep are frequently a bit ashamed of what they're saying or doing. So, we can now be relatively sure that "Lincolnish" means "like Abraham Lincoln." The case of "megamerican" seems to work much like "Lincolnish." The word directs our attention to the existing words "mega" and "American," and we are able to easily conclude that what the word means is American to such an extreme degree that the biggest possible scale of measurement of American-ness has to be employed.

"Freem" is the new Colbert word which is most difficult to define. I can offer only conjecture about its meaning. The way this word sounds when you say it out loud, it appears to be an amalgam of the words "free" and "meme." So, it seems to me that "freem" means something like "freedom which spreads from individual to individual and situation to situation from mere contact." The way that this might refer to the *Colbert Report* is that the show writers are implying that the show is a freem, or that it contains freems, and that by watching the show, freedom will in some way be transferred to the viewers of the program. For a different (and therefore wrong) interpretation of "freem" see Chapter 16 in this volume.

That we have trouble trying to identify the meaning of these words should not be seen as a problem for this view of determining meaning, but rather as support for it. This is because, if a large part of what fixes the meaning of a sentence (and its parts) is the context it appears in, when we have very slim or incomplete contexts, we should expect there to be vagueness and doubt about the meanings of the words. To have a better idea about what "freem" means, we will have to wait for Colbert to actually use the word, and, in doing so, place it in a context.

Conclestions

You might now be thinking that I have only shown that, given that there are literal meanings of words, we can determine the meanings of the strange utterances of Stephen Colbert. If you think this, you're right. This doesn't mean that we need the wordinistas at Webster's, however, because the literal meaning of words does not have to come from them. If you recall, with all of the single-word examples that we have worked through, we have figured out the literal meanings without a dictionary. Many philosophers argue that we come to know the literal meanings of all words and sentences in a similar way. We hear new words or sentences used (preferably more than once) and we reason to the meaning based on the context or contexts in which they appear.[7]

So what now? Even though you now know there is no need for the wordinistas at Webster's, this should not end your contemplation of the subject, as there are several issues to consider which stem from this conclusion. First, the discussion of Colbert's "new words" should affect how we respond to those people we run into every day who we might call grammar Nazis, and who Colbert would call wordinistas. If "truthiness" and "freem" are legitimate words with legitimate meanings, is it right to tell others that there is no such phrase as "for all intensive purposes"?

---

[7] For any reader who wants to know more about how we establish meaning with nothing but context, here are some works I recommend that you read. W.V. Quine, in an article "Two Dogmas of Empiricism," and in a book, *Word and Object* (MIT Press, 1964), discusses how we might go about translating a language of which we have no knowledge at all. Donald Davidson later builds on this idea in "Radical Interpretation," found in *Inquiries into Truth and Interpretation* (Oxford University Press, 2001). If you're really dedicated you should read *Philosophical Investigations* by Ludwig Wittgenstein (Prentice Hall, 1958). Wittgenstein argues that the meanings of words are determined by how we use them, and that ultimately there can be no explicit definitions given for any word.

Another thing to think about is whether or not you're a responsible speaker. If you're not following Grice's Maxims, the answer is "no," and you now know why people have trouble understanding you at times.[8]

---

[8] I would like to thank Ruth Tallman for her helpful comments on this chapter.

The ThreatDown: Truthiness

6

Truth, Truthiness, and Bullshit for the American Voter

MATTHEW F. PIERLOTT

> Facts are stubborn things; and whatever may be our wishes, our inclinations, or the dictates of our passion, they cannot alter the state of facts and evidence.
>
> —John Adams
>
> Let's face it. John Adams is a sissy, and this kind of defeatist attitude weakens America.
>
> —Some guy in the room after Adams had left

On October 17th, 2005, the world was exposed to the first segment of "The WØRD" on *The Colbert Report*, and "truthiness" has been with us ever since. Undoubtedly, Colbert had the kind of bullshit we see daily in political discourse as his target when he coined this term (the word's pre-existence is irrelevant here, since it was not in common usage, and Colbert's usage has completely eclipsed the former meaning). But perhaps Colbert has confused a few different ideas, thinking bullshit and truthiness amount to much the same thing. I don't think they are the same. Furthermore, truthiness may not be as bad as it sounds.

As a satirist, Colbert's mocking of truthiness has a double edge. On the one hand, his comedy invites us to laugh at those who seem to fit the category he is parodying. If I ever hear someone say, "I don't need to check the references; I can tell you have a good heart," I will be reminded of how Colbert mocked Bush's nomination of Harriet Miers for Associate Justice of the U.S. Supreme Court in that first episode: "We are divided between those who think with their head and those who know with their heart."[1] But this association is the result of an appeal to ridicule; by mocking some person or idea, I am invited to dismiss that person or idea without critical reflection. On the other hand, satire is not merely a mode of ridicule in that it presupposes a level of critical thought. There's a big difference between the schoolyard bully who says "Shut up . . . you're ugly and stupid," and the sophisticated exposure of contradiction or absurdity achieved through satire. So satire may, in fact, invite us to reflect on the issues, and not merely take the satirist's side.

So why does Colbert expose truthiness as a dangerous concept? Out of character, he has said:

> We're not talking about truth, we're talking about something that seems like truth—the truth we want to exist.[2]

> Truthiness is tearing apart our country. . . . It used to be, everyone was entitled to their own opinion, but not their own facts. But that's not the case anymore. Facts matter not at all. Perception is everything. . . . Truthiness is "What I say is right, and [nothing] anyone else says could possibly be true." It's not only that I *feel* it to be true, but that *I* feel it to be true. There's not only an emotional quality, but there's a selfish quality.[3]

The first quote links truthiness to wishful thinking, or perhaps self-delusion: I believe it's true because I want it to be true. The second quote makes it clearer that I take something to be true with either a lack of evidence for it being true, or even in light of direct evidence of its falsity. I then become entrenched such that no one disagreeing with me could possibly be right.

But it's at this point that I think the way Colbert defines truthiness in character diverges significantly from how he defines it out of character. From here on, I'll refer to the out-of-character satirist as Colbert and the on-air character as Stephen to help keep us straight. First let's look at what Stephen has to say about truthiness. Stephen says truthiness is trusting in yourself (in your gut) and

---

[1] Episode 1001, originally aired October 17th, 2005.

[2] Adam Sternbergh, "Stephen Colbert Has America by the Ballots," *New York Magazine* (16th October, 2006).

[3] Nathan Rabin, "Interviews: Stephen Colbert," (January 26th, 2006) A.V. Club, The Onion, http://www.avclub.com/content/node/44705. Accessed 1st December, 2008.

trusting in people who've proven reliable (following the heart, or knowing their heart). Colbert, on the other hand, sees truthiness as an abandoning of truth and fact in preference for a self-indulgent ideology. The problem I see, however, is that anyone who buys into the truthiness as Stephen *defines* it is allegedly engaging in the truthiness that Colbert loathes. The satire can cloud the issue here, since the character of Stephen definitely *engages* in the truthiness the way Colbert views it. We need to keep Stephen's concept of truthiness separate from his own behavior in light of it.

The Gut and the Heart

In character, Stephen defines truthiness in terms of rejecting external authorities (like dictionaries and reference books) in favor of relying on one's gut intuitions and experience. After all, we are supposed to *think* Harriet Miers's is an absurd nomination based on standards of competence set up by powerful know-it-alls, but Bush *knows her heart*. Apparently Bush is less interested in whether she meets formal qualifications set up by others and is satisfied that her character is sufficient to qualify her.

Bush and his ilk are obviously the target of Colbert's satire and he hits his target dead on. But does this mean that every time I go with my heart or gut over my head I am wrong? Maybe not. For one thing, it's not quite clear what 'going with my heart' even means. Colbert implies this means going against the facts, both in the comments above and in his roasting of Bush during the 2006 White House Correspondents' Dinner: "Now I know there's some polls out there saying this man has a thirty-two-percent approval rating. But guys like us, we don't pay attention to the polls. We know that polls are just a collection of statistics that reflect what people are thinking 'in reality.' And reality has a well-known liberal bias."[4] Bush seems to be an irresponsible figure because his political rhetoric and activities dismiss relevant and inconvenient facts. Okay, that's bad. But nothing prevents me from paying attention to facts while still valuing my gut and my heart.

Think of it this way. I have had to make decisions about applicants for jobs based on the pieces of paper that represent them.

---

[4] "Re-Improved Colbert transcript," Daily Kos, http://www.dailykos.com/storyonly/2006/4/30/1441/59811. Accessed 1st December, 2008.

When it comes time to interview a set of applicants, I've found that the people I met are very different than the people on paper. Applications list all sorts of qualifications and accomplishments, which are facts. But they do not fill in other sorts of information that would be important to make the decision. There's another set of facts that the interview is supposed to help provide. What's their character? How well do they work with others? Will they thrive in the actual work environment that I and my colleagues face every-day? But answers to such questions are not opposed to facts. They're just different kinds of facts discovered by different kinds of methods.

When I say I know someone's heart, I probably have evidence for my claim. I've seen them in hard situations; I've talked to them about their most personal opinions and prejudices. Of course, sometimes people think they know someone's heart for poor rea-sons. Imagine someone liking a candidate simply because he keeps self-identifying as a good Christian. Well, we've seen enough politi-cians play that game to know that it doesn't mean very much. In the twenty-fourth installment of the 434-part series "Better Know a District,"[5] Colbert exposed Georgia Congressman Westmoreland's inability to cite the Ten Commandments that the congressman so ardently felt must be displayed in the House of Representatives and the Senate. Westmoreland may or may not be a good Christian, but certainly a person who assumed that he was a good Christian on the basis of his political posturing would be acting foolishly. But this doesn't mean that we should avoid trying to get know some-one's heart altogether. We don't normally trust strangers like we would an old friend because we haven't built up enough experi-ences with them. Our trust grows as our experience builds our sense of their character. We can always trust them too soon or mis-read them, but the method of assessing character isn't itself at fault.

So what does knowing someone's heart really mean? A claim to know someone's heart is a claim to know what they value and how they are disposed to act in certain situations. This is a factual claim (which can always be wrong and unsupported, of course, but need not be).

Similar reflections will lead us to the same conclusion about the gut. If Colbert means something like intuitions, that is, that some-

---

[5] Episode 2074, originally aired June 14th, 2006.

thing *feels* right, these too have an important role to play in decision making. Gut feelings may be the result of repeated experience with similar situations. Think about the last time you got a bad feeling about someone. Maybe you were picking up on body language and subtle signs that reminded you of other bad experiences. We pick up on and process lots of information that isn't at the center of our attention. So gut feelings may be the result of lots of experience being unconsciously processed.

Intuitions may even indicate something like rational 'instincts'. Often people have trouble articulating the line of thinking that leads them to a conclusion. This isn't to say that the brain didn't process information. It's just that the process might not be available for easy recall. A common example is found in introductory philosophy classes: Maybe someone can't "prove" why they think that the existence of an all-knowing, all-powerful God eliminates the possibility of personal human freedom, but this isn't to say that there isn't an implicit logic to it that the person simply has difficulty making explicit.

So a gut feeling does in all likelihood lend itself to some assertion of fact and will be the result of some kind of evidence. We are in the same position again: it's not that gut intuitions are bad in themselves, but that they may be misused. Gut feelings aren't infallible (sorry, Stephen, but the gut is *not* like the Pope of the Torso), but they are worthy components of any deliberation. Truthiness, if understood as the preferring of personal intuitions and experiences over claims to fact coming from others, may not always be bad. Authorities can indeed be wrong (experts often disagree, after all, so some of them must be wrong), and personal convictions need not be baseless. It depends on the situation whether this preference is justified.

Just the Facts, Ma'am

Surely we now see why the out-of-character Colbert understands truthiness in terms of someone abandoning "facts" to privilege her own "selfish" perspective. This is backed up by the examples of the in-character Stephen. While Stephen only defines truthiness in terms of heart and gut, with skepticism of authority, his examples are always of individuals who seem to doubt only the authorities that inconvenience the view they already hold. The character of Stephen is himself one who goes with his gut when the rest of us know that he shouldn't. (I mean, come on, bears aren't really that evil!) So Colbert complains that public discourse is all just perspective now, without any responsibility to objective facts.

But what are the facts? Colbert presupposes that there is a set of objective facts to which we are to be responsible. I think there is too, but it's important to recognize how hard it is to establish these facts and that the easiest ones to establish are the least interesting and helpful. When we're dealing with clashing political ideologies, it becomes very difficult to settle on facts, since the facts are often understood in radically different contexts. Let's look at Colbert's own analysis of the right's attack on media neutrality:

> What the right-wing in the United States tries to do is undermine the press. They call the press "liberal," they call the press "biased," not necessarily because it is or because they have problems with the facts of the left—or even because of the bias for the left, because it's hard not to be biased in some way, everyone is always going to enter their editorial opinion—but because a press that has validity is a press that has authority.[6]

Is Colbert presenting us with a fact? Is this a factual motivation of the right? I wouldn't consider myself to be on the right, yet I want to undermine the validity of the press for my own reasons. Indeed, *The Colbert Report* is a successful indictment of the media as much as it is of politicians. Might the right-wingers actually believe the mainstream press is biased? And wouldn't it be a justified decision, then, that the press should have some of its 'authority' taken away? So the problem with an authority expecting individuals to respect it is that individuals have to grant that authority its legitimacy in the first place in order for the authority to demand respect. Why does the real Colbert trust investigative journalists more than right-wing politicians, while the character Stephen reverses this trust?

Surely there are objective facts that are not so politically loaded. Here's one: There is a copy of *I Am America (And So Can You!)* beside me while I type. No problem. Unless I get all crazy skeptical and ask how I know that I'm not really in the *Matrix*, this is an

---

[6] Nathan Rabin, "Interviews: Stephen Colbert," (January 26th, 2006) A.V. Club, The Onion, http://www.avclub.com/content/node/44705. Accessed 1st December, 2008.

acceptable fact. And I am very confident that it's true. So yes, there are facts that are easier to accept and facts that are harder to determine. And typically the easier to accept facts are the least important. You and I may both agree that the day is sunny, but we may not agree whether *The Colbert Report* is better or worse than *The Daily Show*. The more complex the judgment, the more we may diverge.

So maybe we should take a look at what kind of realism is involved in Colbert's presupposition that there are objective facts. If he's simply saying that there is a reality, some kind of independent way things are that can't be wished away by us, then Colbert is echoing the John Adams quote with which I started. But does this mean we are committed to what those facts are? No. You and I can both admit that there are such things as facts, but disagree about which claims are indeed facts. What matters is how we justify our own personal claims. We use various methods to justify our claims. One way is through gut intuitions, another through rational analysis, another through accumulating sensory data, and there are others. The difficulty is figuring out how reliable these methods are and how far they can really take us even if reliable. Consider an example of gathering statistics to defend the claim that men are by nature more physically aggressive than women. Say I record how different people respond to a panhandler on the street. Let's pretend I do find that the men tended to more aggressively repel the panhandler. Does this really show men are more aggressive by nature? Can't it be that men are allowed and encouraged to act aggressively with their bodies while women are socially penalized for doing so? Statistics are important bits of data, but they are rarely enough to end debate.

So, even if we agree with Colbert that there are facts out there, it doesn't mean any of us know which facts are facts. It's hard work thinking through our justifications for our beliefs. But it gets worse! Since the information we rely on becomes overwhelming and our needs for information outpace our individual ability to process it, we often rely on others to provide it. That means we quite often turn to an authority to tell us what to believe even though we have no direct way of testing the 'facts' they provide. I believe in lots of stuff that scientists say even though my lab experience probably consists of just slightly more than turning a potato into a battery. We have to judge who the good mediators of information are, but we do this either by trusting the word of another authority we've already accepted or by going back to our own personal views and gut feelings. With a wide variety of perspectives then, we should also expect vast disagreement about which 'facts' are even 'facts' to begin with.

Since I share Colbert's and Adams' basic realist attitude, I don't find this too troubling. I'm optimistic that the variety of opinion tends to congregate around approximate facts. But this view means that truthiness is not defined in opposition to the truth or facts, but that truthiness is one part of the *orientation toward truth*, as I will explain below. Indeed, this realist optimism may itself be an example of Colbert's truthiness, of "something that seems like truth—the truth we want to exist." I want to believe that rationality and empirical evidence draw us as a community closer toward reliable objective perspectives, but I do so by explaining away the prevalence of young-earth Creationists as simply being those lagging behind the more progressive pack. "They'll come around, or at least their kids will be a bit closer than they are."

The Politics of Bullshit

So the distinction between what facts there are and what is left over as mere opinion is itself something that emerges from perspectives. One woman's truth is another woman's truthiness. This isn't to say that there aren't clear violations of being oriented toward the truth. Someone is oriented toward the truth if they genuinely want to know the way things are, not just bathe in the bliss of ignorance. And when we *say* things without any care to the truth of the matter, we are just spewing bullshit. Bullshit is far worse than the truthiness of the gut and the heart.

A truth-oriented person, while testing things out to find evidence for her beliefs, is trying to be aware of how she might fool herself. She is cautious about her beliefs, and so would be cautious about her gut feelings and character assessments. And because she's cautious, she engages with others to find out the truth. If she disagrees with someone, she argues her point and listens to the other person's argument. Why? If she's wrong, she wants to know! If you're actually interested in establishing the truth, you ought to take your own views seriously enough to defend them well on reasonable grounds, and take other's views seriously enough to listen to them and test them by the same standards.

On the other side of things, someone who simply denies evidence without giving any explanation as to why has taken himself out of truth-oriented discourse. For example, if I show you a video of me and Stephen fighting with lightsabers, you can't just deny that the video is genuine. You need to explain why. "You just used footage from his famous green screen challenge." Your explanations move the examination from the 'fact' of the video to the evidence for your explanations. Now it's my turn to defend my claim that I really did fight the Sith Lord Colbert. Maybe I compare the footage from the green screen to my video and show that his body movements are inconsistent with the alleged original. Nailed you, didn't I? Well, that's how truth-oriented discourse works.

For those engaged in truth-oriented discourse, some explanations are better than others. Sometimes people say stupid things in defense of their views. Consider Colbert's May 5th, 2008, segment of the The WØRD, "Free Gas." In it, Colbert's satire suggests that both Senators Clinton and McCain were pandering to angry consumers by proposing a summer gas tax holiday. Stephen applauds their courage for standing up to the delicate critiques of "so-called" economic experts, like Krugman's "pointless and disappointing," Shultz's "bad policy," and Friedman's "so ridiculous, so unworthy of the people aspiring to lead our nation." Then Stephen points out the "one favorable review" of Mankiw, who claimed not to know of any prominent economist who favors the idea. For Stephen, that is why the idea is so good! Then we see the clip of Clinton defending her proposal to George Stephanopoulos, who asked her about the total lack of support from economists:

CLINTON: Well, you know, George, I think we've been for the last seven years seeing a tremendous amount of government power and elite opinion basically behind policies that haven't worked well. . . . Somehow elite opinion is always on the side of doing things that really disadvantage the vast majority of Americans.

STEPHEN: Sure. If you *think* about it, lifting the tax will increase demand and ultimately will lead to higher gas prices. But doesn't it *feel* like this is going to help somebody? [text on screen: OPEC?][7]

---

[7] Episode 4060, originally aired May 5th, 2008.

This is a very bad defense, but a great example of the kind of truthiness Colbert mocks. In discussing truthiness on that first segment of The WØRD, Colbert even uses this same tactic in calling books elitist because they are "Constantly telling us what is or isn't true or what did or didn't happen."[8] What makes Clinton's defense so bad is that she dismisses the economists by lumping them into the vague notion of 'elite opinion' and then blames bad policies on those elites. Do we know what Krugman, Shultz, and Friedman have been saying about the various policies over the past seven years? Maybe they have been criticizing those policies too. And what policies are we talking about? Are all government policies responsible for the high gas prices, or only just some of them? Might it also be that the gas prices are not just the result of American policy, but global factors outside the control of presidents and congresspersons?

Notice also that Clinton linked elite opinion with government power. Now, I agree that we should be suspicious of those in power serving their base over the rest of us. But does all "elite opinion" couple with government power? Economists don't always agree and both the right and left have economists on their side. Many economists call their shots one by one without joining a political team. And many other kinds of elite opinion may advise those in government power without having an agenda at all. Should we think that surgeons advising healthcare regulations might try to promote unnecessary surgeries because of their closeness to Big Scalpel? It looks like she's trying to tie any elite opinion with the authoritarian Bush administration. And hey, wait a minute! Isn't the Senator from New York and former First Lady a part of the government establishment herself? When we consider it rationally, Clinton's defense of her proposal allegedly pandering to the angry consumer is itself pandering to angry citizens.

But perhaps Clinton is not very interested in pursuing truth anyway. Perhaps she's more interested in spewing a type of bullshit. Harry G. Frankfurt, professor emeritus of philosophy at Princeton University, started a line of inquiry with his celebrated 2005 essay "On Bullshit." Frankfurt goes to some lengths to show that even a liar has an implicit respect for the truth. A liar must think there is a truth to lie about and thinks he knows the truth when he is lying. Liars and truth-tellers are both truth-oriented:

---

[8] Episode 1001, originally aired October 17th, 2005.

One who is concerned to report or to conceal the facts assumes that there are indeed facts that are in some way both determinate and knowable.[9]

In contrast, a bullshitter is indifferent to the truth. The bullshitter doesn't have his eye on the facts at all. The bullshitter just wants to get away with what he is saying for whatever his purpose is. What he says may be true, may be false. A student who's just trying to pass the test may bullshit through an exam only hoping that the essay appears like it reflects extensive study and forethought. A politician will say whatever it is she has to say regardless of the "facts." So maybe it's better to understand Presidential Candidate Clinton not as stuck in truthiness, but as neck-deep in bullshit. When it suits a politician to say intensive study results in unreliable elitist opinion, they do so; when it suits them to cite intensive study, they do so.

But is Clinton totally full of shit? Well, Clinton pointed out that even a little savings during hard times can make a big difference to those struggling and she said she'd impose a windfall tax on the oil companies to pay for the tax cut. If her real goal is to provide temporary immediate relief, even if it results in raising costs long-term, then maybe her proposal is not so bad. It is a matter of priorities. Maybe she thinks we can handle the higher gas prices better down the line, once we turn the economy as a whole around. For now, let's help the poor drivers. The difficulty here is that the difference between an incompetent truth-seeker, a deceiver and a bullshitter is a matter of intention.

To illustrate the difficulty, let's consider an example. Have you ever wondered whether the triumvirate of Stephen Colbert, Jon Stewart, and Steve Carell all really like each other as much as they seem to? Maybe there are hidden hostilities. Maybe all the wonderful smiling and hugging they do with each other on the shows or at the Emmys are just to keep up appearances for their respective careers. Suppose Jon genuinely adores his colleagues, while Stephen secretly despises Jon for keeping him down all those years and is jealous of Steve whose career is now more fully independent of Jon. As for Steve, he doesn't think much of his colleagues at all anymore, so doesn't really feel one way or the other and hasn't reflected on his relationship. Suppose Mo Rocca interviews them

---

[9] Harry Frankfurt, *On Bullshit* (Princeton University Press, 2005), p. 61.

for a piece, and asks how they feel about each other and they all say "Oh, we're all great friends." Jon's telling the truth (or at least being honest, since it might not be true through no fault on his part); Stephen's lying to cover up his true feelings; and Steve is probably just bullshitting. For Steve, it's not that it's true or false; he's just saying what he thinks he's supposed to say in that kind of situation, or responding habitually.

So, maybe we can't say for sure whether Clinton is bullshitting us since we don't really know what her intentions are. We don't see into her intimate thought processes, so we can't figure out what she really believes and why she really says what she says. But we still can be fairly confident that there is a lot of bullshit out there. Frankfurt claims that bullshit is so prevalent because it is unavoidable whenever the situation forces someone to talk when they don't know what they are talking about. This is why the classroom might be so full of bullshit, from both students and instructors. And this is why politics is full of bullshit. The motives and intentions in the political discourse are often far removed from expressing true descriptions of the world, or even false ones. That's why we are so quick to think that Clinton and so many others are really just pandering and bullshitting their way through the day.

But, of course, Frankfurt isn't exactly right on this. A situation can force me to talk, and I can talk in response, without giving up my respect for the truth. In the classroom, for example, I can say, "Well, I don't know for sure, but I have heard . . ." Maybe I have to fill up the air, but I don't need to fill it up with bullshit. Politicians don't need to bullshit either. They choose to. And it's not necessarily bullshit if they speak falsely, as Frankfurt notes. We can then imagine a world in which the politicians don't speak beyond their most reasoned and honest opinions. So the political forum is not inevitably a shithouse, but the temptation to dump one's share is quite high.

The Truthiness of the Vote

If what I have been saying is true, then something odd results. Colbert the satirist is not really fed up with truthiness, but with bullshit. It's bullshit that's tearing apart our country, not truthiness. The irony is that the prevalence of bullshit actually makes truthiness all the more necessary and preferable. In other words, to wade through the noise we use our guts to figure out who to trust and which leaders will serve us best.

Obviously, we'd all love for interpreting politics to be as easy as our ordinary judgments about whether there is a copy of *I Am America* on the table in front of us. If it were, we'd better be able to distinguish cases of true judgments from deluded truthy judgments. And truthy judgments would *all* be deluded, since one would have to deny fairly obvious truths in favor of any *opposing* gut feeling. So I'd claim to know my lover's heart and deny the videotaped evidence of her affair. Or I'd have a gut feeling that Senator Larry Craig or Pastor Ted Haggard really weren't hiding in the closet behind a door of homophobia or in self-denial, and everyone else around me would know that I'm in as much denial as those two are. There wouldn't be any instances where my gut was the only thing, or even the primary thing, to go on. That would be a great world of clarity for those of us who bother to know what the truth is.

But our political forums are full of politicians who speak with cross-purposes, media outlets that compete for ratings and funding, and special interest groups vying for access amid the ubiquitous commercial messages. There's far too much information from far too many sources for individual citizens to stay on top of it all. And all that information is coming from sources that are sometimes truthful, sometimes deceitful and very often full of bullshit.

So what should we do? Well, if we're truth-oriented, we can either spend the time and energy trying to uncover the truth or rely on others and hope they are doing the hard work for us. Perhaps I can focus all my energy on an issue or two so that my view will be well informed and defensible; but I couldn't focus my attention on every important issue. And how will I pick out reliable sources for those other issues? I'll use my gut and heart. Because it is so difficult to wade through the mixture of truth, falsity, and bullshit, truthiness may often be what we ought or need to rely on in a democracy.

As far as assessing politicians goes, there are often very good reasons to doubt the authenticity of statements made by an office-holder or office-seeker: party pressure, placation of the constituency, response to opinion polls, lobbyists, corporate interests and more. When supporting or voting for a candidate one can only be responding to what feels true, that is, an optimistic trust in the candidate. It is not that 'facts' and 'rational arguments' aren't considered, but that the legitimacy granted to them is a matter of gut feeling. I look at the facts of where the person grew up, the items on her resume and the statements she's made to the press. As I look at the facts, though, I view them differently depending on what I think of the candidate's character. If I do know one or two issues in depth, perhaps I make my decision about what she has to say about those issues and then infer that her views on other subjects (about which I know less) are also well-reasoned. I make a judgment about her heart: she really does value having informed policy! In other words, when we go out to vote for, say, Stephen Colbert in the South Carolina primary, we do so because we know Stephen's heart.

A similar argument can be made about policies themselves. More often than not, citizens do not have the data or the expertise to interpret the data to assess which policies are most beneficial. We rely on experts, but there is a spectrum of expert opinions, and there are so many contingencies in real-world dynamics that expert opinions may often simply be educated guesses. Consider VP Dick Cheney's March 16th, 2003, view (*Meet the Press* interview)[10] for an invasion of Iraq since our soldiers would be embraced as liberators. Now compare that to the 'formidable opponent' AEI Fellow Dick Cheney's April 15th, 1994, view (*C-SPAN* interview)[11] that a war in Iraq to take down the regime would result in our soldiers being stuck in a quagmire, since we wouldn't have anything to put in place of the regime to keep the country together. With such formidable opponents as these, which Dick Cheney should we trust? It would be hard to say before the invasion. In retrospect, it looks like we were greeted as liberators. But that the embrace was short-lived, as it proved difficult to keep the country together and get a new government working well. Both Dick Cheneys seemed to be on to something, yet their advice was geared to steer us in different directions.

We endorse policies or policy-tendencies via our support of parties and particular politicians and advocacy groups. Nonetheless, it seems that undergirding all of this is a basic gut-feeling informing our decisions. We value various things and try to determine what

---

[10] NBC News, *Meet the Press*, 16th March, 2003.

[11] Tim King, "Statement on Iraq Made by Cheney in 1994 Making the News," (August 15th, 2007) Salem-News.com, http://www.salem-news.com/articles/august152007/cheney_1994_81507.php

will promote our values. We try to figure out which sources of information to trust, and who will most likely represent our interests. It's not that we ignore facts; it's that we select which "facts" presented to us we will accept as facts. And we do this not because we already know that they are facts, but because we follow our guts and trust the people whose hearts we feel we know.

Democracy invites the tools of mass persuasion by its promotion of the individual's opinion and these tools generate at least as much bullshit as anything else. When there are too many 'facts' to be accessed, and the situation is too complicated for an individual to understand fully without dedicating his whole waking life to the issue, truthiness seems to be the only thing we have to go on. That said, a recognition of the practical inevitability of truthiness emerging as a useful tool does not require us to abandon a commitment to more objective truth as well.

Wishing and Dogmatism

This is where Colbert's conception of truthiness comes into play. Colbert said that truthiness was about stating things you wish were true, not what you know to be true. And he said that one then refuses to think that anyone else's view may be correct, becoming stubbornly ideological. As already noted, these two out-of-character additions go beyond the on-air definition. But the character of Stephen certainly is self-deluded and dogmatic. So while Stephen defines truthiness in terms of following the gut and heart, while resisting submission to authority, Colbert uses the character of Stephen to show that this rhetoric may be a rationalization for delusional dogmatism. But does this mean that truthiness always dissolves into abandoning the humble respect for objective fact that we noted was essential to the truth-oriented person? Let's look at these two additional elements that Colbert attaches to Stephen's definition of truthiness.

So what about wishful thinking? If by this we mean believing something is true when you know it's not, then all wishful thinking would seem irrational. But is it even possible to know something isn't true, yet believe it anyway? Perhaps. When we speak of self-delusion and self-denial, we speak as if some *part* of the person deceives another *part* of the person. After all, the same part that knows the truth cannot *not* know it at the same time. But the part that knows can't be the conscious part of us, since then we'd be aware of the very thing we are not aware of. I can only delude myself if I'm not really conscious of my act of self-delusion, if I don't consciously know the truth I'm trying to keep hidden from myself. And I can only be in denial of something as long as I am not consciously aware of its reality. It would be a bit of a puzzle to think that I consciously do this to myself. So, maybe it's some unconscious or subconscious mechanism in the brain that keeps information from the conscious part of us. Or perhaps we make conscious decisions to keep things on the periphery of our conscious mind, which successfully keeps us from recognizing the truth of something.

In any case, if this is what we mean by wishful thinking, we all do this in numerous ways, so to this extent truthiness is as much an inevitable feature of the human condition as is bullshit and deceit. But I don't think this is what Colbert is getting at. Maybe he means when someone consciously asserts truths that she knows are in fact false. Consider the example of Bush saying "we do not torture." This is probably an outright lie or, at least, bullshit. Either Bush knows that water-boarding is torture and that it is occurring or he simply doesn't care enough to examine the issue and is just saying what he needs to. On the other hand, perhaps Bush is a true believer. But if he is, then how can we claim that he believes something he wishes to be true but knows isn't true?

So, the wishful thinking component of truthiness might not require that I know that the facts *are* indeed facts yet choose to ignore them anyway. Colbert's out-of-character addition, then, really boils back down to Stephen's in-character definition. I choose which facts I want to recognize as facts, based on my own experience and perspective, with the slight addition that I am often guided by what I want to be the case. Again, I'd say that this is part of the human condition that truth-oriented people and bullshitters share alike. And this doesn't mean we are all optimists. I may secretly or subconsciously wish that I get fired because I really feel more comfortable without the responsibility of my job. So when I think "I'm no good at this . . . they are going to fire my ass," I am actually thinking wishfully. I may be quite capable, but I don't really want to be. If I know that I am good and am just pretending to stink in order to get fired, then I am being deceitful in some way, not truthy. If I *don't* know that I am good, then Colbert would be wrong to think I believe facts that I know aren't true and dismiss facts I know are true.

Good truth-seekers and bad truth-seekers share this tendency to accept the things one would rather be true. What separates the two is that the good truth-seeker is *trying* to overcome the disposition to accept what she'd like to be true, and has some good methods to do just that. And I think this is what leads us to Colbert's other addition of being dogmatic, of selfishly thinking that what I think is true, because I think it, and no one who disagrees can possibly be right.

I think it is insightful of Colbert to identify dogmatism with a kind of selfishness. Dogmatic people can sometimes think of themselves as selfless since they humbly accept the dogma, rather than trying to come up with their own understanding. I've been accused of being selfish because I don't just accept the Bible as literally true, but choose to 'think for myself' ("as if I knew as much as God," they say). But I don't see it this way. After all, who decides that it is true that God wrote the Bible, or inspired its writing in such a way that we must accept it as literally true? Even if it *is* true that God did this, each one of us decides for our own reasons whether we buy this story. The person who accepts must reason through her decision to accept. Maybe it's fear, or a personal mystical experience, or thoughtful metaphysical reasoning that leads us one way or the other. Maybe it has more to do with social circles and tradition for someone else. There is no escaping the fundamental truthiness of it all: we each decide what sources to accept, which methods to use to search for the truth and how much we conform to this or that external influence.

The problem with dogmatism is not its truthiness. In fact, the suspicion of authorities that Stephen advocates rails against dogmatism being imposed on you by others. The problem with dogmatism is that it has cut off future evidence. It is a final decision, or at least semi-final. Perhaps major life-events may shake some people enough so they arise from their dogmatic slumber, but dogmatism provides so much cushioning that nothing short of a major earthquake is going to do the trick. It isn't the preference for one's own experience and belief in people's character that's at fault, but the unreflective devotion to these. Dogmatism isn't bullshit because it cares about the truth. It cares so much, in fact, that it can't handle not having it. So it insists on having it already without having to work for it. Dogmatism is the Dark Side of Truthiness (I now invite the Colbert Nation to post videos of Stephen battling Dogmatism with his lightsaber on YouTube). And this is what

Colbert is getting at with the wishful thinking. It's wishful thinking that overpowers any other source of information one might accept, so that one is stuck in an ideology, rather than navigating through them.

But wishful thinking need not turn bad. And in some cases it is desirable. Believing that people are generally honest and reasonable is not necessarily supported by evidence. Of course, there are many instances of corruption and idiocy. But there are also many instances of honorable and enlightened acts. By being optimistic without sufficient evidence, good consequences may result. I may suffer incidents of corruption and idiocy with more patience. I may attract other people who are genuinely honest and reasonable to my life. I may very well add a whole lot more light to the world myself. Since our beliefs have implications for our behavior, choosing to believe what we want to be true without knowing that it is true may not always be bad. It *can* be bad. But it's not truthiness itself that's the problem. It's the manner in which one is truthy.

So I think we can now appreciate that Colbert the satirist is too hard on the truthy elements in all of us. Truthiness exists on a continuum from the nonsensical to the more rational and objective. Truth is the goal of all truthiness, so it isn't as bad as engaging in mere bullshit, which ignores truth, or purposefully lying, which attempts to subvert it. Moreover, it is a requirement of any life that seeks to establish more than the basic undeniable facts of immediate sense experience, like 'Stephen sure looks dashing in that painting above his fake fireplace.'

Facts that are complicated and removed from my immediate testing must come to me through external authorities. Ultimately it's my own experience and ability to think rationally that I rely on to wade through all the lies and bullshit. So, I'm left with a choice of who I trust in public discourse and who I'll promote to a political platform. With all its potential pitfalls, the path of truthiness is the only way to start your journey, and it won't always lead you in the wrong direction. And if you want to know my opinion, I'm holding out for the Colbert-Stewart ticket for the next election cycle.

7

Truthiness of the Appearances

ETHAN MILLS

I'll admit it. The very first time I saw *The Colbert Report*, I didn't get it. I was uneasy about this funnier version of what I considered to be insidious ideologues like Bill O'Reilly and Sean Hannity. Sure I was laughing, but I laugh at O'Reilly and Hannity too, even if this laughter leaves a sour taste in my mouth. I chuckled at Stephen's tomfoolery, all the while wondering what was so funny about the destruction of journalistic integrity and democratic discourse in America.

After watching *The Colbert Report* a few more times, I "got it," became one in a long line of "it-getters" and realized Stephen Colbert's genius. It wasn't that he was *celebrating* these negative tendencies, but that he was offering a sophisticated (and hilarious) *parody* of such tendencies. And parody is often a much more effective critique than the solemn, preachy condemnations offered by boring old media critic eggheads, elitists and the like.

The word "truthiness," one of Colbert's better bits of genius, refers to those who "know with their heart" rather than relying on facts and evidence. Much has been written on what truthiness portends for the state of political discourse in the United States. If I'm right, truthiness also constitutes a response to an old philosophical problem of skepticism and political commitment: how can philosophical skeptics, who argue that no one knows much of anything, possibly be committed to *any* political persuasion, since it seems that political commitment requires that you *know* that your brand of politics is the right one? If Stephen doesn't *know* that President Bush is the Greatest President, how can he claim that Bush is not just *a* great President? Why would I bother to vote if I admitted I didn't *know* one candidate was better than the others?

If you're not sure about politics, the best thing seems to be to just stay home and watch *The Colbert Report*. Truthiness, however, gives us a way to act politically without having to live up to elitist, egghead ideas that knowledge requires boring old things like facts and evidence. Is this solution a good one? That's an issue reflective members of the Colbert Nation ought to consider and I'll get to it at the end. But first let's think about philosophical theories of knowledge and the number one threat to knowledge: skepticism.

Do You Know the Stuff You Think
You Know? No!

Epistemology, or theory of knowledge, is the branch of philosophy that investigates knowledge. It asks questions such as: What is knowledge? How do you get it? How do you convince people that you have it? Why should we bother trying to get it? Does anyone really have it in the first place?

The most amusing and accurate definition of epistemology comes from a recent book of philosophical jokes: "How do you know that you know the stuff you think you know? Take away the option of answering, 'I just do!' and what's left is epistemology."[1] Epistemologists, or the philosophers who try to answer these and similar questions, are generally not impressed by appeals to truthiness.[2] If Stephen were to tell epistemologists that he "knows with his gut" the epistemologists will ask, "But how do you know that you know with your gut?" If Stephen replies, "I just do!" the smart-ass epistemologists will ask, "Do you have another gut to tell you that your gut is correct? Do cows, having multiple stomachs, know a lot more than the rest of us?" At this point Stephen would probably change the subject by accusing the epistemologists of supporting bovine affirmative action and putting human guts out of work.

In normal English, "skepticism" means something like "disbelief." In this sense, Stephen was skeptical that global climate change is occurring, until of course Al Gore's *An Inconvenient Truth* did

---

[1] Thomas Cathcart and Daniel Klein, *Plato and a Platypus Walk Into a Bar: Understanding Philosophy Through Jokes* (Abrams, 2007), p. 51.

[2] See Chapter 6 in this volume, for an example of how some philosophers don't think truthiness is all bad.

well at the box office and he asserted, "The market has spoken. Global warming is real."[3] In the field of epistemology, skeptics are people who have a pretty dim view of whether people actually know much of anything in the first place. Philosophical skeptics don't just deny that Stephen knows that bears are the number one threat to America or that there's no need for the "wordinistas" over at Webster's. Skeptics in epistemology usually take a much bolder approach and deny that *anyone* (even Stephen) knows *anything* at all, or at least we don't know nearly as much as we think we do.

But why on Earth would anything think *that*? Surely we know some stuff: we know that *The Colbert Report* is on Comedy Central, that Spicy Sweet Chili Doritos are tasty, that Stephen's portrait once hung near the restroom at the National Portrait Gallery and so forth. But *do* we know that stuff? Maybe it's time to better know a skeptic and find out.

Better Know a Skeptic: A Four-Part Series

Many philosophers today stay in business by debating the correct interpretation of other philosophers and philosophical ideas with no end in sight. As soon as one of us comes up with a brilliant interpretation some other smart aleck philosopher comes along to show why it's wrong (and gets published in the process, thus engendering another smart aleck to come along to show why *that's* wrong). Stephen might say that the market has spoken against definitive, once-and-for all interpretations in philosophy.

This feature of philosophy infuriates many people who like to have cut-and-dried answers and seems to give philosophy a bad name, as it looks like we've been talking about ancient philosophers such as Plato for over two thousand years and *still* don't understand them. The problem, however, isn't that philosophers are too dim-witted to get what Plato's saying or pulling a fast one on the academic establishment just to stay in business. Rather, it's that the *problems* of philosophy addressed by the great philosophers are hard. Really, really hard. We shouldn't despair, however, because even difficult philosophical ideas can benefit from the "Colbert bump" and become intelligible enough for purposes of pondering.

---

[3] Episode 4066, originally aired May 14th, 2008.

Skeptics and their philosophical ideas are notoriously difficult to figure out. It would be impossible to say anything about skepticism without invoking some kind of scholarly controversy, so I'll employ a bit of truthiness myself and put forward *my* interpretations "from the gut" (but readers should feel free to inspect the guts of other philosophers as well).

Skepticism isn't just one thing, but rather an "umbrella term."[4] I want to offer brief sketches of four kinds of skepticism that might fall under this umbrella: Pyrrhonian skepticism, Modern skepticism, Indian skepticism, and a fourth kind of skepticism prevalent among Americans today, which I call political skepticism.

Pyrrhonian Skepticism: Belief Is Undesirable

Pyrrhonism is a form of skepticism developed by ancient Greek and Roman philosophers such as Pyrrho (around 360–270 B.C.E.) and Sextus Empiricus (around 200 C.E.). According to Sextus, skeptics are those who continue their investigations of things, which makes sense since the Greek word for skeptic (*skeptikos*) means "inquirer" or "investigator." Skeptics are opposed to "dogmatists," which is their word for people who end their investigation by committing to a belief.

Like most Greeks and Romans, Pyrrhonists thought that happiness is the goal of philosophy. This may sound strange to anyone who's taken a philosophy class, since doing so can make you very unhappy. To see what the Pyrrhonists are talking about, think of a certain kind of unhappiness: mental disturbance. Suppose Jon Stewart of *The Daily Show* has just told you that President Bush is the *worst* President and immediately after Jon checks in with his good friend Stephen Colbert at *The Colbert Report*, Stephen tells you that President Bush is the *Greatest* President. Who should you believe—Jon or Stephen?

You might keep thinking about it so much you're too distracted to enjoy the latest installment of the 435-part series, *Better Know a District*. It might even keep you up at night. Even if you choose one side or the other, your mind will be in turmoil while figuring out how to defend your belief against people who disagree with you. Philosophers seem like a mild-mannered bunch, but philoso-

---

[4] R.J. Hankinson, *The Sceptics* (Routledge, 1995), p. 13.

phy itself tends to induce mental disturbance and turmoil by asking such questions as "Do we know anything?", "Do we have free will?", "Is Stephen Colbert really the 'Socrates of Shred' in the *Rock and Awe Countdown to Guitarmageddon?*"[5]

Pyrrhonism's answer to mental disturbance is to create a situation in which the two sides of any question balance equally, leading a person to suspend judgment on the question altogether. For Sextus this amounts to saying, "I can't say which of the things proposed I should find convincing and which I should not find convincing." From suspension of judgment mental tranquility is alleged to follow "as a shadow follows a body."[6]

Going back to Jon versus Stephen on the status of President Bush, a good Pyrrhonist would weigh-up the two sides so that the pros and cons of each side are in perfect balance. Of course, nonskeptics will insist that either Jon or Stephen must "really" have the better argument and thus one of them must be right and the other wrong. Sextus admits that some Pyrrhonist arguments may not be all that convincing, but for Pyrrhonists an argument just has to be good enough to balance with its opposing argument.[7] If you find one of the opposing arguments less convincing than the other, just leave it to a clever Pyrrhonist to come up some way of making them equal. For instance, if you agree with Jon that President Bush is the *worst* President because you think that Stephen's arguments are weak, a Pyrrhonist might point out that President Bush isn't nearly as bad as Herbert Hoover, that eight years of the Bush Administration will give us a greater appreciation for future administrations and, most importantly, President Bush has given both Jon Stewart and Stephen Colbert such great comedic material that any of his negative political effects on America are outweighed by his positive comedic effects on America.

If you then ask Pyrrhonists, "Is President Bush the *greatest* President or the *worst* President?" they would respond by saying that each side is equally convincing and unconvincing. This suspension of judgment (known in Greek as *epoche*) leads to mental tranquility, because once you give up on grasping at one belief or

---

[5] Episode 2161, originally aired December 20th, 2006.

[6] Sextus Empiricus, *Outlines of Scepticism* (Cambridge University Press, 2000), Sections 1.12 and 1.22.

[7] Sextus Empiricus, Section 3.32.

another your mind is free from the disturbance caused by holding passionately to beliefs. For this reason, I think the sound-bite slogan of Pyrrhonism is "belief is undesirable."

Modern Skepticism: Knowledge Is Impossible

Modern skeptics such as Michel de Montaigne (1533–1592) and David Hume (1711–1776) owe a lot to Pyrrhonism, but developed some new ideas. This is why they are "Modern" skeptics as opposed to the "Ancient" Pyrrhonists. "Modern" in the study of philosophy usually refers to the European philosophical scene from around 1600 to about 1800.

When Montaigne wasn't busy inventing the literary form of the essay, he claimed that we human beings don't know much at all and aren't any better off than animals that rely on their instincts to get through life. Since we're a sorry lot when it comes to actually knowing anything, Montaigne advocates that we adhere to custom and religion. Our animal habits can lead us through life and religion is based on revelation from God, who as a perfect being is a lot smarter than we are. It sounds strange to us today that a skeptic was so keen on religion, but Montaigne took up Pyrrhonist arguments, not for the Greek ideal of happiness, but for cultivating traditional faith in Catholicism. He provocatively describes a skeptical view of "Man . . . annihilating his intellect to make room for faith . . ."[8] Stephen Colbert would probably get along with Montaigne: both are distrustful of "experts," both are Catholic, and both have French names.

Hume, on the other hand, was not religious. In fact, he offered pretty serious skeptical challenges to some of the more popular arguments for the existence of God and doubted whether we should trust people when they tell us about miracles. Hume's also famous (or infamous, depending on who you ask) for denying that we have any substantial knowledge of whether one thing causes another thing. Even worse, for Hume it's unclear whether things like Doritos and portraits of Stephen Colbert really exist outside our minds and even whether we have real, enduring selves underneath all our various thoughts and perceptions about Doritos or portraits of Stephen Colbert.

---

[8] Michel Montaigne. *An Apology for Raymond Sebond* (Penguin, 1987), p. 74.

One of the most famous (or again, infamous, depending who you ask) arguments used by Modern skeptics is called the argument from ignorance. This argument goes something like this: Suppose you're sitting on your couch eating Spicy Sweet Chili Doritos, drinking Diet Cherry Vanilla Dr. Pepper (four drinks in one!), watching *The Colbert Report*, and thinking about the pint of Americone Dream in your freezer. Now, what if you were just *dreaming* that you were sitting on your couch eating Spicy Sweet Chili Doritos, drinking Diet Cherry Vanilla Dr. Pepper, watching *The Colbert Report*, and thinking about the pint of Americone Dream in your freezer, and in fact you were sound asleep in your bed? Or what if you were a nothing but a brain in a vat in some mad scientist's lab or a body floating in a pod as in the film *The Matrix*?[9] Say you just had electrodes plugged into your brain feeding you signals that made it *seem* like you were sitting on your couch? How could you tell the difference between *actually* sitting on the couch and only *seeming* to sit on your couch? Maybe you could appeal to hearing the crunch of the Doritos or seeing Stephen's face on TV. But couldn't your experience of that crunch and that face be part of your dream or the result of electrical stimulation? How could you tell the difference? You can't. If you can't tell the difference, it seems like you don't really know anything about couches, TVs, or *The Colbert Report*. After all, it could all be an illusion! Therefore, knowledge of the world is impossible.

Modern skeptics are *not* arguing that we *actually are* dreaming, but that if we can't even say for sure *whether* we are dreaming or not, then it seems silly to go around claiming to know stuff about sodas and Doritos and whether President Bush is the Greatest President. Take a second to consider this point, since even some really smart philosophers have failed to fully appreciate that Modern skeptics don't use dream arguments to worry about *reality* so much as they worry about what this possibility says about our *knowledge*. Through arguments from ignorance, Modern skeptics claim that it's not possible for anyone to *know* anything about the world of experience. Hence, the sound-bite slogan of Modern skepticism is "knowledge is impossible."

---

[9] For more on *The Matrix* and the argument from ignorance, see David Mitsuo Nixon, "The Matrix Possibility," in *The Matrix and Philosophy: Welcome to the Desert of the Real* (Open Court, 2002), pp. 28–40.

Indian Skepticism: Concepts of Knowledge Are Incoherent

Skeptics in ancient India, such as Nagarjuna (around 200 C.E.) and Jayarasi (around 800 C.E.), didn't try to suspend judgment like Pyrrhonists or deny that knowledge is possible like Modern skeptics. In a sense, they're much bolder than their Western counterparts, since they try to show that the *very concepts* philosophers use to discuss knowledge are incoherent.[10]

India developed its own tradition of epistemology that differs in a few ways from Western epistemology.[11] For example, epistemologists in India worried above all about the "means to knowledge" (*pramana* in Sanskrit). For most Indian epistemologists, identifying the correct means to knowledge is an important task both for regular life and for programs of religious liberation. The two most common means to knowledge are perception and inference. How do you know that Stephen is wearing a red tie in tonight's episode? You see it and are thus using perception as a means to knowledge. How do you know that *The Colbert Report* will be on right after *The Daily Show*? You infer it by appealing to the reason that whenever *The Daily Show* is on, *The Colbert Report* always follows.

One of Nagarjuna's skeptical arguments against theories about the means to knowledge runs something like this: First, he asks how we establish that there are means to knowledge in the first place. Suppose we establish the means to knowledge by appealing to the things we know. But how do we know those things without having already established a *means* to knowledge? We can't assume that the *means* to knowledge tells us what we know, since the existence of these very means to knowledge is what was being questioned. So we can't establish the things we know without means to

---

[10] Note that my interpretation of Indian skepticism may be more controversial than my take on Pyrrhonism and Modern skepticism. Many contemporary scholars wouldn't call Nagarjuna a skeptic, but rather a mystic, nihilist, deconstructionist, or anti-realist. However, the few scholars who notice Jayarasi at all generally do agree he is some kind of skeptic. My gut tells me Nagarjuna and Jayarasi are similar enough to warrant being called "Indian skeptics."

[11] Pyrrho, the founder of Pyrrhonism, apparently traveled to India with Alexander the Great and some scholars hypothesize that there were actual historical interactions between Greek and Indian skeptics. Appropriately enough, we don't really know if such interactions took place, but there may have been East-West skeptics' meetings thousands of years ago.

knowledge and we can't establish the *means* of knowledge without having established the *things* we know. Hence, any attempt at a theory of knowledge in these terms is circular and incoherent. In his own Meta-Free-Phor-All, Nagarjuna claims that this would be to say that the father produces the son *and* that the son produces the father at the same time. If you say that, the very meanings of the terms "father" and "son" break down, because each person would fit both the definition of "father" *and* the definition of "son."[12] Say I told you that Stephen is the father and Stephen, Jr. is the son *and at the same time* that Stephen, Jr. is the father and Stephen, Sr. is the son. Each one would be both father *and* son! Who would be the majestic American Bald Eagle and who would be the majestic American pundit?

Jayarasi belonged to a school of philosophy called Carvaka, which was notorious among Indian philosophers for being vehemently anti-religious. They denied *karma* and reincarnation, called the authors of sacred texts "buffoons" and thought that the mind is the result of the body just as alcohol is the result of fermentation (they were probably fun at parties, too). In a book called, *The Lion of the Destruction of Principles*, Jayarasi went one step further and denied that epistemology itself was even possible (since most epistemologists of his day were religious, this fit nicely with his school's anti-religious sentiment). He denied epistemology by arguing in tremendous detail that no definitions of the terms used by the prominent epistemologists of his day could possibly be made coherent. If no definitions can be coherent, he thought, then the whole project of epistemology is impossible.

Neither Nagarjuna nor Jayarasi advocated suspending judgment in exactly the same way as the Pyrrhonists, but they did both think their more negative arguments could lead to happiness of some kind. As a certain kind of Buddhist, Nagarjuna thought that doing philosophy in his way would cause you to "relinquish all views" and stop grasping at beliefs to live a happy, Buddhist life. Jayarasi was no Buddhist, but did see his arguments as leading to happiness. He ends his book by saying, "Thus, when the principles are

---

[12] This is an approximation of an argument that appears in Nagarjuna's text, *Overturning the Objections*, verses 46–50. This work has been translated in Thomas F. Wood, *Nagarjunian Disputations: A Philosophical Journey through an Indian Looking-Glass* (University of Hawaii Press, 1994), pp. 307–322.

completely annihilated, all everyday practice (or: all thinking, speaking and acting) can be delightful in as much as it no longer has to be deliberated."[13] All this follows from realizing the utter futility of epistemology. Thus, the sound-bite slogan of Indian skepticism is "Concepts of knowledge are incoherent."

Political Skepticism: American Democracy Inaction

If you ask me (and you are, since you're reading this), skepticism is alive and well right here in America. Most Americans aren't pondering the details of Sextus, Hume, or Nagarjuna, but there is a widespread suspicion whether anything as lofty as *knowledge* is possible when it comes to politics. Political skepticism applies some of the tactics of Pyrrhonism, Modern and Indian skepticism to the realm of politics.

We have plenty of *opinions* about politics, but these opinions are far from facts. In fact, I'd say that the strict dichotomy between fact and opinion, so carefully etched into the minds of American students, is one of the causes of political skepticism in the United States. Since we all agree that there are no *facts* about whether conservatives or liberals are right about highly controversial topics like abortion and immigration, all that remains are opinions with no more justification than my preference for Stephen Colbert's Americone Dream over Willie Nelson's Country Peach Cobbler (and this preference itself is based mostly on what Stephen has told me to prefer).[14]

Here many of us unwittingly apply two of the Pyrrhonian "modes" of suspension of judgment: the mode deriving from dispute and the mode of relativity. The mode deriving from dispute is like this: since there is widespread dispute on political matters, who's to say who's right? Political skeptics may, like Pyrrhonists, suspend judgment or, with a more Modern disposition, they may deny that knowledge is possible on political matters. The mode of relativity is like this: since political opinions seem relative to the person holding them (conservatives say one thing *because* they're

---

[13] The text is translated in Eli Franco, *Perception, Knowledge and Disbelief: A Study of Jayarasi's Scepticism, Second Edition* (Delhi: Motilal Banarsidass, 1994), p. 44.

[14] Episode 3038, originally aired March 20th, 2007.

conservatives and liberals disagree *because* they're liberals), we may likewise suspend judgment in a Pyrrhonian vein or deny knowledge in a Modern vein. As most professors of philosophical ethics courses will tell you, something akin to the mode of relativity is very popular with college students. I call this contemporary variant "shoulder-shrugging" relativism, which is the attitude that a shrug of the shoulders and the lackadaisical expression, "it's true *for them*," constitutes the appropriate response to any ethical or political dispute.

Stephen's concept of "wikiality" takes the mode of relativity to the next level and some people might think it provides a way out of political skepticism. Wikiality is the idea that something *becomes* true if enough people say it. This idea is based on the website wikipedia.org, which Stephen praises by saying, "Any site that's got a longer entry on 'truthiness' than on 'Lutherans' has its priorities straight."[15] Stephen doesn't like being told that George Washington owned slaves, but through wikiality it can become true that Washington was not a slave owner!

Wikiality is similar to what philosophers call cultural relativism, which is the idea that truth is relative to a culture. In other words, what Americas say is true is true *for Americans* and whatever is true in Canada (or even in California's Canada, Oregon) is true *for Canadians* (or Oregonians). Instead of cultural relativism, wikiality is *Internet* relativism, since it says that the truth is whatever the majority of Internet users say it is. There's a big difference between forms of relativism like wikiality and various kinds of skepticism. Skeptics say we should withhold judgment or deny knowledge about whether something is true or not, whereas wikiality relativism affirms that there is a truth we can know and that this truth is simply what the majority says it is. As Stephen says, "Together we can create a reality we can all agree on, and that's the reality we just agreed on." It's quite easy to know the truth according to wikiality; you just check Wikipedia!

But wikiality won't derail political skepticism, as there are a lot of tough questions about wikiality and other forms of relativism. Why should we believe the majority? Does it really make sense to say that something is true *just because* people say it is? Sure, we can *say* that *The Colbert Report* is on Comedy Central twenty-four

---

[15] Episode 2096, originally aired July 31st, 2006.

hours a day or create a Wikipedia entry that claims this is the case, but that doesn't seem to make it true. It's obvious that *South Park*, *The Daily Show*, and plenty of mediocre movies are on Comedy Central at various times. And what about issues where there's no clear-cut majority, such as the debates surrounding abortion, immigration and the other contentious political issues? Then we're back to the mode deriving from dispute; with such widespread disagreement, we may despair of ever finding the answer. Also, what's a "majority" anyway—fifty-one percent, sixty percent, eighty percent? And what constitutes a proper group of truth-makers? Who do you have to ask to discover the truth? All Americans? Just the people who edit Wikipedia? Only the viewers of *The Colbert Report*? Or maybe you just ask Stephen, since he assures us, "On this show your voice will be heard . . . in the form of my voice."[16] These are just some of the difficult questions philosophers ask about relativism. While there may be answers out there, most philosophers today have an unfavorable view of relativism precisely because it's hard to see how these questions can be answered effectively. Wikiality and other forms of relativism may seem like easy answers, but political skeptics need not be convinced.

The effect of political skepticism is often cynicism about politics. Just as Indian skeptics deny that concepts of knowledge make sense, many Americans begin to wonder if old-fashioned concepts of democracy and political knowledge are even coherent and if we might be better off without them. Political actions such as voting, writing letters to Congresspeople, and volunteering for campaigns are thought to be based on mere opinion. Also, we wonder how we'll ever *know* that such actions will make a difference anyway. Thus, it's better to stay home, watch *The Colbert Report* and be a hero like Stephen says: "You're doing something right now. You're watching TV!"[17]

Stephen Colbert: Skeptic, Smart-Ass, or Both?

Stephen, a skeptic? It probably sounds strange. Imagine if Stephen had prominent philosophical skeptics as guests on *The Colbert Report*. Sextus would call Stephen a dogmatist, because Stephen rashly adheres to his beliefs. Jayarasi might call Stephen's pro-

---

[16] Episode 1001, originally aired October 17th, 2005.
[17] Episode 1001, originally aired October 17th, 2005.

nouncements, as he did the pronouncements of some Indian epistemologists, "the gesticulations of a fool." David Hume might cast
I Am America (And So Can You!) into the flames for containing
"nothing but sophistry and illusion." Yet I maintain that there is
something deeply skeptical about *The Colbert Report.*

The regular segment, The WØRD, shows that every concept has
an equal and opposite (and hilarious) counter-concept. This makes
our concepts unstable and allows the audience to either suspend
judgment or deny the coherence of such concepts. As fans of *The
Report* know, The WØRD features Stephen's usual pundit-style
monologue on one side of the screen with a written commentary,
usually satirizing Stephen's monologue, on the other. Consider The
WØRD segment on "wikiality."[18] Stephen asks, "Who is Britannica
to tell me that George Washington had slaves?" and the commentary reads, "Wikipedia *can* tell a lie." This opposes a rhetorical
question meant to establish wikiality with a satirical comment
meant to undermine the whole idea of wikiality. According to
wikiality, Wikipedia *can't possibly* tell a lie, since Wikipedia is itself
the standard of truth. To suggest that Wikipedia *can* tell a lie is to
undermine wikiality.

A more blatant example of this skeptical opposition occurs
when Stephen claims that Africa has more elephants today than it
did ten years ago (the commentary reads, "Babar getting busy").
Stephen says, "I don't know if that's actually true" while the commentary simply reads, "It isn't." In another example, Stephen says,
"What we're doing is bringing democracy to knowledge" and the
commentary claims, "Definitions will greet us as liberators." Here
the skeptical intent is a bit more subtle, but the idea is the same:
to deflate the concept investigated in The WØRD by removing the
hot air pumped into it by talking heads such as, well, Stephen
Colbert. Sometimes Stephen means to make us suspend judgment
in a Pyrrhonian fashion, but most of the time I think he has in mind
something more akin to Indian skepticism in showing the incoherence of the concept in question.

But, some astute reader might object, doesn't this just show that
Stephen is a smart-ass rather than any kind of dour philosophical
skeptic? Could anything so serious really be happening at Comedy
Central? Wouldn't the network executives be mad if they found out

---

[18] Episode 2096, originally aired July 31st, 2006. All subsequent quotes in this
paragraph are from this episode.

that viewers were exposed to *philosophy* during prime time? The ratings would plummet!

As a comedian, Stephen's "real" motives are hard to pin down, because his first loyalty is to what makes us laugh rather than any program of philosophical insight or philosophically induced happiness. But then the motives of philosophical skeptics—especially of Pyrrhonists and Indian skeptics—are not always so easy to pinpoint either. Sometimes they deliberately contradict themselves and don't seem to put forward any real positions on anything. To make matters more complicated, it seems that Stephen Colbert the person has different motives than Stephen Colbert the host of *The Colbert Report*. But whether he's a skeptic or not, Stephen (both as a person and as a character) is surely a smart-ass, and a damn funny one at that. Perhaps I will simply take Pyrrhonian advice for now and suspend judgment about the philosophical motives of Stephen's shenanigans.

Skeptical Politics: Where's the Commitment?

Recall that political skepticism denies that we can have knowledge on political matters and often leads to cynicism and inaction. It's hard to see how other kinds of skeptics could have much in the way of full-blooded knowledge about politics either. If we don't know, for example, that *our* political outlook is the *right* one, how could we possibly be committed to any form of political ideals or have a basis for political action? If thousands of South Carolinians didn't *know* that Stephen deserved to be on the ballot for the 2008 Presidential Primary, why would they bother signing the petition to get him on the ballot? If the majority of the South Carolina Democratic executive council members didn't *know* that Stephen wasn't "a serious candidate" then why would they have refused to add his name to the ballot?

This basic problem of skepticism and political commitment isn't new. Pyrrhonian skeptics recognized it as a part of a larger problem of how skeptics can do much of anything given their outlook on belief and knowledge. Non-skeptics thought Pyrrhonian suspension of judgment would lead a person to completely stop doing anything. Most non-skeptics, both in Sextus's day and our own, assume that there is some kind of connection between belief or knowledge and action. Having a particular belief or bit of knowledge seems to cause you to act in a certain way. For instance, your belief that Stephen's adopted eagle son, Stephen, Jr., has flown to

Canada might cause you to stand on the border in Bellingham, Washington waving salmon to entice Stephen, Jr. back to America. If we trust Sextus when he tells us Pyrrhonian skeptics have no beliefs, it's hard to see why skeptics would do anything at all.

Sextus responds to this objection by pointing out that skeptics *do* have a standard for action: appearances. Skeptics may not have anything like firm convictions or strong opinions about how things *really* are, but they do have a way things *appear* to them, and these appearances are enough to go on. It might *appear* to Pyrrhonians that Stephen, Jr. has flown to Canada, based on data from the San Francisco Zoo, but if you ask Pyrrhonians a more robust question, "Did Stephen, Jr. *really* go to Canada?" they will respond by suspending judgment. To pick one side or the other on the question of whether Stephen, Jr. *really did* go to Canada or not would create mental disturbance, while going along with your appearances, not holding on to any of them too tightly, is a perfectly good way to go through life as a happy Pyrrhonist. A Pyrrhonist may well go to the border to lure Stephen, Jr. back to America by waving a salmon, but a Pyrrhonist will not be disappointed if Stephen, Jr. doesn't show up. A Pyrrhonist will shrug, say, "Oh well," and move on to the next appearance.

Concerning politics, non-skeptics thought that if a tyrant tried to compel Pyrrhonians to do something despicable and unjust, the Pyrrhonists would not be able to resist. Sextus says that skeptics may well resist the tyrant on the basis of their appearances and their political customs; in fact, skeptics will be able to withstand suffering and cruelty at the hands of a tyrant better than most people, since skeptics will not feel resentment when comparing their treatment to the way things *really are* or *really should be*. So, skeptics surely *can* act politically, but they do so non-dogmatically by going with their appearances and following political customs.[19]

Truthiness of the Appearances

But what does truthiness have to do with all this? If I'm right (and my gut tells me I am), truthiness is a reaction to political skepticism,

---

[19] A great study of skepticism and political action, and one of my inspirations in writing this piece, is John Christian Laursen, *The Politics of Skepticism in the Ancients, Montaigne, Hume, and Kant* (Brill, 1992). See especially Chapter 3: "Can the Skeptic Live a Skeptical Politics?"

which is no doubt why the back cover of *The Best of The Colbert Report* DVD claims, "In this age of skepticism and not getting it, Americans want the truth . . . iness." Truthiness allows us to recognize that we can't really be sure of anything, but we can *nonetheless* be committed to a political position. Sextus talks about "following the appearances"; Stephen could talk about "truthiness of the appearances," in this case, the appearances of the gut. Where facts cannot lead you, allow your gut to be your guide. This is all you need.

Consider the political debate about whether creationism should be taught in public school science classes. Stephen tells evolutionary biologist Richard Dawkins, "If I just think that God just did it, that I can understand."[20] Your *head* might tell you that there's evidence for evolution and elitist biology textbooks might even call evolution a fact, but doesn't it *feel* right—in the gut—that the world and all of its species must've been created by God less than ten thousand years ago in exactly the way they exist now? This is certainly a lot easier, since your gut is a portable reference source (it's always with you!) and doesn't require elitist things like study and education.

Or consider immigration. If you think about it with your head, it's extremely complicated. Most Americans are the descendents of immigrants so it seems fair to allow immigration today, but on the other hand there are a lot of us here already and we wonder whether we can handle more people. You might be led into political skepticism on this issue, since it's complicated and creates a lot of dispute. But truthiness can give an answer! Consider how Stephen puts truthiness into action in *I Am America (And So Can You!)*.

> So let's take a beautiful idea to its logical conclusion and not only leave the past behind but deny that the past ever happened. Like this:
>
> **America is <u>not</u> a land of immigrants.**
>
> There. Was that so hard to say? It makes sense if you think about it. It *feels* like we've been here forever, doesn't it? Let's just assume we have been. (*I Am America*, p. 183)

And what about general political commitment to liberal or conservative *ideals*? Again, you might be led into political skepticism. Who's to say what the best ideals are? How can we provide evi-

---

[20] Episode 2132, originally aired October 17th, 2006.

dence or facts to support something as amorphous and deep-seated as political ideals?[21] One's basic political framework is thought to provide some kind of knowledge about politics. For instance, the conservative framework of limited government interference and personal responsibility will probably tell you that government-sponsored healthcare systems are a bad idea. On the other hand, the liberal ideal of ensuring equal access to basic needs will tell you that some kind of government-sponsored healthcare might be a good idea, because everyone needs healthcare (or even has a *right* to healthcare) and we ought to help everyone get it.

Since our basic political framework generally purports to give us a *means* to knowing things about politics, a political skeptic might be inspired by the Indian skeptic Nagarjuna in the following way. We can't establish our political framework (the means of knowing) without establishing that government-sponsored healthcare is good or bad (the things we know) and we can't establish that government-sponsored healthcare is good or bad without first establishing our political framework. So it appears there is no way to really make sense of *knowing* whether government-sponsored healthcare programs are a good idea.

Truthiness can help! For Stephen, conservative ideals just *feel* right, which allows him to be fully committed to his ideals. He feels in his gut that a conservative outlook is the right one, without having to appeal to outside evidence or knowledge of any kind. Where "truth" fails to push us to political commitment, "truthiness" delivers commitment beyond the need for pesky things like facts and evidence.

It-Getting: The Truth about Truthiness

Is this Colbertian solution to the problem of skepticism and political commitment a good one for America and for democracy? Ultimately, no. Of course, this is precisely Stephen's point. Through his brand of parody and satire, Stephen may be one of the greatest champions for the traditional values of truth and critical thinking on basic cable today. By relentlessly making fun of truthiness he can incite us to reflect on the direction of our culture, to question truthiness and those who wield it.

---

[21] George Lakoff attempts to provide evidence that liberals' "nuturant parent" model of morality is superior to conservatives' "strict father" model in *Moral Politics: How Liberals and Conservatives Think* (University of Chicago Press, 2002).

Truthiness is meant to answer political skepticism by giving us completely certain beliefs resting on the bedrock of our guts. However, Modern skeptic David Hume tells us that skepticism is unavoidable if you think about philosophical problems long enough. For Hume, skepticism is part of the human condition. Could political skepticism be the same? The kind of certainty we aim for in truthiness seems unobtainable, especially in complicated political matters. As I tell my philosophy students, one of the greatest lessons you learn in doing philosophy is that everything is more complicated than you think it is.[22] Stephen teaches us a similar lesson about politics. Truthiness creates nothing but a veneer of false certainty. If you scratch the surface a bit, all the old complexities are revisited. Political skepticism remains.

But if we're left with political skepticism are we then left with the political inaction and cynicism that usually accompany it? I don't think so. The assault on certainty common to Pyrrhonists, Modern skeptics, and Indian skeptics teaches us that action need not be predicated on certainty, knowledge or even substantial belief. In fact, living a full, happy life may even *depend* on dispensing with philosophical or political illusions of certainty. Many people find this frightening, but skeptics show us that giving up on certainty can be liberating.

Some people feel that you either have absolute certainty *or* completely arbitrary opinion. This commits the fallacy of false dichotomy by asserting that there are only two possible options when there are more than two. We might not *know* with certainty that a particular political action or political ideal is *true*. However we can nonetheless go with our appearances, profess our ideals, and act on our commitments, all the while realizing that we could be wrong. Such political action does not rest on certainty, but it need not be entirely arbitrary either. There is a third option: we can continue our investigations and go on the best evidence we have. Such evidence usually lies somewhere between the false certainty of truthiness and the unobtainable certainty of truth. The attitude I have in mind is exemplified by scientifically minded skeptics such as Carl Sagan and the writers of *Skeptical Inquirer* magazine. Sagan says, "Science is far from a perfect instrument of knowledge. It's just the best we have. In this respect, as in many

---

[22] Including this statement!

others, it's like democracy."[23] Neither science nor democracy can give us perfect, certain knowledge, but they both represent the best we can do. If science can successfully get along without certainty, why can't politics?

Some contemporary philosophers have put this issue in terms of a challenge to "give an argument to show that Hitler was a bad man *that would convince Hitler himself.*"[24] Just because we can't meet this challenge, does not mean that we have to admit that Hitler could've been a decent person. We have good reasons to assert that Hitler was bad, even if we can't prove it to everyone. Yes, there is dispute and controversy about political issues, and, yes, political ideals can't be definitively proven. But none of this relegates politics to the heap of mere opinion. Politics encourages in some people the kind of reckless dogmatism known as truthiness. But we don't need truthiness to pick up the slack when it comes to certainty in politics, because we don't need certainty in politics at all. Reflection on the follies of truthiness can go a long way in helping us be a little more careful and bit more modest when it comes to politics, and may even counteract some of the crippling partisan bickering so effectively lampooned by *The Colbert Report*.

Neither should we give up on politics all together. Skeptics can still be liberals or conservatives and argue for their views. They can vote, volunteer for campaigns, or even run for office. They just do a little bit less yelling about it than their truthiness-spouting counterparts (and probably have lower blood pressure too). They also realize that at the end of the day, their political views and cherished ideals may be wrong or even incoherent. This uncertainty is unsettling for most of us, but with a big dose of skeptical therapy, even Stephen Colbert could learn to live happily skeptically after.[25]

---

[23] Carl Sagan, *The Demon-Haunted World: Science as a Candle in the Dark* (Random House, 1995), p. 27.

[24] Hilary Putnam, "Reasonableness as a Fact and as a Value," *Pragmatism: A Contemporary Reader*, edited by Russell B. Goodman (Routledge, 1995), p. 178. Here Putnam is referring to a conversation with fellow philosopher Robert Nozick.

[25] I would like to thank our editor, Aaron Schiller, from the bottom of my gut, not only for many helpful comments on this chapter, but also for being the It-Getter-in-Chief of this volume.

8

The WØRD: Fearless Speech and the Politics of Language

MICHAEL TIBORIS and KORY SCHAFF

Does *The Colbert Report* promote democratic values in American political dialogue? If so, does it encourage substantive criticism of political orthodoxy? Or does it just encourage the politics of cynicism, like so many other cable news shows?

We're going to show you that Stephen Colbert's style of political satire actually *promotes* democratic values of free, open, and critical speech. Colbert's satire reflects an ethical commitment that evokes the earlier spirit of criticism embodied by the ancient Greek philosophical tradition of *parrhesia*, or "speaking the truth" fearlessly in public.

"The WØRD": *Parrhesia*

The ancient Greek ideal of free speech, "*parrhesia*," focused on promoting criticism of political orthodoxy. We think this notion promotes values important to contemporary democracy. We also think that Stephen Colbert's style of satire promotes these values in something like the *parrhesiastic* tradition. So what is *parrhesia*?

Parrhesia is not just saying what is true; it is saying it *because it is true*. This notion of free speech promotes democratic values, in part, by defining the proper means of critiquing political orthodoxy. There are three conditions of *parrhesia* to consider independently when reconstructing its traditional relationship to the practice of democracy: (1) *speaking* the truth freely, (2) *criticism*, and (3) the *duty* to speak the truth.[1] These three aspects capture

---

[1] This division of ideas is based on Foucault's lectures on *parrhesia*. Michel

the external, interpersonal, and internal conditions of free speech that give content to the idea that *parrhesia* is the purview of responsible democratic citizenship. Thought of this way, *parrhesia* is a central ideal of freedom that democratic institutions intend to support, but might rarely achieve.

Free Speech Means Never Having to Say You're Sorry

Speaking the truth freely refers to the external conditions in which individuals engage in political dialogue with one another. Freedom to speak is obviously threatened by direct prohibitions like state censorship, suppression of free press, and threats of violence against those speaking out. Such restrictions may be explicitly articulated by the state, but they may also be implicit to an ethical way of life in which social norms encourage complicity and acquiescence. An example of this would be a deeply entrenched caste system that denies some people access to political dialogue, thereby restricting their ability to speak freely about conditions within the caste system. This doesn't mean *parrhesia* can't be practiced at all in such a society, because privileged classes might not face such restrictions on their ability to speak. So while *parrhesia* is contextual with respect to the conditions under which individuals may speak freely, it makes no claims about who has this power or why. The concept itself is not committed to any particular viewpoint or political interest.[2]

The relationship of the speaker to the truth is another external condition of *parrhesia*. Individuals fail to be *parrhesiastes*, truth-speakers, when they lack sufficient access to the truth, or are otherwise provided with false information. The fact that this external condition is an obstacle to free speech suggests that *parrhesia* might be thought of as positive freedom, requiring more than negative liberty.[3] Rather than protecting individuals from obstacles to

---

Foucault, *Fearless Speech* (Semiotext(e), 2001).

[2] Even though the notion is not committed to any particular political order, the centrality of *parrhesia* in democracy is more pronounced than in other forms of political organization. To borrow a term from John Rawls, *parrhesia* is the "first virtue" of democratic institutions. It is not so for other types of political organization.

[3] See Isaiah Berlin, "Two Concepts of Liberty," in *Four Essays on Liberty* (Oxford University Press, 1969). Negative liberty is basically the absence of

speak freely, *parrhesia* implies that they actually have something to speak about.

The ancient Greeks believe that proof of access to the truth is provided, in part, by possession of a good moral character. This presupposes a relationship between knowledge and virtue that is not widely accepted in the modern scientific worldview, where facts and values are distinct. Like the Greeks, we believe that free speech requires more than just being allowed to speak. But modern speakers see access to information, from multiple reliable sources, as a credential for truth speaking. How much access to good information one requires (and what counts as good information) is not always clear. But individuals who "speak freely" might be doing so without certainty, or they might be offering an opinion freely without being properly informed of the subject matter. Thus, *parrhesia* requires that some external conditions obtain, such as individuals not being physically prevented from speaking or otherwise denied reasonable access to facts. However, as the next few conditions of *parrhesia* make clear, access to "the Truth" is not always necessary to fulfill the obligation to engage in substantive criticism of political orthodoxy.

Talking Is a Gateway to Thinking

The second condition of *parrhesiastic* speech is its function as a form of criticism aimed at political authority or majority sentiment. French philosopher, sociologist, and social critic Michel Foucault (1926–1984) claims that

> The function of *parrhesia* is not to demonstrate the truth to someone else, but has the function of *criticism*: criticism of the interlocutor or the speaker himself. 'This is what you do and this is what you think; but this is what you should not do or should not think'. (*Fearless Speech*, p. 17)

Such criticism is frequently associated with democracy and challenge to political authority. However, there's more to *parrhesia*

---

constraint ("freedom from"), while positive liberty includes the freedom to achieve relevant goals and purposes ("freedom to"). Positive freedom may require substantial material support in order to provide people with the power or ability to speak freely.

than simply pointing out deficiencies of the status quo. *Parrhesiastic* criticism challenges majority opinion, but is also *dialogical* and *risky*. It requires dialogue with or about political authority. In particular, the social role of a *parrhesiastes* requires engaging in a "game" where one positions oneself with respect to others in an argumentative space. While this space is primarily conceived as oppositional, not all critiques of authority are instances of "fearless speech."

Bumper stickers that criticize the president may be a kind of critique, but they are not necessarily *parrhesiastic*. This is because the function of a bumper sticker is to state one's position *without* entering into dialogue with others. Our modern concept of "free speech" is thus wider than that of *parrhesia*, but the latter, contextual, kind of dialogic speech is more suited to promote democratic values. Anyone can slap bumper stickers on their car affirming their own beliefs, but *parrhesia* requires individuals to engage in a certain kind of relationship between themselves and the objects of their critique.

In addition to this dialogical engagement with authority, *parrhesia* emphasizes the risks involved in speaking freely. In his discussion of the "riskiness" of this kind of speaking, Foucault focuses on how such criticism of authority can lead to marginalization and even execution. In modern democracies this risk in speaking freely is rarely as explicit as the threat against Socrates during his trial and execution in ancient Athens. However, it's simply wrong to say that it's never risky to speak freely in modern democracies. Obvious and recent examples from America's political history include controversial figures like Martin Luther King, Robert Kennedy, and former U.S. Surgeon General Joycelyn Elders.

Parrhesiastic speech is risky by its very nature, not simply because of the historical circumstances surrounding the speaker. These risks may come in a variety of forms. In the context of American political dialogue, for instance, individuals take a special kind of risk when criticizing political orthodoxy publicly. They take the risk of having their fundamental views challenged, and perhaps openly defeated, by others. Genuine dialogue thus requires being open to challenge and possibly to being convinced that one is wrong. This arises naturally out of the *parrhesiastic* idea that people engaging in discussion are *talking to* one another rather than *at* one another. In doing so, there's always the risk of discovering that the opposing view is more convincing. It's the fact that one takes this risk that makes democratic dialogue valuable, for without it even individuals who are speaking the truth are either shouting into the void or being shouted down.

Speaking from the Gut

The final aspect of "fearless speech" concerns the relationship of the truth-speaker to moral *duty*. Foucault uses the example of a criminal forced to confess as an example of someone who does not speak *parrhesiastically*, even though he is speaking the truth in admitting his crime. By contrast, *parrhesiastic* speech arises from the obligations of moral conscience. The conception of freedom embodied by practices of *parrhesia* is more than the freedom to do what one wants. Instead, it is the power to act for reasons that one knows are right. For some, the concept of "duty" calls up images of authoritarian obligation, not images of freedom. However, the possibility of democratic discussion depends on individuals viewing themselves as duty-bound to act from their well-considered values as best they can. This ethical commitment to the *truth* as well as the *duty* of truth-telling constitutes part of what it means to speak *parrhesiastically*. The duty to speak freely defines the relationship the speaker must have to herself: she must speak from well-considered values for the purpose of speaking the truth as well as discharging her civic duty.

American Democracy, Mass Media, and the Politics of Language

Does contemporary media exclude "speaking truthfully," *parrhesiastically*, in American politics?

The manipulation of language in political dialogue is an obvious obstacle to substantive criticism of political orthodoxy. Part of the power of Colbert's style of political satire is contextual; it relies on the general dissatisfaction of voters with contemporary media and politics. *The Colbert Report* is modeled on the cable news show with disaffected "talking heads" slanting the news in a partisan direction. This kind of cynical dissatisfaction is expressed on cable news programs that engage their viewers with news "analysis" already constructed for partisan audiences. These pundits represent the worst excesses of partisanship, "framing" information in ways that reinforce such dissatisfaction and detract from informed political dialogue.

In journalism, this practice is called "slanting," while in politics it's called "spinning." Framing, via slanting and spinning, is standard operating procedure in media presentations of information. And it severely inhibits critical and substantive analysis of the status quo. Since both media practitioners and politicians frame political issues in language that promotes affective, emotional, or otherwise irrational analysis for its audience, this tends to promote dissatisfaction with both media and American politics. The excessive reliance on framing, spinning, and slanting information on cable news networks and by politicians is the primary target of Colbert's political satire.

This "politics of language" controls the outcome of communication between media, politicians, viewers, and voters. For example, media practitioners and politicians rely extensively on sound bites developed for popular consumption by political marketers using focus groups. Individuals participate in such focus groups with the good intentions of civic-minded voters, but the outcome of this market-driven political medium is the self-fulfilling prophecy of an impoverished political dialogue.

Both media practitioners and politicians engage in the manipulation of language in order to emphasize particular controversies that highlight strengths, downplay weaknesses, and castigate the opposition. Media-driven politics elicits information from viewers and voters alike, but closer analysis reveals that manipulation, distortion, and outright falsification actually describes the relationship between media and its representation of public sentiment. Voters often provide feedback to both media and politicians through focus groups that allow political marketers to develop a "language" that connects politicians with the interests and attitudes expressed by their constituents.

Political marketers create the language of politicians from the very words used by voters in these focus groups.[4] Yet voters consistently complain that politicians cannot be trusted because they say only what they think will be popular with voters. They call politicians "flip-floppers" but themselves rely on the very same sound bites and slogans given to them by media practitioners and politicians. Either voters are "flip-floppers" and politicians merely

---

[4] Frank Luntz, *Words that Work: It's Not What You Say, It's What People Hear* (Hyperion, 2006).

reflect their inconsistencies, or politicians "flip-flop" because they want to engage different voters who want different things at different times, or even incompatible things at the same time! Either way, the relationship between media practices and American democracy suffers from inconsistency, incoherence, and intellectual schizophrenia.

Media Culpa

Substantive criticism of political orthodoxy is increasingly frustrated by the material conditions of late capitalism, which create a monopoly of information providers. The more media is concentrated in the hands of fewer and fewer owners, the easier it is to control and manipulate the language that is used to describe and evaluate political reality. Since there are fewer owners of media outlets, pundits and politicians are more easily able to frame political reality in ways that favor their view, while excluding real criticism. By extension, mainstream viewers and voters are less able to think critically about the status quo and, more importantly, to think beyond it. In the last twenty years, globalization has strengthened this monopoly on information and, by extension, on American political dialogue.

The majority of media sources are currently corporate-owned. The concentration and accumulation of capital in larger firms has been deleterious to competition among different media sources.[5] The more corporations have consolidated, the more formerly competing media outlets have become owned by the same parent corporations. Although the exact ratio of media outlets to corporate ownership is disputed, it is clear that several corporations, including General Electric, Viacom, News Corporation, and Time-Warner, own the majority of cable news networks and newspaper syndicates.

One consequence of this consolidation is that the monopoly of the market correlates with the "monopoly of meaning" so to speak. The less diversified the sources of news are, the less diversified the language for describing and evaluating news events and politics becomes. Media practitioners, especially "talking heads" and partisan pundits, frame information in almost identical ways

---

[5] C. Edwin Baker, *Media Concentration and Democracy: Why Ownership Matters* (Cambridge University Press, 2007).

as fewer news wire services limit the terminology reproduced by subscribers. News agencies and reporters then repeat this language over and over, and thus fewer and fewer critical alternatives exist for describing and evaluating these events. The result is that you can hear the same discussion in nearly the same words wherever you look. This encourages the belief that what you're hearing is the *authoritative* view, even if it's just the most repeated one.

Another consequence of corporate consolidation of media is the intensification of the news cycle, so that all media outlets simultaneously and continuously report on events. This inevitably frames events in ways that restrict alternative perspectives from being introduced to viewers. A widely discussed example in studies of media and cognition is the so-called "crack" crisis of the 1980s, which was perpetuated by media relying on false and falsified information.

> Where was the press's information coming from? Surveys of media's report on crack reveal that the vast majority of experts cited in news reports of the drug were taken from law-enforcement communities and politicians, followed by interviews from punters on the street. The single *least*-cited sources were academics—the people who had actually studied the drug. The reason? Academics tend to be less sensational and more circumspect. They don't launch into vitriolic condemnations of crack the way police and politicians do. In short, their sound bites aren't as good.[6]

More recently, the ubiquitous phrase "weapons of mass destruction," which was used by the Bush Administration in the build up to the invasion of Iraq in 2002, led the American Dialect Society to vote "WMD" as "Word of the Year." Such examples demonstrate that the "bottleneck" of corporate ownership over media outlets has immense influence over the meaning of news events, in effect controlling the political impact of these events through sensational language, repetition, and selective use of sources. Furthermore, there is increasing evidence that information also has to be approved for audiences in advance, further restricting the diverse dissemination of transparent information. Whistle-blowers point out instances of

---

[6] Dominic Streatfield, *Cocaine: An Unauthorized Biography* (Macmillan, 2003), p. 309.

censorship inside newspapers and cable news programs in an effort to expose the fact that partisan politics increasingly influences the dissemination of information.[7]

Finally, the "loyal opposition" has largely failed to appreciate that the battle of ideas is covertly influenced by the politics of language, and therefore have come late on the scene to counter the language of political orthodoxy with alternative formulations. They have relied on the naive view that "good" ideas eventually replace "bad" ideas in the free marketplace of ideas. Not true. Herbert Marcuse (1898–1979) used the phrase "one-dimensional" thought to describe the assimilation of organized opposition, even formerly "critical" ideas, in ways that support the reproduction of status quo politics.

> The result is the familiar Orwellian language ("peace is war" and "war is peace," etc.), which is by no means that of terroristic totalitarianism only . . . Relatively new is the general acceptance of these lies by private and public opinion, the suppression of their monstrous content. The spread and effectiveness of this language testify to the triumph of society over the contradictions which it contains; they are reproduced without exploding the social system. And it is the outspoken, blatant, contradiction which is made into a device of speech and publicity. The syntax of abridgement proclaims the reconciliation of opposites by welding them together in a firm and familiar structure. . . . the "clean bomb" and the "harmless fall-out" are only the extreme creations of a normal style.[8]

Even as early as the 1950s, it was apparent to Marcuse that the rise of mass media in the context of the growing collusion between politics and corporate ownership would lead to decreasing substantive criticism of political orthodoxy. The very idea of "one dimensional thought" for Marcuse is that political dialogue lacks the "fearless speech" characteristic of *parrhesia*. Between the material conditions of late capitalism—media consolidation and expansion—substantive criticism and opposition to political orthodoxy have been made largely ineffective.

---

[7] See the recent documentary *Outfoxed: Rupert Murdoch's War on Journalism*, which exposes the politics of language inevitably involved in corporate-owned media outlets like that of the Fox News Network.

[8] Herbert Marcuse, *One-Dimensional Man* (Beacon Press, 1964/1991), p. 89. Contemporary examples are abundant: "clean coal," "energy independence," "market correction," and "war on terror."

Given that particular words like "flip-flopper" and "evil-doer," as well even such seemingly innocuous words like "freedom" and "marriage," increasingly influence the interpretation of political events and figures, linguist George Lakoff recommends a principled approach when engaging in political debate with the opposition: "Do not use their language."[9] However, it's precisely Colbert's capacity for appropriating the dominant rhetoric of political orthodoxy that makes his style of political satire a contribution to democratic political dialogue. Colbert uses the language of media practitioners and politicians to subvert many of their core beliefs. He engages in framing, spinning, and slanting all the time. But viewers are in on the joke, which exposes such practices for what they are, and brings to light the ways that they undermine democratic values of free, open, and critical speech.

Much of the power of Colbert's humor lies in the fact that contemporary media and politics, especially on the cable news networks, are failing to address substantive issues in favor of preserving preposterous language-games. These language-games of weak and duplicitous reasoning provide a target-rich environment for Colbert's political satire.

"The WØRD": Reading Between the Lines

In the recurring segment "The WØRD," Colbert satirizes contemporary news analysis through a familiar visual presentation employed by cable news shows. These shows place the face of the "talking head" next to a panel of text, which outlines, emphasizes, and even highlights the content of the analysis being presented. Mimicking not only the visual style of this cable news staple, Colbert takes up their way of talking as well. He speaks in the language of political orthodoxy, and repeats its main points in the terms that they have chosen to frame them. Colbert happily throws around terms like "flip-flopper" and never misses an opportunity to discuss the most recent "number one threat facing America." Meanwhile, the bullet points beside him visually lay out the critical viewpoint, which is aimed squarely at viewers and voters.

Beyond its comedic value, the segment is also quite effective as *parrhesiastic* speech, and not just to the extent that it works as a

---

[9] George Lakoff, *Don't Think of an Elephant: Know Your Values and Frame the Debate—The Essential Guide for Progressives* (Chelsea Green, 2004).

critique of conservative "talking heads." The WØRD segment is just as much a critique of the current role of TV in political dialogue. To see what we mean, consider that, for better or for worse, TV is where most of the public dialogue about American politics takes place. The news media's presentation of political arguments is meant to supplant our own participation in such discussions. They carry on these discussions for our sake, and with the help of expert guests, data, polls, and staged arguments between representatives of different viewpoints. The result is a kind of play-argument where the critical political speech is acted out for us, leaving us the passive role of viewing the discussion.

Contrary to this kind of presentation, Colbert enters a critical dialogue with the news media itself by explicitly mimicking, and implicitly mocking, this form of presentation. Colbert tells us "this is what they say and think," while the bullet points tell us "this is what they should not say or should not think." To this extent, the segment models a critical form of dialogue by individuals who present different viewpoints to us, but the point is to call into question the language that is used to articulate and defend these viewpoints. The bullet points provide viewers with a critical subtext that challenges what is being spoken. Thus, the satirical presentation of political dialogue in "The WØRD" segment in fact suggests the form of political speech we should strive for: *active* criticism of political viewpoints and the language used to articulate and defend them.

An Out of Control "Fact Insurgency"

The idea of truthiness is particularly relevant here since, all too often it seems, the goal of speakers in media and politics is to *appear parrhesiastic*, rather than actually to be so. As Colbert demonstrates time and again, truthiness often comes in the form of language designed to avoid critique by making it hard to deny, or even understand, the claims made by the speaker. Colbert recently exposed such a strategy in Republican presidential candidate John McCain's attempts to separate himself from President Bush's war doctrine, in spite of McCain's ongoing public support for both Bush and the War in Iraq. Where President Bush has previously used words like "existential threat" to talk about international terrorism, McCain chooses the word "transcendental" to emphasize the importance of the conflict. Colbert analyzes this contrast of terminology in "The WØRD" segment (the bullet-point critique is emphasized in brackets).

> Folks, language is very important in politics, particularly when it comes to war. [Weapons of mass description.] For years the Bush Administration used the phrase "war on terror" which was replaced with the phrase "the global war on terror." [Bush loves nicknames.] Then it was "the global struggle against extremism," then briefly it was "the long war" before they settled on the new name, "hey, maybe we should bomb Iraq." [The "Maybe" proves they're diplomats.][10]

On McCain's new word for describing the conflict, Colbert has this to say:

> That's right. The war is now 'transcendental.' [Transcends voter approval]. No surprise. After all, Toby Keith's anti-terrorist lyric 'We'll put a boot up your ass. It's the American Way' originally appeared in Henry David Thoreau's *Walden*. (Episode 4081)

He goes on to show that this word makes little sense in the context, which suggests that it may have been chosen merely to sound impressive, or perhaps to make it impossible to pin down McCain's actual view.

> Does he mean "transcendent," which according to *Webster's* means "exceeding usual limits"? Because the war has certainly exceeded the time limit. [And the constitution] Or, is he intentionally using the word "transcendental," which is defined by *Webster's* as "of or relating to experience as determined by the mind's makeup," in which case he's saying the war on terror is all in our heads? [Along with Cheney's buckshot.] (Episode 4081)

Colbert makes the criticism explicit by changing other ways President Bush has described his policies into other religious-sounding plays on words. This rephrasing tactic doesn't just color the arguments of politicians. It's done to disengage them altogether from responding to and accepting criticism. Rather than engage in real dialogue about their (lack of) substantive disagreement, McCain's strategy is to linguistically reframe his views so that they

---

[10] Episode 4081, originally aired June 18th, 2008. The WØRD was "Lexicon Artist."

no longer look similar to Bush's. Of course, this is not real democratic speech, as Colbert points out, in what he presents as a winking *endorsement* of McCain's tactics: "Using language to turn failed policies into ideals that transcend debate is the best way to get people to think of you as 'transcen-presidential'."

Sometimes the suppression of criticism is not done by using opaque language, but by distorting the relative importance of the claims being made. As Colbert so often shows, media cover non-stories with the same kind of seriousness that they cover important news topics. When these less serious issues get serious attention, they appear to be more significant than they are. Thus, they take on an air of "factiness" as Colbert says.

In a recent episode, Colbert discussed a CNN story about Democratic presidential candidate Barack Obama, which compared Obama's style of dress (collared shirt, no tie, dark blazer) with that of Iranian President Mahmoud Ahmadinejad. He criticizes both the reasoning of the story and its representation as information that is *factual* and therefore news worthy.

> It is a *fact* that Barack Obama dresses like Mahmoud "Ahmedinefrere-jacqueijad." It is also a *fact* that Mr. Obama is a carbon-based life form. Just like Osama bin Laden. If Obama *really* wanted to separate himself from our enemies, wouldn't he try to be one of those sulfur-based tubeworms that live in the volcanic vents off the coast of Chile?[11]

These things are true statements or "facts," but the implied conclusion is absurd nonetheless. The very presentation of such "facts" by a credible news source misrepresents the relative significance of *all* the claims being made. Is Barack Obama intellectually, politically, or religiously like President Ahmadinejad simply because they both eschew ties? Distorting the relative importance of a claim is often as effective as obscuring access to the truth itself, because the former blocks one's access to dialogue about substantive political issues that matter to democracy. Colbert calls this common strategy of treating all "facts" as equally important "fighting facts with 'facts.'":

> Until now, folks, my job has been to protect you from the facts. Now my job is to bring you the *selected* facts that will protect you. These

---

[11] Episode 3001, originally aired January 8th, 2007. The WØRD WAS "FACTS".

will be real facts that I can prove, or you can't disprove. To give you the real sense, the "factiness" if you will, of what's going on in Washington. (Episode 3001)

Framing, slanting, and spinning further predispose viewers to respond favorably to the claims of purported truth-speakers. Use of affective language in particular reduces complex arguments to simplistic and emotionally-charged caricatures. If all terms of debate are reduced to emotional reactions rather than judgments informed by critical reasoning, then real debate cannot exist. These emotions may be powerful, filling viewers with fear or nationalistic pride. But under these conditions, the best we can do when confronted with others who disagree is assert opposed emotions, shame them, or otherwise terrorize them into agreement. To the extent that the news media adopts these argumentative tactics they stifle free debate.

If real, *parrhesiastic* criticism of political orthodoxy requires reliable access to good information and open discussion, then it is clear that media and political control over language frustrate this access. Either this control obscures the meaning of terms, misrepresents their relative importance, or cloaks them in affective language. This encourages the presentation of claims as "facts" when they are merely "facty." Colbert's critique in "The WØRD" amounts to pointing out that media and politicians alike undermine reasonable access to the truth and diminish the democratic values of free, open, and critical speech through the manipulation of language.

Finally, Colbert uses "The WØRD" segment to critique the media's self-perception that they are dutiful speakers of the truth for their viewers. Media sources work very hard to suggest that they can be trusted to present accurate information and representative, balanced debates about issues. Such claims depend on the authority of the news reporter or visual graphics suggesting both authority and truthfulness. The intense graphics and music which open news programs, and often punctuate segments within them, are meant to reinforce the authority of the news source while invoking a particular emotional reaction in the viewer. Colbert mocks this strategy directly by pushing it to absurdity in the beginning of his show. Both the opening credits and the set are saturated with stars, flags, bald eagles, and other totems of American patriotism.

Media practitioners do more than just suggest their truthfulness though their visual graphics, however. They must show that they have special access to the truth which, as we suggested above, means presenting themselves as authoritative and unbiased, with a kind of "duty" to bring out the truth. But for all the reasons we have discussed so far, this can only rise to the level of appearances, a kind of fake-dutifulness. Colbert points this out by frequently mentioning his "duty" to "protect" his viewers from information that challenges beliefs they already have. He is simultaneously and ironically claiming to be impartial and biased. This is, of course, the position of all news analysts, and Colbert's critique lies in making this conflict conspicuous.

But Does Political Satire Promote Democratic Values?

There's no more clear evidence that Colbert's style of political satire promotes democratic values, including criticism of status quo politics, than "The WØRD" segment. It attacks both the content and the visual format of American political discourse, and it raises substantial challenges to media, politics, and the claim that any one of its defenders speaks truthfully in support of free, open, and critical political dialogue.

Colbert's satire succeeds because it models substantive critique in the media's own language. He exposes the failure of the media to support democratic values allowing criticism of political orthodoxy by identifying the ways framing obstructs or altogether evades critique and debate, and he derides the efforts of both media and politicians to appear engaged in real debate. In this respect, by speaking in the very words of political orthodoxy, then ridiculing them with bullet points and ironic commentary, Colbert shows how political satire can act in the service of promoting democratic values in political dialogue.

But is Colbert's style of political satire sufficiently similar to the practice of *parrhesia* to justify our claim that it promotes substantive criticism of political orthodoxy? Or is it just the politics of cynicism played out as satire? One objection to the point we have been making is that Colbert's political satire is ill-suited to promote informed political dialogue. Even though he criticizes media and politicians, it can be objected that this doesn't mean that Colbert himself promotes either democratic values or *substantive* kinds of criticism. After all, a major goal of the show is poking fun at the status quo and making his audience laugh, not improving political dialogue. While we acknowledge the limitations of both television and satire for improving the impoverished dialogue of American politics, there are still features of Colbert's style that are uniquely *parrhesiastic* in their criticism of political orthodoxy.

Colbert's focus on the dominant rhetoric of media practitioners and politicians, the demands he makes on his audience, as well as the risks he takes as a commentator all work to qualify his speech as "fearless." His satire is aimed at media as well as viewers, who are complicit in the poor quality of political dialogue in America. This is the kind of critique that makes it nearly impossible to view "actual" news media in the same way ever again. In this respect Colbert's style of political satire has the *function* of critique. "The WØRD" segment makes this clear: Colbert exposes the collusion between media practitioners and politicians who frame news and information in ways that subverts access to truth in politics. Colbert forcefully exposes viewers' and voters' responsibility to critically assess the quality, sources, and motivations of media practitioners and politicians.

And that's "The WØRD."

9

Philosophy in the Age of Truthiness

DAVID DETMER

We live in an age of advertising, public relations, and political propaganda. It seems that the cynical manipulation of belief is increasingly replacing rational fact-and-evidence-based discussion as the dominant form of discourse in all areas of public life. The result is not pretty. The President of the United States makes false claims about weapons of mass destruction; the mainstream media play along and decline to challenge him; the country wages war as a result; and the likes of Rush Limbaugh, Ann Coulter, and Bill O'Reilly successfully masquerade as serious political analysts despite their utter contempt for factual accuracy and total disregard for even the most minimal standards of logical cogency, intellectual honesty, and simple fairness.

One of Stephen Colbert's greatest achievements is to have satirized this phenomenon brilliantly by coining the term "truthiness." Whereas a claim is "true," in the old-fashioned sense, only if it accurately states the way things actually are (as determined by a careful and scrupulous examination of the relevant evidence), truthiness has nothing to do with facts, evidence, reason, logic, or correspondence with the way things really are. Rather, truthiness has to do with what is "felt in the gut." If you *believe* something strongly enough, even if that belief is merely based on wishful thinking, then it *is* true (or, rather, "truthy"). The old-fashioned belief in objective truth is rejected as oppressive and bullying. As Colbert puts it, "Who is *Britannica* to tell me that George Washington had slaves? If I want to say that he didn't, that's my right" (*The Colbert Report*, July 31st, 2006).

In a rare, out-of-character interview, Colbert has made it clear (perhaps for the benefit of those who don't quite "get" satire), that he deplores truthiness, indeed that he thinks that "truthiness is tearing apart our country."[1] Philosophers, who generally see themselves as champions of logic and reason, should applaud. And they certainly must see themselves as exempt from Colbert's critique.

But are they? Many philosophers rely rather heavily on "intuition." That is, they claim that some truths are self-evident, and can be known simply on the basis of direct inspection of them, without the intermediary of evidence or reasons. For example, in ethics, theories are often "tested" by seeing how well they conform to what we allegedly know intuitively to be true (for example, that torturing young children for the sheer fun of it is morally wrong). Is this reliance on "intuition" really any different from what Colbert so deftly skewers as "truthiness"?

The Age of Truthiness: How Did We Get Here?

Before turning to that, however, let's consider a bit of history. The twentieth century brought two innovations that have helped to usher in the age of truthiness: (1) the application of scientific methods to the practice of manipulating opinions and attitudes (leading to more effective techniques in advertising, public relations, marketing, and political propaganda) and (2) the development of electronic media, such as radio, television, and the internet (facilitating the rapid and prolific distribution of the fruits of all that cutting-edge scientific research). The result is a culture that is thoroughly saturated with corporate-sponsored messages and relentlessly indoctrinated into the worldview those messages cumulatively promote.

But why should improvements in the techniques of persuasion and in the distribution of information lead automatically to deterioration in intellectual standards? After all, might not advertisers, politicians, and others in the business of persuasion put these improved methods and technologies to the service of communicating cogently reasoned, fact-and-evidence-based messages in support of conclusions that they find to be true?

---

[1] This interview is available at http://www.avclub.com/content/node/44705, accessed April 20th, 2008.

How Do You Sell a Mediocre Product?

Occasionally they do, but generally not, and for several reasons. First, while sellers of a genuinely superior product need not resort to deception in order to persuade potential customers to buy it, the truth will not serve sellers of inferior products nearly as well. And very few advertisers, whether they are selling toothpaste, lite beer, automobile insurance, or what have you, are blessed with the advantage of backing a product that significantly differs from its major competitors. The sad truth is that most products consist of basically the same ingredients in roughly the same proportions as are found in the products with which they compete. Those in the selling business have learned that it is easier, and more cost effective, to differentiate their products from those of their competitors by marketing them differently than by actually making them different. Creating a superior ad campaign, though neither easy nor inexpensive, turns out to be a more economically sound strategy than creating a better product. And if you're trying to peddle an inferior or indistinguishable product, facts, evidence, reasoning, and the truth are not your friends. As a result, such reasoning as one finds in contemporary advertising tends to be fallacious, rather than cogent.

Advertising and the Avoidance of Reason

But a more significant result, and one that entails an even more drastic rejection of the norms of cogent reasoning, is that modern advertisements tend to avoid reasoning entirely. One would not go far wrong in thinking of modern advertising as an attempt, on a gigantic scale, to create a world in which concerns about issues of meaning and truth do not arise. Handsome people, perhaps celebrities, are shown using the product and smiling with enjoyment; animals speak; humorous incidents are depicted; catchy tunes featuring the name of the product are sung; but, typically, no specific claims or arguments are made. The advertisements seem designed to drill the name of the product into viewers' minds, and to cause the audience to associate that name with pleasant sounds, images, and thoughts, thus predisposing these "consumers" to want to buy the product. Only an occasional commercial (and generally a very badly constructed one) provokes viewers to ask themselves what the claims in the commercial might mean.

One can readily see the utility of this attempt to bypass rationality. Cogent arguments cannot lend support to a decision to purchase an inferior or mediocre product. But fallacious arguments, when scrutinized by a public critically engaged with questions of meaning and truth, are likely to be seen through and rejected. The best solution, then, is to sell through non-rational means, that is, to persuade without engaging the audience's rational faculties. Thus, to the extent that we are inundated with advertising, we are immersed in a world in which the concept of truth is a stranger.

Contemporary Politics

In the realm of politics, truth and the norms associated with it are enemies to those who back indefensible programs and policies. Politicians whose primary concern is to please their corporate sponsors, even at the expense of the general welfare, are hardly in a position to defend their actions with rationally compelling arguments. Little wonder, then, that contemporary political "debate" and "discussion" is carried out at such an appallingly impoverished intellectual level. Politicians are sold in the same way that toothpaste, dishwasher detergent, and fast food hamburgers are sold. Indeed, political advertisements, if anything, tend toward even greater heights of irrationality than those achieved in their non-political counterparts, due to the prevalence, in politics, of "negative" advertising—that is, commercials in which the candidate offers no concrete policy proposal, issue-oriented argument, or even positive statement about his or her own achievements or values, but rather instead viciously attacks a wildly distorted caricature of the opponent's character or record.

Elitism

Regardless of where they began, modern advertising and politics have spread their way around the world. But there are certain other typically American ideas that have helped to facilitate the emergence of the age of truthiness. One such idea is the rejection of elitism. Consider the following two quotations from Stephen Colbert's book, *I Am America (And So Can You!)*:

> [This book is] not just some collection of reasoned arguments supported by facts. That's the coward's way out. This book is Truth. My

truth . . . like our Founding Fathers, I hold my Truths to be self-evident, which is why I did absolutely no research. I didn't need to. The
only research I needed was a long hard look in the mirror. (*I Am
America*, pp. viii–ix)

. . . science is elitist . . . who gave some lab-coated pipette wielder per-
mission to act like he knows more than I do about mitochondria, just
because he spent twenty years of his life studying them in a laboratory? PhDs and 300-page dissertations don't make his opinion any
more valid. (*I Am America*, p. 194)

Americans are very suspicious of elites, often for very good reason.
There is indeed something offensive and disturbing about the idea
that some people should be considered better than others, or given
more authority or credibility than others, merely on the basis of
some arbitrary characteristic. Moreover, we have the idea, which
fits naturally with the ideals of democracy, that thinking about serious matters is everyone's business—an arena into which everyone
is entitled to enter.

But Colbert's satire exposes the downside of these ideas. While
it is laudable to withhold deference to those who have not demonstrated any special excellence, the case is quite different with
regard to those who have. Americans seem readily to acknowledge
this point in some spheres of life. No one sneeringly dismisses
champion athletes as "elitists." But while appeals to authority are
indeed a genuine affront to science (and not merely to Colbert's
feigned anti-elitist sensibilities), the reason is that, in science, what
counts is *evidence*, not credentials.

So while Colbert's persona is technically right in saying that the
scientist's PhD, three-hundred-page dissertation, and twenty years
of research experience do not guarantee that his opinions on mitochondria are more cogent than are Colbert's own, he goes dramatically wrong in thinking that the relative merits of the differing
opinions can be decided without reference to evidence. Thus, anti-
elitism, which in the context of scientific practice results in a refusal
of the lazy method of deference to credentialed authority, is turned,
in the hands of Colbert's persona, into the lazy claim that one's
own opinions should be afforded equal status to opinions that have
survived numerous vigorous attempts at refutation in the scientific
laboratory.

Having the Right to Believe Doesn't Mean that Your Belief is Right

Another truthiness-enhancing idea is the conflation of the fact that I have the right, in the legal-political sense, to hold a certain opinion with the very different claim that my opinion is therefore *substantively* right (in the sense of "accurate" or "correct"), or at least *as* right as any other opinion. As Colbert puts it, "Who's Britannica to tell me the Panama Canal was built in 1914? If I want to say it was built in 1941, that's my right as an American!" (*I Am America*, p. 223). This conflation thus trades on at least two equivocations. Not only are two senses of "right" conflated, but also the very different ideas of legal equality and the equality of different pieces of "evidence." Colbert lampoons this confusion by asserting: "It's natural to be curious about our world, but the scientific method is just one theory about how best to understand it. We live in a democracy, which means that we should treat every theory equally" (*I Am America*, p. 193).

Colbert's very good at making fun of this all-too-common idea that popular opinion, democratic processes, or market forces, should be extended far beyond their proper domain, so as to determine the truth or falsity of matters that can be legitimately settled only by reference to evidence and reasoning:

> [S]cience is elitist. Making rules, setting boundaries, constantly telling us what is and isn't flammable—all without input from the very people who are expected to abide by these laws. I know I never consented to Gravity Without Representation. (*I Am America*, p. 194)

> Some say [physics] is fundamental; I say it's a bunch of unnecessary regulations. Physics is the ultimate Big Government interference—universal laws meant to constrain us at every turn. No staying in motion if acted on by a net force. No thermodynamic systems without entropy. Hey, is it wrong that I sometimes want to act without having to deal with an equal and opposite reaction? . . . We'd be a lot better off if we took physics off the books and just let the free market decide what was possible for matter. (*I Am America*, pp. 201–02)

Objectivity

Finally, consider the journalistic ideal of "objectivity." According to it, mass media journalists are to strive to keep their reporting "objective," in the sense of presenting only "the facts," while specifically avoiding the inclusion of conclusions, opinions, and value-judgments. To be sure, opinions and value-judgments are to be given their place, in letters, editorials, and commentaries. But these are to be clearly labeled as such and kept strictly separate from the main business of journalism—the straight, objective, reporting of hard news. Opinion columns, by contrast, are said to be "subjective." Accordingly, they seem not to be held to any discernible standards of logical cogency or factual accuracy.

From a philosophical standpoint, this doctrine is open to multiple objections. For example, the distinction between facts and conclusions appears to be untenable. Facts are not simply given, but rather must be reasoned to on the basis of evidence. One must *conclude* that a given claim is, indeed, factual. It thus makes no sense to try to include facts while excluding conclusions. Similarly, it's difficult to see how anyone could write an article about anything without making value-judgments about what is or is not worthy of inclusion in the article. And these value-judgments, in turn, would depend on other value-judgments concerning whether or not a given item is important or interesting or relevant or significant.

Perhaps the biggest problem with the journalistic doctrine of objectivity, however, is that it seems in practice to lead away from an engagement with evidence and reasoning. For in determining whether or not a given claim is factual, journalists tend to turn to the question of whether or not there is a consensus of opinion in the "right" circles in support of the claim. If a claim is supported across the spectrum of mainstream U.S. political opinion, it can safely be affirmed as a fact, even if the evidence, or the rest of the world, or the findings of scholars, would strongly suggest otherwise.

For example, it frequently happens that both Democrats and Republicans in positions of power favor giving diplomatic, economic and military support to governments with abysmal human rights records. Abysmal, that is, if you listen to scholars of human rights issues, and independent human rights monitoring organizations, such as Amnesty International, Americas Watch, The International Committee of the Red Cross, and The International Council of Jurists. When this happens, the U.S. mass media tend to present the Democrat-Republican consensus as the factual, uncontroversial and objective truth. The alternative view, that of the scholars and human rights organizations, on the rare occasions when it is mentioned at all, is dismissed as nutty at worst, or biased at best.

It is as if the point of the doctrine of objectivity were to avoid offending two constituencies: corporations (since media outlets do not wish to undermine their own interests, or those of their corporate sponsors) and the audience for mass media journalism (which is overwhelmingly concentrated within the spectrum of mainstream opinion described above). So the upshot of the doctrine of journalistic objectivity is that claims that are universally affirmed within the right circles are treated as facts; claims that are universally rejected within those same circles are dismissed as falsehoods; and claims that are controversial within those same circles are treated as subjective, as matters of opinion—to be dealt with in editorials and opinion columns.

The Coming of the Gasbags

This state of affairs allows truthiness to flourish. It also helps to explain the otherwise inexplicable rise of such factually-challenged pundits as Bill O'Reilly, Ann Coulter, and Rush Limbaugh, whose repeated bombastic insistence that ludicrous falsehoods be accepted as facts is so deftly satirized by Stephen Colbert.[2] As funny and entertaining as Colbert's character is, it's almost sad that his comedy has such wide appeal. It means that Limbaugh and O'Reilly, with their total disregard for the truth, have a profound degree of influence over the course of American civic discourse. Their success is evidence that the critical norms associated with a concern for truth are not enjoying robust health in America right now.

But this should worry us. Truth matters. Just as a brain surgeon will be unlikely to perform successful surgery without an accurate understanding of the physiology and functioning of the brain, so

---

[2] On Limbaugh, see Steven Rendall, Jim Naureckas, and Jeff Cohen, *The Way Things Aren't: Rush Limbaugh's Reign of Error* (The New Press, 1995); and Ray Perkins, *Logic and Mr. Limbaugh* (Open Court, 1995). On Coulter, see Michael Scherer and Sarah Secules, "Books: How Slippery Is *Slander?*" *Columbia Journalism Review* (November–December 2002), http://cjrarchives.org/issues/2002/6/slander-scherer.asp, accessed April 20th, 2008; Bryan Keefer, "Throwing the Book at Her," *Spinsanity* (July 13th, 2002), http://www.spinsanity.org/columns/20020713.html, accessed April 20th, 2008; and Bendan Nyhan, "Screed: With *Treason*, Ann Coulter Once Again Defines a New Low in America's Political Debate," *Spinsanity* (June 30th, 2003), http://www.spinsanity.com/columns/20030630.html, accessed April 20th, 2008. On O'Reilly, see Peter Hart, *The Oh Really? Factor* (Seven Stories, 2003).

will we be unable to solve the major social and political problems facing our society without genuine knowledge concerning both the functioning of our culture and the likely effects of various changes that might be implemented. What we need, in short, is real truth. We need an accurate understanding, based on careful, responsible, logical analysis of the relevant evidence. Ignorant opinions emanating from the gut just won't cut it.

Intuition

But don't philosophers also make extensive use of unsupported opinions precisely in the same way that Limbaugh, O'Reilly, and Colbert do? After all, many philosophers appeal in their work to "intuition." They claim that it's possible to know the truth of some statements merely through a careful, close-up inspection of them, without making use of any supporting evidence, arguments, or reasoning of any kind. This gives rise to the suspicion that perhaps a philosopher's claim to know self-evident truths intuitively is no different from Colbert's insistence that he can justify his assertions by referring to the way they feel in his gut. And if it's appropriate to reject the latter claim (and, indeed, as Colbert's performance indicates, to ridicule it satirically and to laugh at it), why doesn't the philosopher's assertion warrant the same treatment?

The answer lies in noticing the ways in which the philosopher's appeal to intuition differs from Colbert's appeal to his gut and Limbaugh's or O'Reilly's uncritical reliance on their prejudices. To see this, let's consider the ways in which some philosophers use intuition.

Perhaps the most important use of intuition flows from the idea that without intuition there can be no knowledge at all. To see why this is so, consider what it would mean to deny that we can know anything intuitively. Such a denial amounts to the claim that there are no self-evident truths and that all knowledge claims must, therefore, be backed with reasons. But notice that this leads to an infinite regress. I cannot know A unless I have a reason, B, that supports A. But I can't claim to know B unless I have a reason, C, that supports *it*. But then C needs support from D, and D from E, and so on endlessly. So it seems that I can't legitimately claim to know anything, since each attempt to demonstrate the truth of a claim merely puts in place a need to demonstrate the truth of the reason that supports it. Thus, either we don't know anything, or else we must know some things intuitively.

Let's consider an example, from the domain of ethics. Suppose I make the claim that torture should never be used as an interrogation technique. You, appropriately enough, ask me to provide reasons in support of this claim. I then produce evidence that torture is an ineffective interrogation technique—many people will not talk, no matter how much they are tortured, while others are so desperate to make the excruciating pain go away that they will say anything, even if they have no relevant knowledge to impart. I also produce evidence suggesting that any policy attempting to mitigate the potential horrors of a torture policy by setting in place strict controls and limits concerning its proper use are likely to fail. Given certain facts about human psychology, and about how bureaucracies work, any policy sanctioning torture will almost certainly be abused in horrific ways. This will in turn lead to the infliction of massive amounts of pain on many innocent people, even though very little if any reliable information will be yielded as a result. Now, you might well dispute any of these claims, perhaps backing your judgment with evidence and arguments of your own. But suppose you accept my supporting claims and yet remain unconvinced of the truth of my conclusion. I, after recovering from my profound surprise, point out that cruelty is a bad thing—that it is wrong to inflict intense suffering on people needlessly. Should you demand evidence for *that* claim, however, I would be stumped. The wrongness of cruelty seems evident on its face, which is to say that it can be known intuitively.

If one is suspicious of knowledge claims in ethics, it must be pointed that the same logic that leads to intuition in ethics does so in every other field as well. Even fields employing the strictest and most exacting standards of precision and proof, such as mathematics, must rely on intuition. For example, Euclidean geometry rests on a very small number of self-evident "axioms" or "postulates," from which all of its other findings are deduced. Examples include "It is possible to draw a straight line from any point to any other point," and "It is possible to describe a circle with any center and any radius." One can no more prove these claims than one can demonstrate that any object having size must also have shape, but they are no less obviously true for that.

This is enough to show that the philosopher's appeal to intuition differs greatly from the conduct of O'Reilly, Limbaugh, and Colbert. The claims that "whatever is colored is extended in space," that "things which are equal to the same thing are also equal to one another," and that "happiness is better than misery" are plausibly regarded as self-evident. We have a kind of *insight* into them. They appear to be not only true, but *necessarily* so, in the sense that their denial seems unthinkable or inconceivable.

The same is obviously not the case with regard to such historical claims as that George Washington had slaves, or that the Panama Canal was built in 1914. It is quite easy to imagine such claims as either true or false. Neither their affirmation nor their denial generates any insight or sense of necessity. Their truth or falsity depends on what actually happened in history, and we cannot know that merely by thinking about it. We must, instead, consult the relevant evidence. Similarly, complex, many-sided issues, such as the question of why a particular verdict was reached in a highly publicized jury trial, the question of whether or not the U.S. mass media is fair and even-handed in its coverage of white and black anti-Semitism, or the question of whether the United States is a uniquely generous nation, cannot be decided by intuition. That is why no philosopher, even in ethics, would attempt to arrive at a position on a multifaceted moral issue such as abortion, euthanasia, or capital punishment on the basis of intuition. Rather, the role of intuition would be to justify the most elementary moral principles (such as that cruelty is bad) underlying the complicated arguments swirling around those issues.

Philosophers also sometimes use intuition as a way of probing the coherence of their ideas. In ethics, for example, even those who doubt that there are moral truths that we can know often will agree that we ought to be consistent in our moral beliefs and practices. Thus, for example, we might test a proposed general moral rule ("promises should always be kept") by seeing whether or to what extent it coheres with our considered judgments about particular cases. For example, what if you promise to return your neighbor's guns to him, but he goes mad in the interim? Should you keep your promise then? Or what if you promise to meet your friend for lunch, but on the way you encounter a drowning child who requires your immediate aid? Should you rescue the child even if it means breaking your promise to your friend? Similarly, we might test a proposed judgment about a particular case ("same-sex marriage should not be allowed") by considering it in the light of general principles we endorse ("we should not cause needless suffering"). I trust it is by now clear how different this is from Colbert's procedure when he proclaims, "If you *think* about it, maybe there are a few missing pieces to the rationale for war, but doesn't taking Saddam out *feel* like the right thing right here—right here in the gut?"[3]

Philosophy in the Age of Truthiness

Keeping in mind the differences between the philosophical concept of intuition and Colbert's concept of truthiness enhances the appreciation of the power of his critique. The problem is not merely that politicians and pundits base their conclusions on gut feelings and unexamined prejudices, but rather that they do so in connection with precisely the kinds of claims where inferential reasoning and an appeal to evidence are most clearly necessary. What is perhaps even more disturbing is that the rest of the culture, for the most part, lets them get away with it.

On the other hand, there are some indications that the time might be ripe for change on this front. It is now widely understood that the principal claims that the Bush administration advanced as justifications for waging war on Iraq were untrue and that the U.S. mass media did a miserable job of subjecting those claims to critical scrutiny.[4] A war is hardly a trivial matter, and the carnage and economic cost of the present one has served to clarify the need for high critical standards in connection with evaluating claims relating to significant matters of public policy. Moreover, the success of *The Colbert Report*, in which the truthiness that got us into this mess is subjected to ridicule on a nightly basis, further indicates that this message resonates with a significant percentage of the public at the present time.

The idea that we should subject all of our fundamental beliefs to critical scrutiny lies at the heart of philosophy. Indeed, if one had to pick one historical slogan as best illustrating what philosophy is all about, it might well be Socrates' famous dictum that "the unexamined life is not worth living." The disasters of this most unphilosophical age—the age of truthiness—therefore may, with the help of Colbert's satire, begin to demonstrate the value of philosophy to a public that has historically rejected it. That is an irony that I think Stephen Colbert would appreciate.

---

[3] Episode 1001, originally aired October 17th, 2005.

[4] Even Bush's former press secretary, Scott McClellan, has now confirmed this from an insider's perspective. See his *What Happened: Inside the Bush White House and Washington's Culture of Deception* (PublicAffairs, 2008).

Better Know a Philosopher

10

Is Stephen Colbert America's Socrates?

MARK RALKOWSKI

> STEPHEN COLBERT: I want to change the world, change it a little bit every
> day. Not much, but give me the wheel. Give me the ball, God. I'll
> run it down the line.
> CHARLIE ROSE: But how can you change the world?
> STEPHEN COLBERT: By catching it in the headlights of my justice.

—Colbert on *Charlie Rose*, December 8th, 2006

Socrates (470–399 B.C.) was famous for wandering the streets of
Athens and asking prominent politicians, artists, and craftsmen
questions they could not answer without embarrassing themselves.
This made some people angry. Socrates was convinced his unpop-
ularity was the ultimate reason Athens brought him to trial and sen-
tenced him to death in 399 B.C. "I am very unpopular with many
people," he told his jury. "This will be my undoing, if I am undone"
(*Apology*, line 28b). Others were entertained by the spectacle. Some
say Socrates made philosophical argument into the new wrestling
match, the new contest that appealed to the competitive impulse of
Athenians.[1] And, in this contest, he was the champion whom the
young admired and nobody could defeat.

> The young men who follow me around of their own free will . . . take
> pleasure in hearing people questioned. (*Apology*, line 23c)

> They enjoy hearing those being questioned who think they are wise,
> but are not. And this is not unpleasant. (*Apology*, lines 33c3–4)

---

[1] See "Homer on Competition," in Friedrich Nietzsche, *On the Genealogy of
Morality* (Cambridge University Press, 1994), pp. 187–194.

Socrates would ask lawmakers to define justice. Surely *they* must know what it is if they distinguish good laws from bad ones, or are they just making it up as they go? He asked similar definitional questions to all Athenians with great reputations for wisdom. The poets were supposed to know the nature of beauty, but they did not. The military leaders were supposed to be able to define courage, but they could not. The sophists didn't possess sophisticated educational philosophies, despite their claims to expertise in education. And, perhaps most famously, a self-proclaimed religious expert named Euthyphro could not define a religious concept as elementary as piety, even though he claimed expertise in all spiritual matters and offered to be Socrates's teacher.

Euthyphro is one of Socrates's many victims, but he is a special case in Plato's dialogues because his character flaws are so exaggerated. He insists on acting in the face of the gravest moral controversy, despite the fact that he cannot adequately explain his reasons for doing so. He feels he *must* act, but he cannot say why. On the one hand, he says piety demands that he take legal action against his father. But on the other hand, he has no idea what "piety" means and cannot explain why it requires him to do one thing rather than another. Socrates has no patience for Euthyphro's lack of self-reflection. He subjects him to a barrage of questions and arguments intended to help him recognize the limits of his deliberation and the gravity of his situation. But Socrates might as well be talking to a wall. Euthyphro is ignorant, ignorant of his ignorance, and yet stubbornly committed to taking action. Nothing will persuade him to think or act differently because he isn't really thinking, and he certainly isn't guiding his actions with reason.

Euthyphro may have been particularly bullheaded and especially unaware of Socrates's heavy-handed irony. But he was not alone in being stumped by Socrates. *Nobody* could answer Socrates's questions satisfactorily and Socrates would expose these weaknesses in front of audiences who took pleasure in watching the city's authority figures fail. We can think of Socrates's "street philosophy" as an ancient precursor to the *Colbert Report*. Just like Socrates, Colbert uses loaded questions and irony to expose the contradictions and gaps in his guests' reasoning, and to expose *them* as superficial blowhards and stewards of a broken culture and value system. If he talks to a conservative about the place of women in society, for example, he will go even further to the right than her to test the sincerity of her beliefs and expose their extremism. If he talks to a liberal about his opposition to the Iraq war, he will ask his guest whether he'd support the war if President Bush promised to bring back Saddam's rape rooms.

This ironic rhetorical strategy is often very effective as refutation. When the audience laughs in recognition of Colbert's ploy, he has won the argument with his guest without actually articulating an objection. In some instances Colbert's incisive and ironic interviewing style has caused alarm in Washington D.C. Back in 2006, Nancy Pelosi was so concerned about her candidates suffering political damage from appearing on the *Colbert Report*, she advised them not to go on his show. "I wouldn't recommend that anyone go on the show," she said, not unless "you want to be made a fool of." More recently, Thomas Schaller wrote a piece on "How to Survive a Colbert Interview" for *The New Republic* (April 15th, 2008). He calls Colbert "the toughest interviewer in television" and lists several basic principles to follow in order to avoid falling into Colbert's various traps.

In light of these similarities, it's worth asking: Is Stephen Colbert America's Socrates? Or, as Colbert would no doubt prefer us to ask, was Socrates *Athens's Stephen Colbert*? As much as Colbert might insist on the second question because it suggests that he is more important than Socrates, some might disagree. They might even reject the comparison altogether. For one thing Socrates seems to have had more "balls," Colbert's own ironically chauvinistic metric for measuring a person's worth. How so? Simple: Athens executed Socrates because the Athenian political establishment considered him a threat, whereas Colbert was President Bush's invited guest and entertainer at the 2006 White House Correspondents' Dinner. Moreover, as most Colbert fans are well aware, James Fowler recently discovered that political guests have received a considerable "bump" in campaign contributions after appearing on the *Colbert Report*.[2] Socrates was never so cozy with Athens's power brokers. He was considered more of a heretic than a must-do pre-election interview. If Socrates was "a gadfly on the neck of man," as Friedrich Nietzsche once said, Colbert seems to be a fluffy Pomeranian curled up on the lap of Uncle Sam, a Hamlet who loves Claudius. The point of this chapter, then, is to

---

[2] For details on the Colbert "bump," see Fowler's "The Colbert Bump in Campaign Donations: More Truthful Than Truthy," *Political Science and Politics* 41:3, pp. 533–39 (July 2008).

figure out whether Colbert has enough "balls" to be compared to Socrates.

Socrates the Social Critic

Let's look more closely at what Socrates was all about: the kind of philosophy he was interested in, the point of his inconclusive conversations with others, and what he ultimately wanted for Athens. Once we know the answers to these questions, we will be in a much better position to compare Socrates with Colbert and figure out who has more "balls."

Before Socrates, ancient Greek philosophy was mostly concerned with grand metaphysical questions. What is reality? What is it made out of, and where did it come from? These questions were revolutionary and exciting for their time: they broke away from traditional Greek religious beliefs and myths, and they seemed to promise omniscience to anyone who answered them. If you could know the most basic material constituent of the cosmos (what Aristotle called the *archê*), you could know what reality is made of, where it came from, and how it came to be what it is. You could literally know everything. Or so the pre-Socratic philosophers hoped!

Socrates wasn't so sure. In Plato's *Phaedo*, a dialogue about death and immortality, Socrates says that as a young man he was extremely interested in these early philosophical questions about the nature and origins of the cosmos. Initially he was captivated by the pre-Socratic philosophical view that the entire cosmos was governed by a divine mind. But the more he considered the idea, the less confident he became that it could help him discover answers to the questions he cared about most, questions such as: What is the best life to live? What is happiness, and how does one go about becoming happy? No amount of metaphysical speculation about the ground of being could provide the answers Socrates sought. A new kind of philosophy was needed, a practical philosophy that aimed to make our lives better, to inform and *transform* us. Socrates produced this new philosophy. He lived it. He made his *life*, a life committed to the cultivation of self-knowledge and self-transformation, the philosophy he sought. And he encouraged others to follow suit.[3]

---

[3] For the best discussion of the idea that philosophy was a way of life in the ancient world, and that Socrates established this tradition, see Pierre Hadot's inimitable *Philosophy as a Way of Life* (Blackwell, 1995).

I shall not cease to practice philosophy, to exhort you and in my usual way to point out to any one of you whom I happen to meet: "Good Sir, you are an Athenian, a citizen of the greatest city with the greatest reputation for both wisdom and power; are you not ashamed of your eagerness to possess as much wealth, reputation and honors as possible, while you do not care for nor give thought to wisdom or truth, or the best possible state of your soul?" (*Apology*, lines 29d–e)

For Socrates, philosophy was not a purely theoretical discipline reserved for specialists, and it didn't aim to describe the metaphysical structure of reality. It was a kind of work on the self, the purpose of which was better living, not just deeper understanding. This was something new for Western thought. Socrates had shifted the focus of philosophy from the nature and origins of the cosmos to the good life, from metaphysics to ethics. As Cicero (106–43 B.C.) put this point, Socrates "brought down philosophy from heaven to earth."

The image that Plato uses to illustrate the life transformation that Socrates sought to achieve with his students is known as "the Allegory of the Cave." At the beginning of *Republic*, Book VII, Socrates asks Glaucon and Adeimantus to imagine people who have lived in an underground dwelling since childhood. Their legs and necks are chained so that they must look forward. Their light comes from a fire burning above and behind them. Between them and the fire, "puppeteers" walk along a wall carrying wooden and stone models of all sorts, producing an elaborate play of shadows on the cave wall directly in front of the prisoners.

It's a system of thought control, and it couldn't be more effective. The prisoners can't turn their heads, so they don't see the puppeteers. From their perspective, the play of shadows in front of them is the extent of reality. They literally cannot imagine that anyone is manipulating the images they see, or that the world they consider so real is just an illusion, a bit of theater used by the powers that be to hold their minds captive. From their perspective, such a possibility is as unimaginable as the color red is to a person blind from birth. They are "at home" in their shadow world. It is their everyday environment. To them nothing could be more real. They are so comfortable, in fact, they resist anyone who comes to free them.

When one of the prisoners *is* unshackled and turned around to face the fire, his first reaction is to return to the comforts of the shadows. The light of the fire is blinding, and the new kind of objects is disorienting. None of it makes any sense. Instead of appreciating his newfound freedom, he is overwhelmed with a longing for the tranquility and familiarity of the shadows that he understands. Everything changes, however, when his liberation is completed and he is taken out of the cave into the light of day. At that point he can finally understand that the cave is a prison. He sees it in a new light, as if for the first time. Suddenly his old world collapses. He has no desire to return to it. What used to be so important suddenly seems revolting. He pities his old friends who are still lost in the dark. They attach meaning and significance to the shadows, but it's all a lie. Their desires and beliefs are manufactured through and through.

This is where the story of Socrates reappears. Although he would rather not bother, the freed cave dweller returns to the cave to liberate his old friends and neighbors. It isn't easy for him, however. The transition from the sunlight outside to the darkness inside is as blinding as the original journey in the opposite direction. At first he stumbles and struggles to see things clearly, and the others think he has gone mad. But when his eyes readjust to the dark, he can see better than ever before, and much better than anyone else in the cave. He is in an ideal position to help the other prisoners, but they despise him, resist his efforts to unshackle them, and kill him, just as the Athenians killed Socrates for asking them to adopt a new way of life.

Socrates worried that Athenians were "swollen and festering" with feverish ambitions and a perverted standard of excellence. They measured their city's power and well-being by the size of its navy and the strength of its economy (*Gorgias* 519a). For Socrates this was a tragic mistake. We should be more concerned, he said, with truth and wisdom and the care of our souls than we are with wealth, glory, and imperial conquest. He told his fellow Athenians they were attached to mere shadows on the wall of the cave— wealth and glory were fool's gold compared to virtue and knowledge—but they couldn't understand him and didn't like the alternative lifestyle he recommended. In the end it cost them their empire. At the height of the thirty-year Peloponnesian War, instead of moderating their passions as Socrates recommended, Athenians overreached. Thucydides says Athenians greedily wanted everlasting pay from Sicilian slaves, and access to Sicily's trees for their navy. When they failed to conquer Sicily in 415 B.C., they lost their resolve in the war and never recovered.

Socrates encouraged Athenians to adopt new ideals for their city because he hoped to change the mindset that led Athens into war with Sparta in the first place. Their failures in war, he thought, were a product of their excessive consumption at home. Part of what Socrates was up to, in other words, was the re-education of Athenian desire.

Writing on the Walls of the Cave

If Socrates started the philosophical tradition of critiquing and emancipating culture, and if Stephen Colbert is America's Socrates, then we need to determine what Colbert is critiquing and what he is suggesting we change to make our lives better. Is Colbert, like Socrates, critiquing his country's values and pointing beyond them toward higher ones? Is *that* how he shares in the Socratic tradition of philosophy? Provided we can trust the sincerity and accuracy of Colbert's out of character remarks, then yes. Consider what he said out of character in a revealing interview with Charlie Rose.

> Jon deconstructs the news, and he's ironic and detached. I falsely construct the news and am ironically attached. . . . Jon may point out the hypocrisy of a particular thing happening in a news story or the behavior of somebody in the news. I *illustrate* the hypocrisy as a character. (Colbert on *Charlie Rose*, December 8th, 2006)

This tells us a lot. Jon Stewart and Colbert share an interest in unveiling the hypocrisy of the media and the culture that the media helps create. Their notorious downplaying and suggestions to the contrary are just ironic posturing. If we put this in terms of Plato's cave allegory, Jon Stewart is among the cave dwellers *talking about* the shadows on the cave wall and inviting everyone to look beyond the charade, while Colbert *is on the wall*, as a shadow, trying to cause the charade to come unraveled by undermining it from within.

If Colbert is "ironically attached" to the "false" news he constructs, and "illustrating" the hypocrisy of American culture as a character, doesn't that suggest he is critiquing all things American by embracing them? He *is* America, after all. If he's an ironist, embodying the hypocrisy he wants to expose and undermine, doesn't that mean his professed loves are a direct but inverted reflection of his true loves? And if so, doesn't that mean he *secretly hates America*? Could it be? Could it be that Stephen Colbert, America's favorite son, actually hates America?

If so, new questions arise here. Colbert says he illustrates hypocrisies *as a character*. But which hypocrisies, and how does he illustrate them?

Let's watch Colbert in action and take a closer look at how his character "illustrations" work. In his interview with Caitlin Flanagan, the anti-feminist author of *To Hell with All That: Loving and Loathing Our Inner Housewife*, Colbert employs one of the ironist's most piercing argumentative tools—the mirror. Instead of directly confronting his guests' beliefs and arguments, he adopts them as his own, develops them by following their logical implications, and tests his guests' commitments to their extreme positions by pushing them to possible breaking points. Consider this exchange.

> **FLANAGAN:** The original subtitle was, "How Feminism Shortchanged a Generation," but the publisher said that wouldn't sell. So we have a softer title. But I think it's the notion that feminism sold a lot of women out, and sold us a bill of goods, and a lot of women are unhappy because they're not valued at home the way they once were.
>
> **COLBERT:** Right, I mean it used to be you were valued at home because if mom wasn't at home taking care of stuff, dinner wouldn't be on the table when you came home, right?
>
> **FLANAGAN:** You're darn right about that. You're darn right.
>
> **COLBERT:** I mean there was a time when if you were my wife and you weren't giving it up, I could say, "She's crazy. Lock her away, right?"
>
> **FLANAGAN:** If I was your wife and I wasn't giving it up, I would be crazy.
>
> **COLBERT:** But you know those were the golden days. In this hazy, misty time you're talking about, I could have you lobotomized just by saying that you were unbalanced, right?
>
> **FLANAGAN:** Absolutely.
>
> **COLBERT:** When women who needed money had to depend on their husbands because even if their relationship wasn't good they weren't independent.
>
> **FLANAGAN:** Right.
>
> **COLBERT:** And this is the golden age you're talking about.
>
> **FLANAGAN:** Yes, it's an eternal golden age, really. Yes.

COLBERT: So better for you for women to be dependent on their husbands no matter what the situation.

FLANAGAN: Well, certainly you press the point when you put it that way.

COLBERT: I'm trying to press the point.

FLANAGAN: And you'll not find any refutation from me. More or less you're on target there.

COLBERT: Really?

FLANAGAN: Ya.

COLBERT: You are a perfect woman.

FLANAGAN: I've been told that.[4]

Colbert's strategy here is clear. He invites Flanagan to state her thesis, and then he proceeds to implode it by pretending to agree, only to reveal its untenable logical implications as he develops the idea in ways she does not. As long as it's in her mouth and dressed up in anti-feminist rhetoric, Flanagan's view can seem reasonable: feminism may have caused women unrecognized harm by leaving them unappreciated at home. But once Colbert gets this idea in his clutches, the charade immediately comes undone.

Flanagan says Colbert "presses the point" when he puts it this way, but she ultimately accepts his development of her view. And the audience can't believe it. Several men erupt with deep-throated growling praise, while the women are either silent or openly disgusted. If you listen to this interview closely, you can hear one young woman in the audience groaning with disapproval—"Oh my," she says viscerally—as Flanagan agrees that women ought to be dependent on their husbands no matter what the situation. Colbert's ploy has worked: he has revealed the anti-feminist's view to be male chauvinism in disguise, a celebration of women's traditional subservience to men and a rejection of gender equality.

Colbert's interview with noted conservative and Harvard professor Harvey Mansfield is similar. First he asks Mansfield to state his thesis. Then he adopts it as his own belief in order to reveal its weaknesses. We live in a gender-neutral society, Mansfield explains. Gender matters as little as possible. It doesn't give us our rights, our duties, or our place in society. His book, *Manliness*, is "a challenge to the gender-neutral society."

---

[4] Episode 2050, originally aired April 19th, 2006.

COLBERT: What is that quality of manliness? What best defines manliness?

MANSFIELD: I would say confidence in a situation of risk. It could either be danger, or it could be a situation where your authority is contested or disputed.

COLBERT: President Bush must be the most manly man of all. Because he's taken all kinds of risks over the last five years. It takes some real confidence to go into Iraq without an exit strategy, right?

MANSFIELD: Right.

COLBERT: That's some cajones!

MANSFIELD: Right.

COLBERT: Who's the least manly man in Washington, in politics?

MANSFIELD: John Kerry.

COLBERT: I agree with you. I agree with you there. First of all, "Kerry" is a girl name. Right? Second of all, we know one of those purple hearts was fake. I think it was chocolate or something. But here's what I don't understand. I know he's a wuss, but how does a wuss get the other two purple hearts? I don't understand.

MANSFIELD: I don't either. He must have done something to deserve them.

COLBERT: What is most wussy about him to you?

MANSFIELD: He vacillates. He says one thing one time, and another thing another time.

COLBERT: So he changes his mind occasionally.

MANSFIELD: Yes, or even frequently.

COLBERT: See, that's what I like about President Bush. No matter how the facts change, his opinion doesn't. [*Mansfield nods*] That's what we need.

MANSFIELD: That's right.[5]

Colbert's strategy here is the same as it was in the Flanagan interview. As soon as he adopts Mansfield's position and applies it to President Bush's supremely confident but tragically ineffective execution of the Iraq war, manliness suddenly appears to be a vice, not a virtue. The same thing happens when they shift from President Bush to Senator Kerry, Bush's opponent in the 2004

---

[5] Episode 2046, originally aired April 5th, 2006.

presidential election. Mansfield suggests Kerry is the least manly man in Washington because he often changes his mind. Never mind the fact that he was a war hero in Vietnam. Instead of showing confidence in situations of risk, Kerry shows indecision and timidity. This was one of the most devastating arguments used against John Kerry in the 2004 presidential election. Once his opponents successfully defined him as a flip-flopping decision maker, his campaign was doomed. However, when Colbert explores the converse of Mansfield's value, it is Bush's stubbornness that seems like the real vice, not John Kerry's openness to new information. No matter how the facts change, Bush's opinions do not, Colbert says. Put that way, manliness appears to be a celebration of ideology over reason, hardly the quality one would want in a leader.

Of course, Colbert doesn't just go after conservatives. He has compared Howard Dean, the Democratic National Committee chairman, to Robert Mugabe, Zimbabwe's brutal dictator, for suggesting that the popular vote would not matter in determining his party's nominee for president in 2008.

> When it comes to ending the fierce Clinton-Obama primary rivalry, Democratic National Committee Chairman Howard Dean is finally showing some sack. Listen to what Dean told the *Financial Times* about who the superdelegates will choose for the party's nominee. "I do not think in the long run it will come down to the popular vote." Exactly, popular vote is a stupid way to settle an election. . . . Just ask President of Zimbabwe, Robert Mugabe. He's on your side, Howard![6]

This is classic Colbert, more of the same ironic mirroring. Instead of directly challenging Dean's reasoning, he adopts Dean's position and then reduces it to an absurdity by explaining what it implies: the leader of the democratic party doesn't believe in democracy, the popular vote is "a stupid way to settle an election." What could be more ridiculous? To top it off he assures Dean he's right because Robert Mugabe would agree with him. That's what one might call stinging praise. Yes, it is a rhetorical analogy, and not at all a fair comparison. Dean is no Mugabe. But if you know anything about the current state of Zimbabwe, you know Dean is in trouble if his position on an election outcome *in any way* resembles Mugabe's

---

[6] Episode 4056, originally aired April 28th, 2008.

stranglehold on Zimbabwe's democratic institutions. In the end, Colbert's ploy works again. His audience gets it immediately. And this time one of the country's most important leaders is exposed as a sophist.

Colbert doesn't just go after individuals. He also attacks institutions, especially the "opinion making" branch of the mainstream media. He openly admits that many of these men provided him with the paradigms for his character. "I don't watch O'Reilly," he said, "but certainly he, Sean Hannity, Aaron Brown, Anderson Cooper . . . Stone Phillips, Geraldo Rivera—all of these guys I should give a royalty check to." The more passionate the pundit, the more committed he is to "emotion and certainty over information," the better. Colbert says he admires Geraldo Rivera, for example, because "he has a sense of mission . . . I read once that when he goes jogging in Central Park he's like a battleship on patrol" (Colbert on *Charlie Rose*).

Colbert's character is a parody of this general attitude, but sometimes he addresses specific behaviors or stories in the media as exemplary of truthiness and thus worthy of special attention. He subjected ABC to withering criticism for its moderation of a debate between Hillary Clinton and Barack Obama. As usual, his method is ironic mirroring.

> STEPHANOPOULOS: Can you explain that relationship [with William Ayers] for the voters?
>
> OBAMA: This kind of game in which anybody who I know, regardless of how flimsy the relationship is, is somehow—somehow their ideas could be attributed to me—I think, the American people are smarter than that.
>
> COLBERT: Smarter than that? No thank you . . . Consider this: Senator Obama has been endorsed by Ted Kennedy. Ted Kennedy is a Catholic. Catholics are led by the Pope. The Pope was a Nazi Youth. Ergo, Barack Obama loves Hitler. Check . . . mate![7]

ABC's debate moderation was almost universally criticized. George Stephanopoulos and Charles Gibson, the two debate moderators, spent the first hour of the debate asking Clinton and Obama ques-

---

[7] Episode 4051, originally aired April 17th, 2008.

tions about issues with little relevance to the presidency. Critics described their performance as "shoddy and despicable," "shameful," "embarrassing," "tawdry," "disgusting," "a train wreck." But instead of adding directly to these criticisms, Colbert pretends to side with ABC. "I think ABC did a great job." By doing so, and by developing ABC's reasoning to the point that Obama ends up "loving Hitler," Colbert makes a mockery out of "Gibsonopoulos," reducing ABC's work to a freak show of bad reasoning and infantile guilt by association games. The audience eats it up. They recognize the poor reasoning. They can see the media's obsession with hot button issues and impatience with policy substance, and they find it amusing.

At the end of the day, Colbert elevates his audience to a position of cool ironic detachment and superiority. Their culture, their most exalted institutions, and especially their loftiest authority figures, are all full of it. They are charlatans, and America is a cesspool of hypocrisy. Colbert illustrates this. He lets his audience in on his clever deconstructive insights, and he lets them take pleasure in unmasking the pretenders to wisdom and moral authority as nothing more than ordinary phonies.

There's no question that Colbert "wins the battle." He embarrasses many of his most confident guests. He refutes the bad arguments made by politicians and members of the media. He goes after higher education, the Catholic Church, modern science, and many others. And he exposes American culture in general as an increasingly irrational society awash in a sea of truthiness. Maybe the Democratic Party isn't very democratic. Maybe manliness is foolhardiness. Maybe anti-feminism is chauvinism in disguise. Maybe our system for choosing our presidents is broken and our media is deadening our democracy. These are serious topics, not just light entertainment. But to what end? Does Colbert achieve his aims as a critic of American culture?

Colbert's War on Truthiness

Colbert may achieve some influence *within* the system of political punditry, but he doesn't appear to be winning his war on truthiness. If anything, he may be reinforcing its grip on us—why should we worry about truthiness if it's good for a few laughs every night?

In this respect Colbert and Socrates share at least one thing in common: they're both failures. Socrates failed to convince

Athenians of their inverted priorities. He warned them of the dangers of avarice, and they ignored him, waged a war of conquest in spite of his warnings, lost their empire as a consequence, and in the end blamed him for their losses. Colbert's failures are no different. He wins the battle—he refutes his extremist guests and reveals his various targets, in the media and politics and religion, as hypocrites—but he loses the war: his audience is persuaded in theory, but not in practice. The jokes go down easy, and nothing *really* changes.

In the 2008 election coverage, for example, we've spent most of our time talking about Barack Obama's missing flag pin and the beliefs of his pastor, John McCain's age and the names he calls his wife, and Hillary Clinton's pantsuits and whether she cried in New Hampshire. Forget about climate change, war, energy, health care, and a steadily weakening dollar. Those issues don't sell magazines or garner strong ratings.

Consider Colbert's famous speech at the White House Press Correspondents' Dinner. He went after the president on illegal wiretapping, the Iraq war, his low approval ratings, his exploitative photo ops and political posturing, his stubbornness, his denial of global warming, his reliance on a timid and complicit media, the leaked identity of Valerie Plame—and the next day none of the major opinion makers said a word about it, or if they did it was to critique Colbert for failing to be funny. The mainstream media ignored the content of his speech with a nation-wide collective yawn, even though some of his jokes were downright blistering in their condemnation of the president.

> I stand by this man. I stand by this man because he stands for things. Not only for things, he stands on things. Things like aircraft carriers and rubble and recently flooded city squares. And that sends a strong message: that no matter what happens to America, she will always rebound—with the most powerfully staged photo ops in the world. (White House Correspondents' Dinner)

This is extraordinary. Colbert told the President *to his face* on national television that he was a failure in the Iraq War, the defining issue of his presidency. "I believe the government that governs best is the government that governs least. And by these standards, we have set up a fabulous government in Iraq." Then he blamed the president's own bullheadedness for his failures. "The greatest thing about this man is he's steady . . . He believes the same thing Wednesday that he believed on Monday, no matter what happened Tuesday. Events can change; this man's beliefs never will." Biting stuff, the type of attacks one would expect to be newsworthy, maybe even paradigm-shifting in the national media, but nobody other than the marginalized blogosphere blinked an eye.

Charlie Rose discussed Colbert's "failures" in his December 8th, 2006 interview. Comedy can be insightful, persuasive, even visionary, he said. Often it's more revealing than journalism because it operates under fewer constraints. But in the end it's a toothless tiger. It never manages to effect the change it envisions. "Cabaret satire had never been better than it was pre-Weimar," Rose said. "And it just stopped Hitler in his tracks!" Colbert didn't miss a beat. He admitted that his jokes were politically impotent. "I would say that in the lead up to the Iraq war, *The Daily Show* was highly dubious of the idea. And it didn't seem to stop it." But he also suggested that he never expects anything more. "You can't be disappointed if you don't actually change things because it can't have been your intention." In comedy you go for the laugh, he said, not for social justice.

This may sound like Colbert is denying that he has a political agenda, much as Jon Stewart has done.[8] But it's more than that. There is a paradox here. Colbert (i) intends to illustrate hypocrisy as a character, but (ii) he doesn't expect to change things. This says something about *us*, Colbert's audience. He intends to tell or show us the truth, but he doesn't expect us to do anything with it. *We* are the ultimate targets of Colbert's condescending irony. America is Colbert's Euthyphro, the self-satisfied one who is ignorant and ignorant of his ignorance, the target of Socrates' thinly veiled scorn.

Or perhaps we're even worse than this. Alexander Nehamas distinguishes between Socratic and Platonic irony, and he suggests that Platonic irony is deeper, darker, and more disdainful. The target of Socratic irony is the person with whom he speaks. The target of Plato's irony is his audience, his readers, the self-deceived ones who listen to Socrates and share his values but do not change their lives. They understand his condemnation of the shadow world, but they devote themselves to it no less vigorously.

---

[8] For instance, in his now infamous *Crossfire* interview (October 15th, 2004) or when he went on *The O'Reilly Factor* and said explicitly, "We don't have an agenda to influence" (*The O'Reilly Factor*, September 17th, 2004).

Plato lures the readers of his early dialogues into a cunningly induced state of confident ignorance. He instills confidence by lulling us into believing that we know better than Socrates' interlocutors. He makes us presume that, unlike them, we see Socrates' point; he makes us imagine we agree, if not with every single one of Socrates' views, at least with his general outlook on life. And he displays our ignorance by showing that we do nothing of the sort . . . Plato turns us into participants in his dialogues, almost into characters of his own fictions. The dialogues' final audience, watching all watchers, is Plato himself, who stands behind the most distant observers of Socrates' dialectic and follows ironically the dramatic action he has created.[9]

Are *we* the ultimate targets of Colbert's irony, and is he the final audience, watching all watchers of his show? He seems to admit as much when he discusses the origins of *The Colbert Report*. Bill O'Reilly is one model for his character, he says, but not the only one. When he developed his character and planned his show, he "was thinking of passion and emotion and certainty over information," he said. "Passion and emotion, what you feel in your gut," what Colbert famously calls "truthiness," "the thesis statement of the whole show—*that* [truthiness] is more important than [true] information to the public at large, *not just the people who provide it*" (Colbert on *Charlie Rose*). This is a stunning revelation. Colbert intends to mock all things truthy, the peddlers *and* the consumers of truthiness, ABC news *and* the people who watch it, our broken election system *and* the people who accept it, our sophistic political representatives *and* the people who vote for them.

Colbert is not just parodying Bill O'Reilly and the others who "provide" America with her truthiness. He's going after us as well. There's something deplorable about a society that embraces truthiness as a way of life, as we do. But there's something even worse about us, Colbert's audience, because we identify with Colbert's critique of American culture but embrace that culture no less vigorously. We accept its profound flaws and injustices with a shrug of the shoulders and a few laughs. We want the revolution, but only if we don't have to do anything or make any real sacrifices.

---

[9] Alexander Nehamas, *The Art of Living* (University of California Press, 1998), pp. 46–47.

Colbert Is (the Tragedy and Comedy of) America, and So Are We

That's one possible interpretation of Colbert's irony. There is another, and it attributes less disdain and more loving concern to Colbert.

At the end of Plato's *Symposium*, it's dawn following a long winter night of drinking and debauchery. Socrates is seated between Agathon, Athens's great tragedian, and Aristophanes, Athens's great comic playwright. The three of them are passing a large bowl of wine from left to right, drinking and following the trail of the night's argument. Everyone else has either left the party or fallen asleep. Socrates, who is unaffected by alcohol, eventually outlasts everyone. Aristophanes falls asleep, and he is followed by Agathon, but not before being told by Socrates that the greatest poet ought to be capable of writing a single work that can be read both as a tragedy and as a comedy. One classic question here is: How if at all does this formula apply to Plato's philosophy? Does he think the human condition is both tragic and comic, and did he hope to illustrate the human tragicomedy in his dramatic dialogues? Was his philosophy the work of art that Socrates describes to Agathon?

There are many ways to answer these questions, but here is one that might teach us something about Stephen Colbert and Socrates equally. It is possible that, for Plato, the tragedy of the human condition is our inbuilt, predetermined resistance to those who might liberate us from our ignorance and existential shortcomings. In the cave allegory the liberator is "destined" to fail, but he tries anyway, and he loses his life because of it. The people he intends to help rise up and kill him to preserve their ignorance and prolong their imprisonment. This is comic because the liberator is like Sisyphus: he is condemned to a task he *cannot* complete but is determined to complete it anyway. And it's tragic because the cave dwellers' conditions could improve unimaginably but don't improve at all. Nobody needs help more than they do. Their bodies and minds are trapped. Everything about their condition is controlled. Socrates reaches out to his friends and neighbors in an effort to turn them around, away from imperial conquest toward virtue and philosophy, but they ignore him. And they end up losing their freedom to Sparta and their liberator to their own madness.

In Colbert's case, the pattern is the same. He illustrates America's various hypocrisies. He points out his guests' flaws. But, in the end, they sell more books or raise more money after appearing on his show. In some cases this doesn't matter, but in others it couldn't matter more. For example, it is a tragedy for us and for the rest of the world that we don't act on something as serious as Colbert's diagnosis of our broken presidential election system, or that we don't demand that our media produce better, less truthy journalism. Our inverted priorities are unjustifiable. Our bland disapproval of our corrupt institutions is inexcusable. But there is something amusing about our failures when Colbert enters the picture. How can one not laugh at people (us) who are laughing at others (Americans) for the ignorance they (we) exhibit in their (our) laughter? This is the joke Colbert tells about us, his audience. When we laugh with him, he laughs at us, because we are the consumers of the truthiness he disparages.

Alexander Nehamas suggests Plato's irony is deep, dark, and disdainful. He despises his audience for their self-satisfaction. But if the Colbert-Socrates comparison is apt, shouldn't we imagine Plato wringing his hands *and* laughing at Socrates' unsuccessful attempts to lead Athenians out of the cave? Doesn't he regret Athens's failure at the same time that he takes pleasure in observing and mocking its absurd self-satisfaction? And isn't this just what Colbert is doing for America with his show? If so, perhaps we should revise the question in the title of this chapter and ask whether Colbert, the real Stephen Colbert behind the ironic mask on *The Colbert Report*, is America's Plato: he is condemning us at the same time that he makes us laugh, and he is trying to turn us away from the shadows on the wall of the cave despite knowing that he is predetermined to fail.

Perhaps Colbert is America's Plato, and not America's Socrates, or perhaps he is both. Either way, we must admit it takes some "balls" for him to bite the hand that feeds him by telling his audience some bitter truths. Whether his "balls" measure up to Plato's or Socrates's, however, is still an open question, and it will probably *remain* open unless Colbert meets Socrates's fate. Only then would we know for certain that he had really challenged his country.

Well, Stephen, if you are reading, consider yourself *on notice*. In the meantime we'll be waiting to see just how big your "balls" really are.[10]

---

[10] I would like to thank Elijah Moyo, Alyson Lynch, Katherine Veach, Brian Wright, Andrew Bleiman, Maureen Melnyk, Misha Chkhenkeli, and Ratna Ralkowski for their thoughtful feedback on earlier drafts of this chapter. And I would especially like to thank Aaron Schiller for his extremely helpful and meticulous revision suggestions.

11
Why Is Stephen Colbert So Funny?

SOPHIA STONE

The Colbert Report maintains a huge following for its comic parody of cable news bloviating, but what is it exactly that makes Stephen Colbert funny? His Wit? His Insight? His Wicked Neil Diamond Impersonations?

Can the question of what makes something funny be answerable through a philosophical account of humor? Through the lens of the philosophy of Ludwig Wittgenstein (1889–1951), we can come up with a robust theory of humor that will answer these questions and many others, but not, unfortunately, why my Uncle Larry insists on wearing his trench coat to dinner.

Café au Laugh

On Tuesday, February 26th, 2008, Starbucks closed its shops for three hours to retrain their baristas to perfect the making of espresso shots. This event from the ubiquitous coffee conglomerate made the headlines. While reporters mentioned what went on in the training sessions, talked about the press release from Starbucks CEO Howard Schultz, or how the closing impacted local mom and pop coffee shops, *The Colbert Report* did something a little different.

The Starbucks event was declared the number one threat facing America.[1] Stephen Colbert reported how the closing personally affected him—a special, self-interest report. At five thirty we see a frustrated Stephen Colbert trying to open a door to a closed

---

[1] Episode 4026, originally aired February 27th, 2008.

Starbucks. Then we see him drinking out of a *café au lait* coffee cup with ten tea bag tags dangling from the sides. The next clip shows a sweaty Stephen Colbert on an exercise machine, exaggerating his movements and then posing as if in slow motion.

The camera zooms in on the clock that now says six. Stephen Colbert digs through the trash and finds a used Starbucks coffee cup, throws his head back and attempts to drink any last drop. Failing, he takes the end of the paper cup and burns the edge, using his cupped fingers to wave the burning aroma into his nostrils.

Next scene, we see a disgruntled Stephen Colbert at the office, yelling "I hate you" to a fellow co-worker. As he walks down the hall towards the camera, he pushes anyone aside who gets in his way. Camera shot to the clock now says quarter to eight. Stephen Colbert is in an undisclosed basement, tied up and choking, acting like a rabid man. Clock now says eight-thirty and we see Stephen Colbert finally entering a Starbucks.

Last scene: Stephen Colbert taking a shower, about to drink from a Starbucks coffee cup, and instead, he pours it on his head. He takes another Starbucks coffee cup, takes off the lid, dips his four fingers in the cup and takes out whipped cream, and smears it all over his chest and presumably his genitals. Finally, he takes a shaker of pumpkin spice and sprinkles it all over his chest.

Three Overused, Outdated, and Overrun Philosophical Theories of Humor

There are numerous theories of humor that could explain why we find Stephen Colbert sprinkling pumpkin spice on his chest funny, but the three main contenders are:

- **superiority theory**

- **relief theory**

- **incongruity theory**

Superiority theory is often attributed to Plato and Aristotle but was first explained by Thomas Hobbes in his *Leviathan* (1651) and *Human Nature* (1650). Relief theory was first described by Sigmund Freud in his book *Jokes and Their Relation to the*

Unconscious (1905). Incongruity theory has its origins in Francis Hutcheson's *Reflections Upon Laughter* (1725).[2]

Superiority theory claims that the cause of our laughter is due to the feeling of superiority we have to the object of our laughter. So perhaps we laugh at Stephen Colbert sniffing the fumes of a burning Starbucks cup because there's nothing funnier than watching a junkie suffer.

Relief theory holds that we laugh because we have repressed desires that need to be released. So maybe we laugh when Stephen Colbert drinks from the many-tea-bagged cup because of our own fear of coffee withdrawal or a grumpy boss. Or, as Freud would claim, we might have some pent up sexual anxiety that is related to caffeine withdrawal and seeing the many tea bagged cup over-stimulates our libido and causes us to laugh.

The incongruity theory explains that we laugh because we expect one thing to happen, and then something else happens. We may have laughed when Stephen Colbert dumps coffee on his head in the shower because we expected him to drink the coffee while showering.

Each one of these theories, however, is limited to a particular kind of humor. The problem is that they try to account for all facets of Stephen Colbert's humor with one explanation. The superiority theory explains why we laugh at how desperate Stephen Colbert becomes in dealing with his withdrawal from Starbucks coffee; we feel elevated to a higher status when we see him suffer. And this explanation carries over to the other examples of his humor. The superiority explanation becomes the only focal point of the humor, while in fact we may laugh for other reasons. If we were to continue with this theory, we would have to explain that the reason why we laugh when Stephen Colbert pours coffee on himself while showering is because we think we are better than that. The theory would not take into account our surprise and the oddity of pouring coffee over oneself in the shower.

The relief theory explains that our laughter is due to some pent-up fear or other emotion in desperately needing coffee and having to continue on without it. The relief theory would explain why we laugh at Stephen Colbert pushing his co-workers out of the way. In this case the reason again is because we too have a secret desire

---

[2] See John Morreall, ed, *The Philosophy of Laughter and Humor* (SUNY Press, 1987).

to be mean to the people we work with, and who wouldn't after what they said about us last week? The theory reduces the reason why we laugh at Stephen Colbert's humor always to some repressed desire we have. The relief theory doesn't give a satisfying account for why we laugh at the ridiculousness of Stephen Colbert on an exercise machine, unless, of course, we say that we have all been there and have done that before, and we are relieved from some sort of hidden anxiety we feel about having to go through it again.

While it's true that in most scenarios what Stephen Colbert does is contrary to our expectation (the incongruity theory), it's not clear that this is the reason why we laugh. Sometimes we laugh because we are surprised, but other times we laugh because of the extent of the ridiculousness. The problem with these theories is that they focus on a single cause while there seem to be multiple reasons for why we laugh. Just as there are varieties of people and paralyzing phobias, there are a variety of ways people can understand humor and different reasons for why they laugh, and why they're afraid of small flightless birds. Sometimes we laugh in a silly way, since what Stephen Colbert says is absolutely true and he is revealing something about the way we live, act, and think. What is needed is a complete theory of humor that can account for all the different ways Stephen Colbert makes people laugh.

The theory should also be able to do more than that, though. It should also be able to explain why some people laugh at Stephen Colbert's humor while others do not. And, while no one comedian can be funny all the time, how can we account for the fact that even when Stephen Colbert bombs his jokes, he can still be funny?

What we need is a theory of humor that does not force us to accept one explanation for all the different kinds of humor. We need a theory that allows for multiple explanations for why we laugh, and the same theory should do the dishes and make us breakfast in the morning.

That Quirky Philosopher Wittgenstein and his Language Games

Ludwig Wittgenstein was an Austrian philosopher who devoted his life to articulating the problems of philosophy that are due to language. He had many innovative ideas in the philosophy of lan-

guage, logic, mathematics, and psychology. Though much philosophical work has been done with Wittgenstein's writings, there is
still more we can gain especially with what he has written on
humor. Keep in mind that in this chapter I'm drawing my ideas
from Wittgenstein and not at all claiming to be channeling him
from his grave.

"Humor is not a mood but a way of looking at the world."[3] This
way of looking at the world is particular to specific cultures and
time periods and also differs from person to person. How we interact with one another, the words and mannerisms we use, are also
cultural and time-specific. One of the "tools" we use to interact with
others is language. In his *Philosophical Investigations*, Wittgenstein
likens the use of language to the using of tools in a tool box—there
are many tools in a tool box, each one has a different job and
works in a different way, just like there are many words and grammatical rules that each have a different use and work in a different
way: some to amuse, some to seduce, and some to scare the beje-
sus out of those pesky kids who keep wrecking my lawn.

Another analogy Wittgenstein gives for language is the example
of the controls on a train. Some levers push and pull, others turn,
and some aren't connected with anything at all. As we speak and
interact with one another, we are constantly learning new words,
finding new ways to use some expressions, and likewise, we leave
some colloquial expressions behind.

Humor is part of language, and it too, constantly changes. Think
of the different styles of comedy and the comedians who have
come and gone. Think of the comedy your grandparents laugh at
compared with what you laugh at. Sometimes the humor carries
over from generation to generation, but most often it does not.
Wittgenstein remarks, "what we call 'wit' and 'humor' doubtless did
not exist in other ages. And both are constantly changing." Part of
this change is context, but also, the 'taste' of humor, this changes
as well. We'll return to these ideas of context and taste in humor
later.

One of Wittgenstein's contributions to the philosophy of language is his idea of a language game; "the term 'language-*game*'
is meant to bring into prominence the fact that the *speaking* of

---

[3] Ludwig Wittgenstein, *Culture and Value* (University of Chicago Press, 1980),
p. 78e.

language is part of an activity, or a form of life."[4] When we communicate with one another, we participate in a language game. Like any game, we need to follow established rules, and like some games, there's an element of improvisation. Among the many language-games that we engage in is making a joke, telling it, and play-acting. Stephen Colbert is often funny because of the way he twists and mixes language games. When we react, laugh, and discuss what we see with one another, we too are engaging in a language game; often we're engaged in more than one game at a time, depending on the situation and circumstances.

Just as there are many tools that we use in a tool box, there are endless variations on how we use language. When we engage in humor, either because we laugh spontaneously at something naturally or we laugh due to something that was fabricated for our amusement, we are participating in language games. The rules for these language games, the tools we use are constantly evolving, are constantly changing. Thus we need a robust theory of humor that allows for the fluidity and flexibility of the language games we call humor.

A Robust, Rotund, and Rofound Philosophy of Humor

As I define it, humor is an aspect change. An aspect change is the thinking of something different when perceiving—the focus could be an object, a situation or an activity. Another name for this is 'aspect-dawning'. Wittgenstein uses this term for 'picture-objects', objects that can be seen under more than one aspect. We could be looking at a face, a face we've seen a hundred times before, and then suddenly we see something new. The face hasn't changed; it's either our seeing or our interpreting that has changed. One time I stared at Uncle Larry's nose until I saw in him Abraham Lincoln. We laugh because we see the world—and then we see it differently. The change of aspect happens to the one who thinks it. For a robust theory though, we will need more than just this concept: we also need a humorous attitude, a shared form of life, an avowal, a good pair of rubber gloves, and a 10 foot pole just for good measure. First, however, we need a discussion on aspect change.

---

[4] Ludwig Wittgenstein, *Philosophical Investigations* (Prentice Hall, 1958), #23, p. 11e.

Wittgenstein was interested in aspect change as an answer to a paradox left by the psychologist Joseph Jastrow, in his book *Fact and Fable in Psychology*, published in 1901. Consider the illustration of a duck-rabbit, where the picture is both a rabbit and a duck. It's one picture with two images, though one cannot see the two images at the same time. Looked at one way, focusing on lines drawn like a very tall 'm' on one side of the picture, the 'm' becomes a bill, the picture is a duck. Looked at another way, focusing on the other side but seeing the 'm' now as a pair of ears, it is a rabbit. What's interesting about the duck-rabbit is that though it's possible to see both images, it's not possible to see them at the same time. The same image looks now like a duck, now like a rabbit. Why is this? How is this? How can we see two different concepts, but one picture? What changes? The picture? The mind? The perception?

Wittgenstein's lectures on aspect-change often began with him reading from Wolfgang Köhler's *Gestalt Psychology*.[5] Gestalt theory says we see two pictures, but not at the same time. The lines that are drawn in the shape of a duck's bill and rabbit ears, distinctive shapes, *cause* our minds to form one picture, then another. The mind perceives a whole picture out of seemingly disparate parts.

Wittgenstein was unsatisfied with the gestalt theorist's answer but it is difficult to say why. It could be that Wittgenstein was skeptical of claims that declared a single psychological cause for human perceptions. Often we think of something because of our surroundings, our past and present experience and perhaps also of things we don't take into consideration, like taste or smell. In his published writings, Wittgenstein never spelled out why he thought the gestalt explanation was inadequate. He was interested in the concept of the aspect-change as something that happens in language. This he discusses in the second part of his *Philosophical Investigations*. He calls this 'noticing an aspect' an experience.[6]

There are two types of seeing. We see Stephen Colbert exercising on an elliptical exercise machine. And we see Stephen Colbert exercising on an elliptical exercise machine *as* a desperate man trying to overcome caffeine withdrawals. The first is seeing, taking in information, seeing Stephen Colbert on television in a particular

---

[5] Ray Monk, *Ludwig Wittgenstein: The Duty of Genius* (Penguin, 1990), p. 509.
[6] *Philosophical Investigations*, p. 193e.

skit. The second is seeing as thinking: the dawning of an aspect. The first claim to a robust philosophy of humor is that humor is an aspect change. We see the world, and then we see it *as* something else. The seeing of an aspect does not have to be a one-to-two correspondence, there can be many aspects *seen* in an object or a situation.

We see the world: a = a, what philosophers call a tautologous relation. Then we see the world differently: a = b, or a = b + c, a revealing relation. When Stephen Colbert visited the Constitution Center in Philadelphia, Pennsylvania during their primary, he noticed that one of the signers of the constitution, Gouverneur Morris, had a peg-leg:

> **COLBERT:** He has a peg-leg.
> **GUIDE:** Yes
> **COLBERT:** How many of the founding fathers were pirates?[7]

In character, Stephen Colbert doesn't ask how Gouverneur Morris got the peg-leg. Rather, he brings in another aspect, an association of a peg-leg and pirates and then assuming in typical Colbert fashion that he is right, asks a question regarding founding fathers and pirates. Stephen Colbert effectively created a change of aspect.

Though we have the ability to see the world differently in many ways at the same time, it is not the case that we do this all the time. There are certain things we just accept as they are:

> It would have made as little sense for me to say, "Now I am seeing it as . . ." as to say at the sight of a knife and fork, "Now I am seeing this as a knife and fork". This expression would not be understood.—Any more than: "Now it's a fork" or "It can be a fork too".

> One doesn't *'take'* what one knows as the cutlery at a meal *for* cutlery; any more than one ordinarily tries to move one's mouth as one eats, or aims at moving it.[8]

Wittgenstein is making the distinction here between normally going about our day and the experience of an aspect change. We're not constantly interpreting what we see in our environment. We see a

---

[7] Episode 4050, originally aired 4/16/2008.
[8] *Philosophical Investigations*, p. 195e.

table and use it as a table and don't question it, unless you're a carpenter or a philosopher.

The comedian shows us a different way of looking at something, a different way of thinking about it. Stephen Colbert is exceptionally good at making these connections. Stephen Colbert's coinage of *truthiness*—feeling with our gut rather than knowing with our mind—shows us another aspect of our culture that has stemmed from the information age and could arguably be attributed to the dumbing down of America.

Wikiality is a term coined by Stephen Colbert to address a growing trend of democratic knowledge where, if enough people agree to it, it becomes a fact: "any user can change any entry and if enough users agree to it, it becomes true. . . . if only the entire body of human knowledge worked this way." Wikipedia is a portmanteau of Wiki, a type of software that allows users to generate and alter content, and the term encyclopedia. The term *wikiality*, is another portmanteau combining Wikipedia, the on-line research resource, and reality. Using wikiality, Stephen Colbert is creating an aspect change in how we think Wikipedia may be influencing our reality.

Stephen Colbert has hit upon a growing trend in this country to use one resource, such as Wikipedia, for the only resource on a subject, taking for granted that if it is stated by an authority, or is in print, and other people agree to it, then it must be true. Stephen Colbert explains this current trend in our culture, "what we are doing is bringing democracy to knowledge. . . . Together, we can create a reality that we can all agree on—the reality we just agreed on."[9]

There Are Forms, and then There Are Forms of Life

Though it gives us a story explaining how humor works, aspect-change alone does not tell us *why* we laugh. What I mean by this distinction is that there can be many reasons for why people laugh, as stupid as they may be, that are particular to their tastes and dispositions, but that the mechanism that allows this to happen, the change of aspect, remains the same. And not all aspect changes are funny. What makes an aspect change funny depends

---

[9] Episode 2096, originally aired July 30th, 2006.

on the circumstances under which the dawning of an aspect was made; the form of life, the humorous attitude, and lastly, an avowal.

We need a Form of Life—a web of shared human relationships, a commonality of everyday life. A form of life is different for humans than it is, say, for lions. Wittgenstein says if a lion could talk, we could not understand him.[10] A lion interacts and communicates with other lions in ways that are obviously different to the way that a human interacts and communicates with other humans. Lions, for instance, never interrupt each other when consuming the still-warm carcass of an antelope, unlike my brother Irving. Even if a lion had a language that was similar to English, the colloquialisms and ways of expressing himself would still be foreign to us. At best, he would be misunderstood.

In order to have a language, we need a shared set of rules for the language. What also comes with these rules are non-speaking verbal cues and a social context that helps us understand the meaning and intention behind every speech activity. The green Starbucks logo centered on a white paper to-go cup is part of our form of life. It represents the coffee conglomerate Starbucks and we associate the cup and logo with mass consumerism of specialty coffee and the tempting aromas of free-trade, cage-free, grass-fed Sumatran Honey-Dragon Blend.

In order to understand the humor in the last scene of 'Threat-Down' mentioned earlier, the shower scene, one would have to be able to recognize the logo on Stephen Colbert's cup as a Starbucks logo and immediately make the connection that the black liquid Stephen Colbert is pouring on his head is indeed, Starbuck's coffee. The Kalahari bushmen in Africa who don't have a concept of to-go coffee or know about the addictive nature of caffeine would not understand the humor that is being portrayed in Stephen Colbert's plight caused by the three hour closing of Starbucks coffee shops because the bushman has a different form of life. Wittgenstein wrote, "to imagine a language is to imagine a form of life."[11] Any human language needs a context, agreed rules, and shared experiences in order for communication to happen; these are all part of a form of life. Though having a shared form of life

---

[10] *Philosophical Investigations*, p. 223e.
[11] *Philosophical Investigations*, p. 8e.

is necessary, it is not a sufficient condition for humor. You can get a group of Californians in the same room but just because they share a form of life does not mean they will find the same things funny.

Yet when the form of life is not shared, the humor attempted to convey is impossible to get. In *I Am America (And So Can You!)*, Stephen Colbert has a whole chapter on religion. At the top, of course, is Roman Catholicism:

> Jesus founded only One Church and it wasn't Unitarian. He took His apostle Simon and made him into a rock and built a church on him. It's called "the Holy Roman Catholic and Apostolic Church," or "Church" for short. (*I Am America*, p. 53)

He goes on to lambaste every major organized religion in America: Protestantism, the Episcopal Church, Methodism, Presbyter-ians, Baptists, Quakers, Mormonism, Judaism. Then, listed under "Other Heathens": Shinto, Hinduism, and Buddhism . . . (pp. 53–59). But when it comes to Islam, though it is still listed under "Other Heathens" it says:

> Islam is a great and true religion revealed in the Holy Koran which was dictated by the angel Gabriel to the final prophet Mohammed, Blessing and Peace Be upon Him.

The entry is followed by footnote 16 which says:

> Islam is a great and true religion revealed in the Holy Koran which was dictated by the angel Gabriel to the final prophet Mohammed, Blessing and Peace Be upon Him.

At first glance, it looks as though Colbert is holding back and that there is nothing funny about this entry. But if one has the background knowledge about the uprising of Muslims all over the world regarding the publication of Muslim cartoons in the Danish paper *Jyllands-Posten* in September, 2005, as well as the many death threats against those who speak out against Islam, one gets the joke. The humor in Colbert's entry on Islam lies in the fact that he is so concerned about Muslim fanatics threatening his life that he doesn't dare say anything negative about Islam. And the fact that he doesn't say anything bad or funny about Islam based on his fear, is, in fact, funny.

The the only way to appreciate the humor here is to have a cultural background where one knows about the on-going conflict of free speech and the Muslim Jihadists. One needs to share in the form of life where this conflict is expressed and talked about.

Humorous Altitude, Aptitude, and Attitude

Humor is an aspect-change, and to understand the humor in our shared cultural community, we need a shared form of life. But these, still, are not sufficient for a robust philosophy of humor.

We also need an H.A.—a Humorous Attitude. Humorous Attitude is what I call an individual's predisposition to find something funny, or the set of things an individual finds funny. An H.A. comes from our lifetime of experience and it shapes the way one thinks. It disposes us towards a certain way of looking at the world. It frames the way we see an aspect-change. It is the "taste" or "palette" of humor. An H.A. explains why some jokes cross cultural and political boundaries and others don't. An H.A. shows how some jokes are tailored to certain political groups and other jokes are apolitical. For example:

> India has one of the most rigid and complex class structures. Based upon their behavior in past lives, all Indians are born into different stratas of society called "castes." These castes forever determine what level of tech support questions they are allowed to answer. (*I Am America*, p. 162)

The people who are most likely to think this is funny are those Americans who have been helped by tech support personnel based in foreign countries and who are also familiar with India's strict caste system. A man in Bangladesh who works for Microsoft is unlikely to find this humor funny, unless he has a very wide, complex H.A., or a wicked sense of self-loathing that he's working on with a therapist. When we find something funny, we ascribe a multi-form *seeing as* property to it that combines our present situation with the history of our garnered concepts.

You may be wondering what is the connection between sharing a form of life and having a Humorous Attitude. Attitudes require a certain surrounding; they don't just happen on their own. There isn't a mental 'cause' to these attitudes but a context that is provided by one's abilities, and is based on what led to the event as well as what happened after, and the social community in which these personal attitudes arise.[12] The background, then, is the form of life, and the H.A. is the individual predisposition one has to finding something funny. That so many Americans enjoy the humor of Stephen Colbert is a testament to his genius in being able to produce an aspect-change of American life that connects to people's H.A.

Avowal, not an Owl

Finally, for our robust philosophy of humor, we need an avowal. An avowal in philosophy is often claimed as an endorsement to what we see. The best example of an avowal for humor is laughter, or a smile. Another avowal can be simply a declaration, "That's really funny," though in some primitive cultures nothing short of spontaneous combustion will do.

But I claim that there are what we might call negative avowals, too. Saying, "That's NOT funny" or divesting yourself of overripe produce are avowals of disapproval over a joke that has fallen flat. One's H.A. is what allows a person to think something is funny and the avowal is what confirms it. Likewise, the H.A. may prevent a person from finding something funny, and their avowal of disapproval, along with their rotting groceries, confirm it.

An odd fact about human psychology is that the more people who express their H.A. through avowals, the funnier the object of their humor becomes. Watching *The Colbert Report*, one will often notice how Stephen Colbert plays on the avowal of the audience, encouraging their clapping and hollering, which in turn, prepares them (and the television viewers) for laughing. Even when a joke bombs, Stephen Colbert is able to turn the audience's disapproving avowal into another aspect-change, thereby creating a new opportunity for humor, as well as impressing the ladies. This, in fact, is exactly what happened when he gave his address at the 2006 White House Correspondents' Dinner.

Attending the Dinner were the elite of the conservative right as well as then President George W. Bush. Stephen Colbert, in character as a right-wing pundit, addressed the President:

> Tonight it's my privilege to celebrate this President. We're not so different, he and I. We get it. We're not brainiacs on the nerd patrol. We're

---

[12] See Hans-Johann Glock, *A Wittgenstein Dictionary* (Blackwell, 1996), p. 128.

not members of the Factinista. We go straight from the gut, right sir? That's where the truth lies, right down here in the gut. (*I Am America*, p. 221)

Throughout his speech, Stephen Colbert used traditional Republican values to criticize the administration:

I believe the government that governs the best is the government that governs the least. And by these standards, we have set up a *fabulous* government in Iraq. (p. 222)

And included an attack on the President:

Now I know there are some polls out there saying this man has a thirty-two percent approval rating. But guys like us, we don't pay attention to the polls. We know that polls are just a collection of statistics that reflect what people are thinking in "reality." And reality has a well-known liberal bias. . . . So don't pay attention to the approval ratings that say sixty-eight percent of Americans disapprove of the job this man is doing. I ask you this, does that not also logically mean that sixty-eight percent approve of the job he's not doing? Think about it. I haven't. (p. 223)

Notice the change of aspect from "sixty-eight percent disapprove of the job he's doing" to "sixty-eight percent approve of the job he's not doing". Implying the criticism many Americans have shared (since the attacks on the U.S. and Hurricane Katrina) that President Bush has done little for the majority of the American population. In fact, Stephen Colbert's next jab directly addresses this:

I stand by this man. I stand by this man because he stands for things. Not only for things, he stands on things. Things like aircraft carriers and rubble and recently flooded city squares. And that sends a strong message: that no matter what happens to America, she will always rebound—with the most powerfully staged photo ops in the world.

There was much more that he said (buy *I Am America* to read the rest) and in the end, his speech was "met with respectful silence." Silence, too, can be an avowal—in this case, an indication that either Stephen Colbert's audience did not think he was funny, or, if they did, they did not feel comfortable admitting that he was funny. And that's funny. The Washington media declared that Stephen Colbert bombed, based on the reaction in the immediate audience. To the blogger media and Comedy Central fans, however, Colbert was a hit. This difference in opinion is a difference in Humorous Attitudes, but also, it shows how one's disapproving avowal can affect another's avowal of approval, as noted on the *Time* blog from James Poniewozik:

> Colbert wasn't playing to the room, if anything he was playing against the room. . . . To the audience that would watch Colbert on Comedy Central, the pained, uncomfortable, perhaps-a-little-scared-to-laugh reaction shots were not signs of failure. They were the money shots. They were the whole point.[13]

The complexity of Colbert humor involves the ability to play on an audience's disapproving avowal for orchestrating an approving avowal for a much larger audience. This playing of avowals in comedy is now achievable with large audiences thanks to the advances of technology. Stephen Colbert possibly is the first comedian to successfully pull it off with the internet.

So, why is Stephen Colbert so funny? First, his humor shows us American culture from the aspect of a stiff, conservative ideologue that allows us to laugh not only at Stephen Colbert, but also his interpretation of particular events. The aspect-change connects to many viewers' H.A, those who either are critical of conservative ideology, or those conservatives who have a wide H.A. and can appreciate the hypocrisy and irony in some of Stephen Colbert's portrayal of American culture and values. That so many people can enjoy Stephen Colbert's humor is a testament to our shared form of life. Finally, that Stephen Colbert is able to incite so many avowals in people—good and bad—is a testament to his ability to affect media in ways that only a brilliant entertainer and bonafide cultural force could.

A larger question that lies outside the scope of this paper is, how long will the comedy of Stephen Colbert last, and will it still pair nicely with a dry chardonnay? Since his humor parodies right-wing conservative pundits, what will happen now, since the

---

[13] James Poniewozik "Stephen Colbert and the Death of 'The Room'," *Time* (May 3rd, 2006), accessed July 25th, 2008.

political shift in the White House? Will Stephen Colbert's popularity wane as easily as it has risen? Or does Stephen Colbert share that special comedic gift that passes down through generations, like Aristophanes, Shakespeare, Charlie Chaplin, and Johnny Carson?

The answers to these questions lie in time, a bottle of wine, and a robust theory of humor.[14]

---

[14] A special thanks to Aaron Schiller, Adam Blodgett, Chris Pincock, and Bodhi Stone for their comments.

12

Where Id Was, There Stephen Colbert Shall Be!

BRAD FRAZIER

In honor of Sigmund Freud, the father of psychotherapy and philosopher of the unconscious, let's have a free association quiz. Please answer with the first name that comes to mind. And don't be ashamed of that answer, guilt-complexinistas. Who is white, apparently racist, and the first woman to be on the short list for joining the ticket of a Democratic nominee for president?

Yes, you're correct, the answer is Geraldine Ferraro. In 1984, Walter Mondale actually chose Ferraro as his running mate. That was long before Ferraro clarified for us how incredibly advantageous it is to run for president in this country as an African-American (C.I.A. director, George Tenet, no doubt would say it's a *slam dunk*). This is especially easy if "Hussein" is your middle name and your last name nicely rhymes with "Osama." Since "b" and "s" are so closely associated in Ferraro's mind, it was an honest mistake.

The Republican ticket of Ronald Reagan and George Herbert Walker Bush (W's daddy) crushed Mondale and Ferraro. Only the communist republic of Minnesota (home of Mondale and Idaho Senator Larry Craig's necessarily wide stance) and the socialist utopia of the District of Columbia (home of the saucy, non-plain-vanilla-man-loving Representative Eleanor Holmes Norton) went for the Defeatocrats. Nation, thank you for pre-supporting our president in a time of pre-war. However, if you voted or would have voted for those who favored pre-appeasing the evildoers, I accept your apology.

Now if initially you were tempted to answer "Hillary Clinton" in response to the impromptu quiz above and you suppressed that idea because she *isn't* a racist, then shame on you for letting facts and common decency intimidate (and assassinate) you. It appears that you don't have Stephen Colbert's balls (tucked away in Jane Fonda's lockbox).

Colbert's Id-ish Improv and Irony

The fact that Colbert gets away with so much on *The Colbert Report*—ironic jabs and controversial riffs and associations that might shipwreck lesser talents—is no mean feat. Consider the double-barreled challenge he faces, as a sharp-edged ironist and improvisational humorist, from the Moralityites (ancient foes of the Sodomites).

Going all the way back to Socrates's Athens, there have been "moral majorities" out to condemn and silence smarty pants like Colbert. Socrates, unlike some of his fans in the Middle Ages, didn't lose his tongue for his ironic and philosophical send up of the moral and religious beliefs of his fellow citizens. Instead, at the ripe old age of seventy, when his prostate undoubtedly was good to grow, the Athenians generously gave him all the hemlock he would need for the rest of his (gurgling, convulsing) life.

But those were the good old days, right? Not quite. Even in our own culture, where we used to pride ourselves on having the freedoms of speech and conscience, moral censuring of irony isn't relegated to rednecks like little Jerry Falwell (the proudest cock of his upright flock—before he went to be with the great Rooster in the sky). For example, Alasdair MacIntyre, an admirer of Socrates and a world-renowned ethicist, argues in his book, *Dependent Rational Animals*, that irony has long worn out its welcome. According to MacIntyre, irony is a corrosive and destructive force in our culture. From this perspective, Stephen's stardom is a surface-level lesion indicative of a pervasive cultural sickness.

That's one moralistic angle from which Colbert's biting brand of humor is criticized. Another pertains to the very conditions for the possibility of Colbert's brilliant spontaneity. According to Jedi masters of improvisation, Keith Johnstone and Del Close (Colbert's own mentor) the basic principle of improvisational humor is to accept *everything* that happens or is said to one in the moment of a spontaneous performance (good rule for other all too brief performances as well). Think of Colbert's off-the-cuff responses in interviews, his reactions to his own gaffes, or the jam sessions of writing that yield "The WØRD." In such moments, to seize on openings for creativity and humor, moral qualms that might block or hinder them have to be relaxed. To invoke Freud again: superego, the uptight, hyper-moralized voice of the internalized parent and other authority figures, has to be shunned in favor of id, the devilish, unsocialized, aggressive adolescent constantly perched on one's shoulder (who always giggles at "caucus").

So those of us Colbert manages to entertain, provoke and even inspire with his distinctive fusion of quick-witted improvisation and deeply ironic humor, are we simply his zombie nation of libertines and immoralists? What redeeming values, if any, does Colbert promote? What are the moralizers missing? To begin to answer these questions, it helps to have a stretch on the couch.

Balancing the Balls

Apparently human beings suffer from a hangover in our hippocampus from a long, tooth-and-claw bender with evolution. As a result, even a normal person's mind teems with uncivilized thoughts. Freud argues that a well-adjusted person blocks or keeps out of her conscious awareness many of these socially unacceptable ideas, wishes, and fantasies. He refers to the mental activity of suppressing such thoughts, which often occurs on a hidden, subterranean level of the mind, as repression. If Freud is right, it turns out that we all need some repression in our lives (especially if we're serial killers). Otherwise there would be many more people in jail (unless they're as clever as Dexter), and all of us would be much more frustrated than we already are (thereby joining the club of all Cubs fans).

But too much repression also is unhealthy. If repressed infantile thoughts and wishes are deeply rooted and powerful enough, they can invisibly exert control over a person's life, thereby robbing her of autonomy. They also can keep a person alienated from healthier versions of herself and render her a prisoner of destructive emotions, such as fear and crippling anxiety, whose origins are obscure (maybe in the basement where the gimp is kept in *Pulp Fiction*). Furthermore, it takes considerable psychic energy to keep an overwhelming number of thoughts and wishes repressed (unending war on mental terror).

The upshot is that human flourishing is a matter of psychic balance. Some people need therapy to achieve such balance (read:

some people can afford therapy). The end game is to develop a civilized self that reasonably manages the various conflicts between superego and id and adeptly navigates the external social world—a kind of Joe Torre of the mind, which Freud refers to as a healthy ego. Freud's way of summing up this goal of mental health is: where id was, there ego shall be.

Talk Dirty to Me: Tell Me You Want My Geneva Conventions

Freud's perspective raises an interesting question about our culture. Are we too repressed overall or not repressed enough?

It might be more helpful to break this question down into two more specific ones: 1. Are we too prone to physical aggression and violence or not aggressive and violent enough? 2. Are we too sexually liberated and permissive or not uptight enough about sex?

If Freud were with us today and not simply haunting our psyches, he surely would find it curious but unsurprising that so many Bible-thumping members of the religious right think that our culture is far too sexually explicit. But they also support the bellicose, warmongering approach of the Bush administration. For instance, James Dobson, a big fan of W's blustery foreign policy, heads Focus on the Family. This evangelical organization seeks to put sex back in its proper place: in the missionary position in a heterosexual, patriarchal, church-sanctioned home (prompting a crisis in foreclosures on foreplay). One of Dobson's cohorts, the right reverend John Hagee, routinely fantasizes from his Texan pulpit about violence in the Middle East as a providential tool in God's overarching strategy to herd Jews back to Jerusalem to hasten a final bloodbath, at which point a Ted Nugent-looking Jesus finally returns. Like many other fundamentalists, Hagee sees a divine formula at work as well in natural disasters such as Hurricane Katrina: in case of too little homosexual repression, expect the Gloryhound's wrathful aggression. (Duck, San Francisco!)

On the other hand, there are many people—usually *significantly* to the left of the religious right—who exhibit the opposite pattern. Arianna Huffington, author and founder of *The Huffington Post*, filmmaker Michael Moore, and Jon Stewart (not to mention Spongebob Squarepants) strongly oppose our bloody occupation of Iraq. But they also believe that we're a bit buttoned-up about sex. During her recent appearance on *The Colbert Report*, for example, Huffington alluded to the psychological dynamic noted above when she observed that the Iraq war is John McCain's Viagra. Colbert quickly replied, "I guess the warning on that should be: if your erection lasts more than one hundred years, you should pull out."[1] (Colbert also has noted that McCain's grandmother is Eve.[2] The Garden of Eden is thought to have been in the Middle East. Hmm, note to self: McCain desires relentless penetration of the Middle East in search of grandmother?)

The patterns of the opposing positions that emerge on these issues are so clear, predictable, and symmetrical (like dueling circumcisions), it's tempting to conclude that the more sexually repressed persons and cultures are, the more likely they are to favor physical aggression as a way of solving conflicts, and *vice versa*. (Simple hippie party platform: can't we all just get along—by having more sex?)

Clearly, however, there are many exceptions to these striking patterns. The Amish manage to combine a pacifist stance on violence with an extremely conservative view of sex and sexual liberation. In addition, as the sex scandals that have rocked the Republicans in recent years demonstrate, there are not a few hawkish conservatives who have had to defend not only Bush's policies on war and torture but also their own family-values-flouting sexcapades. (Of course, Freud has taught us not to be shocked by such inconvenient, unorthodox libidinal spasms.) Colbert would remind us not to overlook (as opposed to looking over) as well those persons he deems the most vulnerable members of our society: the bikini-clad assassins who need their automatic weapons to protect themselves from being objectified.[3]

Still, despite these exceptions and the evident complexities to which they point, there's surprising psychological depth behind the slogan: make love, not war.

Colbert Catharsis

What we make of our country's recent levels of sexual repression and zeal for violent aggression might deeply influence our perspective on the emergence of Stephen Colbert. Is his rise a sign of

---

[1] Episode 4063, originally aired May 8th, 2008.
[2] Episode 4061, originally aired May 6th, 2008.
[3] Episode 4065, originally aired May 13th, 2008.

cultural resurgence—a symptom of a return to health via the salve of therapeutic humor and ironic dissent? Or is it a sign of decadence, nihilism, and imminent apocalypse? (Or is it just an uncomfortably long cultural erection—one of those that lasts more than four hours? Better enjoy Stephen while he lasts.)

Suppose that Huffington, Moore, Stewart, and others in the blame-humans-first crowd are on to something. Stephen Colbert nightly articulates the pubescent fantasies and faith-based wet dreams of some of the most sexually repressed, irrational and blindly nationalistic elements of our culture. But he's an *ironic* pubic Papa Bear. So his Peabody worthy performances, as Freud would tell us, can be profoundly therapeutic.

The Colbert Report is cathartic. By ironically play-acting both the role of the American Id and its fundamentalist Christian superego, Stephen Colbert helps us to cope with some of our worst hang-ups as well as defuse violent, uncivil tendencies through laughter. In turn, we're better able to deal with some of our most troubling traits.

Many Americans are rightly horrified by the surge in mean-spiritedness and aggression in our country's policies and politics, especially since 9/11. The Bush administration cynically exploited our fears in order to justify a tragically stupid invasion of Iraq; a policy regarding torture that is grossly un-American and inhumane; warrantless invasions of our privacy; and the unethical suspension of *habeas corpus* corresponding to the shameful construction of military prisons at Guantanamo Bay.

At the same time, during every election year since 2000, Karl Rove and other Republicans have manipulated the homophobia and xenophobia of significant swaths of voters to gin up support for their candidates. To add insult to injury, they've also implied that American citizens who disagree with them are voters without values. This is logical, in their view, since to lack faith in Jesus is to lack values, and not to be a political conservative is to lack faith in Jesus. And in case there was any doubt about Jesus's own political views, we know for certain that he was a conservative because, as Stephen tells us, he ascended to heaven by his own bootstraps.[4] The fact that Rove himself is agnostic about Jesus simply makes his Machiavellian gambits all the more cynical.

---

[4] Episode 2151, originally aired December 4th, 2006.

Enter Stephen Colbert. In this character we have an O'Reilly off-spring who is so righteous and repressed that he visits the zoo in the spring just to make sure that the animals there aren't engaging in premarital sex.[5] Colbert is so scandalized even by the sex lives of bugs and insects—as chronicled and illustrated in Isabella Rossellini's *Green Porno*—that he's had to give up fishing. Apparently he can't stomach the "invertebrate Caligula," otherwise known as a worm orgy, which occurs in bait buckets.[6]

Of course, Colbert's holy hang-ups extend to *human* sexuality as well. With his own bullhorn in Manhattan, from atop the wreckage of progressive politics, he bombastically but brilliantly announces to all of us the otherwise implicit phobias that Rove and others crassly exploit—as subtly and silently as they can—for political gain. After it was clear that the "Cowards" were going to reclaim the majority in the House of Representatives in the 2006 midterm elections, an exasperated Colbert intoned: "Don't think you're off the hook, voters. You're the ones who made this bed. Now you're the ones who are going to have to move over so a gay couple can sleep in it." He then angrily warned us about the brave new world coming, "where the Constitution gets trampled by an army of terrorist clones created in a stem-cell research lab run by homosexual doctors who sterilize their instruments over burning American flags; where tax and spend Democrats take all your hard earned money and use it to buy electric cars for National Public Radio, and teach evolution to illegal immigrants. Oh, and everybody's high!"[7]

During his recent interview with legendary rock band R.E.M., Colbert immediately moved to protect himself (specifically, his jewels) when lead singer Michael Stipe got a little fresh. He placed the jacket of R.E.M.'s new compact disc, *Accelerate*, over his crotch, thereby creating a cock shield.[8] With this move, Colbert signaled that one cannot be too careful in the presence of a gay man who is not convulsed with guilt over his sexual orientation. Perhaps a Freudian clue to the origins of Colbert's dread of any form of nontraditional sex lies in his proud assertion that he watches *Psycho* on Mother's Day every year.[9]

---

[5] Episode 3043, originally aired March 28th, 2007.
[6] Episode 4064, originally aired May 12th, 2008.
[7] Episode 2140, originally aired November 7th, 2006.
[8] Episode 4042, originally aired April 12th, 2008.
[9] Episode 4064, originally aired May 12th, 2008.

Of course, it's one thing to *play* a homophobe and sexual puritan, it's quite another to *be* one. Stipe knew that he could flirt with Colbert. He clearly was comfortable in Colbert's presence because he knows that the man behind the balls is *not* frightened and repulsed by him and his sexuality. That's also why Colbert's response was not offensive, but humorously instructive. This moment on *The Colbert Report* is a case study in Colbert's subtle deconstruction and diffusion of a right-wing superego with which we are all too familiar.

Give the Id a Chance

A similar effect occurs when Colbert embodies and gives ironic voice to the hyper-aggressive bent of the United States under the chicken hawk leadership of Bush and Cheney. At the beginning of the twentieth century, when we were stuck in that pre-pre 9/11 mindset, our country took a more subtle and less hostile approach to the use of military force, which President Theodore Roosevelt summed up in the maxim, "speak softly and carry a big stick." Many recall this as advice to *walk* softly, but no one bungles the big stick part, of course (as Sigmund smiles). Bottom line: carry a big stick but be gentle—use the oft-neglected lubricant of negotiation and diplomacy.

In his interview with Congressman Joe Sestak, Colbert captured the profound difference between Roosevelt and Bush when he attempted to conflate their perspectives by misstating Roosevelt's quip as follows: "hit them with the big stick and walk softly away." When Congressman Sestak respectfully corrected Colbert, his response was "semantics."[10] This spontaneous exchange was funny but also enlightening. Colbert prompted us to notice that there's a profound difference between *having* an impressive and intimidating military and *using* its deadly force. This difference is even more pronounced when military force is *flaunted* by inviting enemies, as Bush did, to "bring it on"—seemingly welcoming and reveling in the horrible violence of war. Of course, the humbler "big stick" approach is not an option for a hawk like Colbert, who less than a month later, while defending Papa Bear's profanity-laced tirade on *Inside Edition*, twice confessed that he has a "tiny, tiny penis."[11]

---

[10] Episode 4053, originally aired April 22nd, 2008.

Unlike Bush, however, Colbert has the imagination to extend his testosterone-filled patriotism beyond the borders of the United States to Earth itself. In the first place, he's not skeptical about or slow to take seriously global warming because "the market has spoken," that is, Al Gore's *An Inconvenient Truth* was a commercial success.[12] What this means for the id-ish Colbert, however, is that we show our support for our planet, which is in crisis, by talking trash to other planets. So on Earth Day 2008, after leading his audience in an "Earth is #1" chant, Colbert took W's cowboy diplomacy to the cosmos. He bravely reduced the hot-tempered Mercury to a suck-up sissy: "If you were any further up the sun's ass, you'd be pure hydrogen." And that aloof, midget planet, Pluto, got put in its place too: "You're so small, there's a bigger gravitational field being generated by my left nut."[13]

When Colbert belches forth this seventh-grade bravado, he not only amuses us (which is pleasing and therapeutic itself), he also underscores the childish, bullying tendencies of our policies and the silliness of what now passes for patriotism. In turn, we gain greater recognition of and critical distance from these regrettable features of our culture and our politics. Furthermore, although the folly of our extreme overreaction to 9/11 is painful to acknowledge, Colbert helps us to face up to it through the sleight of hand of his embracing, and even oozing, of it. (Call this an honorable dishonorable discharge, if you will.)

The Unbearable Lightness of Being Absurd

Just about everything on *The Colbert Report*—the atmospherics, the symbols and images, Colbert's unflagging machismo sacramentally contained in his conservative white male appearance—screams American exceptionalism and blind nationalism. As we have seen, there is a method to this stars-and-stripes madness. So that we might better grasp the *ethical* thrust of Colbert's irony, let's dig even deeper beneath the thick red, white, and blue surface.

Ironists and satirists have long understood that one subtle but effective way to critique an absurd or problematic, but nonetheless

---

[11] Episode 4065, originally aired May 13th, 2008.

[12] Episode 4066, originally aired May 14th, 2008.

[13] Episode 4053, originally aired April 22nd, 2008.

widely-held, view is to heap ridiculous, over the top praise and attention on it. The idea behind this strategy of going overboard in fake, fanatical support of a position is that it helps to expose hidden problems and inconsistencies, but in a stealthy, roundabout way. In cases where a belief or view is crucially tied to a person or community's self-image and sense of importance, this form of critique may be the only practical one available. The incongruities revealed in the process often are humorous and painless to observe. As a result, the criticism goes down easier and has a better chance to get past the mental defenses that we set up to protect our beliefs and buried prejudices.

Søren Kierkegaard (1813–1855), a Danish philosopher who was very intrigued by irony and was a highly skilled ironist himself, helpfully explains this approach:

> It is the most common form of irony to say something earnestly that is not meant in earnest. . . . Either the ironist identifies himself with the odious practice he wants to attack, or he takes a hostile stance to it, but always, of course, in such a way that he himself is aware that his appearance is in contrast to what he himself embraces and that he thoroughly enjoys this discrepancy.
>
> When it comes to a silly, inflated, know-it-all knowledge, it is ironically proper to go along, to be enraptured by all this wisdom, to spur it on with jubilating applause to ever greater lunacy, although the ironist is aware that the whole thing underneath is empty and void of substance. Over against an insipid and inept enthusiasm, it is ironically proper to outdo this with scandalous praise and plaudits, although the ironist is himself aware that this enthusiasm is the most ludicrous thing in the world.[14]

Ludicrous enthusiasm is an apt way to describe a crucial component of Colbert's shtick. This phrase calls to mind Colbert's interview with feminist and social critic, Naomi Wolf, who appeared on *The Colbert Report* to discuss her book, *The End of America: Letter of Warning to a Young Patriot*.[15] Wolf's book offers a sobering analysis of the fascist bent of our ever expanding executive branch. When she attempted to share her perspective with Colbert, however, his knee-jerk "refutation" consisted of his boisterously leading

---

[14] Søren Kierkegaard, *The Concept of Irony* (Princeton University Press, 1989), pp. 248–49.
[15] (Chelsea Green, 2007).

the audience in a "U.S.A.! U.S.A.!" chant.[16] But the briefly bemused Wolf comfortably stood her ground. She knows the drill. In an unscripted moment, Colbert had managed to capture the essence of years of frustrating (lack of) dialogue in our culture about freedom, tyranny, terrorism, and true patriotism. He also had offered a vivid illustration of one of Wolf's major concerns.

Ironic Inquisition

Especially during interviews with liberals or progressives, such as Wolf or Huffington, Colbert frequently pushes back tenaciously with cartoonish right-wing talking points. In addition to entertaining us, his goal, as he once remarked to Senator John Kerry in a behind-the-scenes glimpse, is to be disabused of his ignorance or, to put it more aptly, neutered.[17] Sometimes not a little barking occurs before Colbert's balls are clipped. Occasionally, when the Republican Rottweiler encounters a person who is determined to treat all animals ethically, he barks all the way through the interview, until he gelds himself.

Presumably, most people who watch *The Colbert Report* are "in the know." We're aware that Colbert simultaneously occupies both an earnest, defender-of-the-American faith persona within the space of the interview and also a zone of ironic distance outside of it, to which he repeatedly calls our attention with hilarious effect. So we're not watching to see a heretic cross-examined and burned at the stake. Rather, we're in on the irony of the inquisition and that is part of the fun of watching the fake interrogation unfold.

What may not be as obvious is that when Colbert veers blindly to the right, he subtly creates *more* space for opposing views to be sympathetically articulated in a comical give and take. He also deftly undermines the ground on which he ironically stands.

Consider, for instance, Colbert's recent interview with Paul Helmke, president of the Brady Campaign, which is a gun control lobbying group.[18] Colbert began the segment by casting gun control advocates like Helmke as anti-American hypocrites—they hate

---

[16] Episode 3117, originally aired September 19th, 2007.

[17] This revealing backstage glimpse was provided by the left-leaning blog *Talking Points Memo* and can be found on YouTube at http://www.youtube.com/watch?v=DfiL2hpnmZ0

[18] Episode 4065, originally aired May 13th, 2008.

guns, but they "have no problem blasting holes in the Constitution." Then he mentioned the Brady Bill, which established background checks and a five day waiting period for the purchase of handguns. Many consider this bill a model piece of legislation, but *not* Colbert, of course. In his view, it "takes away all the spontaneity of hunting" because "by the time you go through all the red tape and get your gun, that deer will have untangled itself from your swing set."

The image of shooting a deer stuck in a swing set, like a good stage prop, offers a sneaky cue as to who the real cowards are. In the context of the interview, it was a harbinger of things to come, but not just yet. Colbert proceeded to challenge Helmke to defend the Brady Campaign. When Helmke calmly replied, "we want sensible gun laws," the game was on.

For Colbert, this was tantamount to Helmke's "coming for our guns" and "infringement." In fact, during a significant stretch of the ensuing examination, the man-child Colbert constantly resorted to "infringe, infringe, infringe" as his mantra of defense in response to Helmke's patient attempts to explain the debate about the meaning of the constitutional right to bear arms. Later, after Colbert failed to goad Helmke into conceding that he'd use a gun to defend himself if Colbert came at him with a knife, Colbert himself admitted that a gun wouldn't help him anyway "because I'm hopped up on screamers."

Seemingly feeling that he was losing ground in the debate to the unflappable Helmke, Colbert eventually trotted out the ultimate weapon: Jesus. You see, we may insanely want to keep guns out of the hands of mentally unstable persons. But, as Colbert noted, the problem with this stance is that many people thought *Jesus* was crazy. Colbert had finally found his trump card: "Now imagine how much more hopeful the story of the gospels would be if Jesus had a gun. You agree that the idea of Jesus with a gun is a good image? . . . I'm picturing it. . . . I had a great picture of Jesus with a pistol."

Helmke couldn't quite agree. For some reason, the image seemed discordant to him. So he whipped out his own trump card: James Brady, the person in whose honor the Brady Bill was named. Brady was an aide to Reagan. In 1981, John Hinckley, Jr. shot Brady in the head as he tried to assassinate Reagan. Although Brady survived, he was seriously and permanently injured.

Now usually Stephen Colbert the comedian wields his ironic wit not as a blunt instrument of cruelty but one of entertainment, therapy and indirect instruction. But there are moments when he reaches, and sometimes even crosses, a borderline of cruelty. It was at this point in his exchange with Helmke that he arrived at one:

> How long is he (Brady) going to hold that up like 'I know more about being shot than you do because I got shot'? Wouldn't it take more courage to be shot and go, 'no, I'm not going to infringe other people's rights just because something bad happened to me.' *That* would be bold. . . . (Brady's being a hero is) just a card you're playing to win an argument as opposed to listening to the issue here, which is people want guns.

Yes, if you're juiced up on crank and fantasizing about Jesus holding a pistol, you might think that the fact that "people want guns" means that there shouldn't be sane restrictions of any kind on our being able to have them. You also might be likely to say something you shouldn't.

Comedians with less talent and heart might have rushed to conclude the interview at such a moment. To his credit, Colbert was as quick to perceive the overreach and pull back from it as he is to see an opening for comedy. Indeed, he turned it into one. The segment concluded with the hard-core but ultimately humane inquisitor ironically improvising a compelling case for gun control:

> And if you say, hey, guns kill a lot of people: look at what happened at Virginia Tech; look at what happened at Columbine; look at our leaders who have been assassinated; look at how many children are killed every year by playing with guns that were not locked properly; look at how many couples kill each other; look at how many people in individual families are murdered by members of their own family; look at how more likely you are to be killed by a gun that you are keeping in your house than to be able to defend yourself; look at how hard it is even for policemen to defend themselves when they are attacked by someone with a weapon—I mean, I think people are tired of the 'a lot of people have been killed by guns' card.[19]

Checkmate.

---

[19] Episode 4065, originally aired May 13th, 2008.

ThreatDown: Taming the Bear Within

As Freud has taught us, it isn't easy to find a healthy equilibrium where our animalistic desires are adequately met while we tend to the moral and social obligations that make possible the civilized community that we share. We're apt to lose our balance and find ourselves suffering from completely avoidable forms of misery, or worse.

Recognizing, coping with, and rooting out of ourselves harsh traits and deeply ingrained shortcomings is necessary for personal and societal moral progress. Critics of *The Colbert Report* who argue that it mainly fosters greater cynicism in our culture crucially fail to see how it helps us with this difficult task, often by clever subterfuges of irony. As we've seen, Colbert is masterful at getting us to laugh at ourselves and some of our worst tendencies and most ridiculous hang-ups, which is a less painful but still effective way of helping us not-so-rational animals have a look in the mirror.

As a final example, consider how Colbert handled the remarkable story involving the women's softball teams from Central Washington University and Western Oregon University. In the final inning of a game between the two schools, a player on Western Oregon's team hit a game-winning home run. However, she was unable to round all the bases after she seriously injured her knee rounding first base. Substituting in a pinch runner by rule would have reduced her home run to a single. So, several players from Central Washington decided to carry their hobbled opponent around the rest of the bases, thus ensuring their loss and Western Oregon's victory. It was an inspiring act of sports*woman*ship.

Colbert introduced the story in a ThreatDown segment. Of course, the specific threat he initially invited us to see in it was a threat to the nature of competitive sports. According to Colbert, the "softball softies" demonstrated by their behavior that "women are a threat to sport." For sexists: so far, so good. Except not a few of us were laughing *at* Colbert's crass sexism and the stereotypes he proceeded to invoke.

The ruse worked. Seconds later Colbert had everyone, sexist and non-sexist alike, in stitches over the Neanderthal attitudes on display in sports—the precise attitudes that make the story of Central Washington's sportsmanship all too unique. As he observed, sports offers us "the last socially acceptable place to express violence and blind regional hatred." Woohoo! "Go, team that lives near me. Destroy that team from nearby town. My team is the best team and always will be the best, until I move."[20]

Moving On

Here's where I think things stand. George W. Bush claims to be a true patriot. In fact, he's so full of it (patriotism) that his administration is able to offer authoritative judgments concerning which Americans have it and which don't. It turns out to be a relatively simple task: everyone who agrees with Bush's (and McCain's) policies is a patriot. As for the rest of us: not so much.

Stephen Colbert, on the other hand, simply *plays* at being a patriot. He can only fantasize about dropping bombs on Iran as he flies across the Middle East on that bald eagle that swoops down each night as his show begins.

To avoid the kind of critical self-reflection that could leave him horribly depressed, perhaps suicidal (like the rest of us), Bush often has stated that history will have to be the judge of his presidency. Well, I'm not a historian or the son of one. Still, I think that when historians look back on this period in American history and culture, they will render an ironic verdict. The man who merely played the true patriot was the more authentic American.

---

[20] Episode 4064, originally aired May 12th, 2008.

13

Why Mr. Colbert Should Be President

NICOLAS MICHAUD

As anyone who has had the pleasure of watching Mr. Colbert on *The Colbert Report* already knows, Mr. Colbert is a super-man. He's the host of his own top-rated news show, the author of the best-selling *I am America (And So Can You!)*, and a paragon of excellence in every aspect of his life. Why else would there be both an ice cream flavor created in his honor and a Hungarian bridge named after him? Mr. Colbert's best-selling book won the very prestigious "Stephen Colbert Award for the Literary Excellence." And he even coined the 2006 Merriam-Webster word of the year: truthiness. Clearly, everything graced by Mr. Colbert's touch turns to gold.

Yet one question eats away at me incessantly: As Mr. Colbert is the most excellent and most American of all Americans—in essence a "Super-American," if you will—why is he not the proud leader of the United States of America? How is it that the most American of us all is not the President of the United States of America?

Now Mr. Colbert did *try* to become president. It was his intention to run for President in 2008. As he announced in a special appearance on *The Daily Show* on October 16th, 2007, Colbert planned on competing for a place on both the Republican and the Democratic tickets in his home state of South Carolina. After a series of setbacks, however, Mr. Colbert's ambition was thwarted once and for all when he was *denied* a place on the ballot by the South Carolina Democratic Executive Council. In what's clearly their least democratic of decisions, South Carolina denied its favorite son the opportunity to become what he so richly deserves. In so doing, they also denied us as Americans that from which we would so greatly benefit. So, why would these so-called "Democrats" deny Mr. Colbert his rightful place on the ballot? The answer is obvious . . . *jealousy.*

I will admit that even I, the most ardent of Mr. Colbert's supporters (I like to think of myself as a "Colbertite""), feel the occasional twinge of jealousy when I consider his amazing gifts. Many of us have experienced this—isn't it natural? How could we not wish we were more like Mr. Colbert? But, would we deny him the opportunity to rule the greatest country in the world just because we are jealous? I hope not. Obviously, there are those who would. After much research, I have found the deep philosophical and psychological explanation for why some lesser men try so hard to hold back great men, and try even harder to hold back the greatest of men—Stephen Colbert.

Why They Try to Keep Our Man Down

Now, first, a quick disclaimer: the philosophical ideas that I am about to explain to you were thought up by a *German*. To be specific, a *not American*. But even "not Americans" can come up with a good idea on a rare occasion. So don't be dissuaded just because it is unlikely! More importantly, remember that just because someone has one good idea doesn't mean he has more than one good idea. In this case, though, I think, and you'll agree, that this "not American" did get one thing right.

Now who am I talking about? I am talking about Friedrich Nietzsche. But that isn't important. What matters is what Nietzsche has to say about our hero—Stephen Colbert. Okay, okay, Nietzsche did not actually write about Mr. Colbert specifically. As he I am sure would regret, Nietzsche died before he had the opportunity (1844–1900). Nevertheless Nietzsche's work is clearly about Mr. Colbert. A central idea in Nietzsche's philosophy is that of the super-man. He is the man who, because of his *overwhelming power*, stands apart from and *above* other men. Nietzsche didn't think that the super-man was alive during the latter-half of the nineteenth century. Indeed, he didn't even think that *he himself* was the super-man. Rather, he believed that the super-man was *a man for the future*, a higher-man who was yet to come.

Well, Nation, the future is now! Finally, Nietzsche's words can be put to the test. And we can look to Nietzsche to explain what Mr. Colbert is currently facing. So now we'll turn our attention to

Nietzsche's ideas about the super-man so that we may better understand the overwhelming power that is Stephen Colbert!

Nietzsche's Super-Man Philosophy

For all of you Colbert fans out there, I want you to bear with me. Although *you* may understand truthiness, there are those readers who don't. Chief among these are the philosophical-types. For them, truthiness is not enough. They (sickly) also want reasons and explanations. So, here I will take a little time to help those philosophical-types understand what I am saying by explaining Nietzsche. Don't panic. We'll get back to the truthiness A.S.A.P. You'll notice that when I say something like "according to Nietzsche" I am going to be giving reasons, thus avoiding truthiness, so as not to scare off those philosophers. (Colbert fans, just plug up your ears and hum the National Anthem whenever you feel like the truthiness is getting bogged down by "reasoning.")

Alright, Colbertites, begin humming! According to Nietzsche, a man is "super" when he is better than other men. He is better because he is stronger physically or mentally. Either way, the key point is that he knows what he wants and he knows how to get it. Nietzsche argues that his super-man has the "will-to-power." The super-man does not let anything get in his way. The super-man is simply superior—better at getting what he wants—and those lesser than him find themselves having to do his will. Some men, like Stephen Colbert, are just better than the rest. "For men are not equal: thus speaks Justice," Nietzsche tells us in his text *Thus Spake Zarathustra*. Philosophers usually interpret Nietzsche as dismissing the very popular belief that all men are created equal. Equality is not the case, says Nietzsche, since some men are simply stronger, faster, or smarter than others. But even beyond this, what really puts the "super" in super-man for Nietzsche is a superior *will to power*.

The will to power is an idea that has its beginning in the idea of the will to live. The will to live is essentially the belief that everything that is alive strives to live—everything is built to try to keep living. Similarly, every living thing has the will to power. But Nietzsche thinks the will to power is even stronger than the will to live. He thinks this is proven by the fact that we will sometimes even risk our lives for power. The will to power can be thought of as just the will to dominate others, but most philosophers think it is a deeper idea than that. For example, Mr. Colbert does not seek dominion over others by being President just for power. He is seeking something more. Rather, he recognizes that because he is as great as he is, he would be the best president. And, importantly, what is clear about Mr. Colbert is that if he wasn't already perfect, he would strive to become the perfect Stephen Colbert that he is. Self-perfection is the goal of super-men.

Granted, as we Colbert fans will admit, there is very little to improve about Mr. Colbert. But it is this "self-overcoming" that best describes the will to power. By this I just mean that super-men seek to grow beyond themselves, they overcome their weakness and thus become stronger. The fact that this causes the super-man to inevitably be better than other men, and thus achieve dominion over them, is just a side-effect.

To be clear, the super-man is not the goody-goody that we might think of when we think of a really good person. The super-man does not show things like compassion and pity. Instead he exhibits the qualities that best lead one to success in the will to power. In seeking this kind of perfection, traits like courage, open-mindedness, and truthfulness best bring one to power. The super-man can identify what he desires and then strive for it without allowing compassion or other emotions to get in the way.

This might seem cold to you. But, remember, when we think about men like Mr. Colbert, compassion could get in his way. It's not as if Nietzsche believed that we should all go around hurting each other. But we should be wary of how emotions like compassion are used to keep power in check. Nietzsche believed that weak people use compassion and pity as a way to keep the powerful from achieving their ends. The reason for this is simple. As a super-man begins to reach self-perfection, the weak around him often must bend to his will. This can lead to servitude for those who are weak-willed. So the weak seek pity from the master in an effort to avoid the burdens of servitude.

Nietzsche argues that in religions like Christianity, compassion and pity are developed as virtues as a way for the weak to hold back the strong—as a way to prevent having to serve the super-man. Now obviously, Mr. Colbert would disagree with this and we will see why very soon. (Don't worry, Colbertites: the truthiness is almost back!) But Nietzsche had very little respect for any religion or institution that encouraged others to hold themselves back. Imagine what would happen to lions if they felt compassion for gazelles. Lions would die off. Instead, the lion is constantly trying to achieve its own success and, in doing so, he achieves dominion over the gazelles. We don't chastise the lion and say, "Bad lion!" So why should we tell he among us who is stronger or smarter, "Bad person"? Nietzsche argues that the super-man is motivated by his will to power, as we all are—his will is just that much stronger, so we resent him or fear him. To quote Nietzsche,

> That lambs dislike great birds of prey does not seem strange: only it gives no ground for reproaching these birds of prey for bearing off little lambs. And if the lambs say among themselves; "these birds of prey are evil; and whoever is least like a bird of prey, but rather its opposite, a lamb—would he not be good?" . . . [T]he birds of prey might view it a little ironically and say: "We don't dislike them at all, these good little lambs. We even love them: nothing is more tasty than a tender lamb."[1]

But did the lambs accept the fact that they were weaker and not as worthy to rule? No! Instead, they tried to overthrow the super-man. But of course that wouldn't work, so they did something far more insidious—they made it a bad thing to be the super-man.

According to Nietzsche, the weak (or what are sometimes referred to as the "sheep") have developed what he calls a "slave-morality." This morality is entirely based on the fact that such a morality is a good way to prevent others from reaching super-man status. This morality is adopted because the weak—the slaves—are jealous of the super-man and because they don't want to have to serve him. Nietzsche has no respect for these slaves. Instead of seeking their own self-overcoming, instead of trying as they should to become "super" themselves, they spend their time trying to hold the super-man back. But even worse, they don't try to stop him by being stronger or smarter. They try to stop him through subtle manipulations, a kind of behind-the-scenes scheming.

When we think about those around us, it seems that Nietzsche might have at least one thing right. We do seem to revel in mediocrity. Ever notice how children will make fun of a child who's smarter than they are, or ostracize a child who is stronger than they are? It seems that we do this in the adult world, too. As soon as someone is better than everyone else, we try to take him down.

---

[1] Friedrich Nietzsche, *On the Genealogy of Morals* (Vintage, 1989), p. 44.

There's one thing we like more than building a hero up—tearing him down afterwards.

Okay, so let's summarize Nietzsche's concept of the super-man before we get back to Mr. Colbert. The super-man has overwhelming power. He is faster, stronger, smarter, and so on. But he wasn't just born this way. The super-man is all these things because of his super-sized will to power. He seeks, first and foremost, to perfect himself. Surely this is a laudable goal. But the pursuit of perfection leads him to become faster, stronger and smarter, which, in turn, leads him naturally to positions of dominance over those less concerned with their own perfection. Those dominated come to resent the super-man and attempt to tear him down. They use many tactics to do this, but their most significant and insidious tactic is to actually *define* weakness as strength—meekness as power. In other words, they make being super "bad," and make being weak "good." In the end, the perfection-seeking super-man is defined away as evil because he is stronger and the weak pat themselves on the back for being meek and mediocre.

The Sheep (aka The South Carolina Democratic Executive Council)

Okay, so let's get back to the truthiness of the matter. What does Nietzsche—a "not American," after all—really have to teach us about Mr. Colbert? We've already determined that Mr. Colbert is the super-man. Mr. Colbert clearly recognize this. And we were *ready* to vote Mr. Colbert into the highest office in America, and thus the world when he tried to run for President! Why didn't we get the chance to do this? Why wasn't the super-man given the reigns of power that he so richly deserves? The Answer: The sheep (aka The South Carolina Democratic Executive Council).

On November 1st, 2007, less than two and half weeks into Colbert's historic bid for the U.S. Presidency, the South Carolina Democratic Party Executive Council voted thirteen to three to prevent Mr. Colbert from appearing on the ballot. "The general sense of the council was that he wasn't a serious candidate and that was why he wasn't selected to be on the ballot," said John Werner, the director of the council. The sheep had spoken. The super-man had been held down, just as Nietzsche had predicted.

Well, "perhaps the Council was right," a godless liberal might object. What a silly objection. Obviously, if Mr. Colbert was not serious, he would not have paid the $2,500 required to run in the first place! "He was only trying to draw attention to himself," they might whine. But if he did not actually want to be President, he would not have sought election . . . think, Nation! But, we cannot expect logic like that from sheep, now can we?

Or, how about this: Did the council members bother to run themselves? No, of course not. Like all sheep, they sought only to prevent others from gaining power because they know they cannot attain it themselves. The Council feared Mr. Colbert's success because they knew they couldn't match it. In short, that council in South Carolina stopped Mr. Colbert from being on the ballot not because they truly believed that he didn't want or deserve to be on the ballot, but because they knew how much better than them he really is!

What Mr. Colbert Got Right and Nietzsche Got Wrong

We have established that Nietzsche was pretty right about one thing. It does seem that when a super-man appears, the weaker resent him and try to make it bad to be a super-man. What's happened to our super-man is a prime example.

But Nietzsche also makes at least one big mistake. He argues that Christianity epitomizes this slave morality. First off, he claims that, "God is Dead." Then he says that God is an idea that *we* created to popularize the slave morality. This is clearly wrong. God can't be dead. How else could Moses have spoken to him? And surely it's wrong to say that Christianity is a religion for the weak, because we know God isn't weak. If you read the Bible—and obviously Nietzsche didn't—you know that God goes around being strong all the time! How weak can you be when you turn people into salt, burn cities to the ground, and open the Earth to swallow people whole? Those of you philosophical-types probably have some issues with this argument, but you had your time already.

Clearly if Nietzsche had really thought about it, he would have realized what the slave morality is actually epitomized by—the Liberal Media. As Mr. Colbert points out often on his show, the liberals in the media spend much of their time trying to corrupt our young people with their ideas of weakness. They talk about "open-mindedness" and "dialogue," but what is really happening is that they are trying to make weenies of us all. For example, since they are not strong enough to become super-men themselves, they try to make us feel bad about the war on terror. Stephen Colbert tells us that we should bring the war to them! But the Liberal Media is too weak for that. So weak, in fact, that they try to make us think that war is a *bad* thing. To quote Mr. Colbert, "The greatest threat facing America today—next to voter fraud, the Western Pinebark Beetle, and the memory foam mattress—is the national news media" (*I Am America*, p. 152).

Now, Nietzsche may have failed to realize that it wouldn't be Christianity, but Liberal Media, that would be responsible for the proliferation of the values of the weak when the man of the future—the super-man—finally arose. But Nietzsche was formidable enough to identify the mindset that the Liberal Media would appeal to in order to do its dirty work. Think about how much the media loves a good story about someone great taking a fall. When a good and noble celebrity gets into some unfortunate trouble, the media make sure that we know it is good to be nobody special. Nietzsche describes their mindset perfectly:

> They will discover, these keen observers idlers, that things are quickly going downhill, that everything around them is turning to decay and causing decay, that nothing lasts past tomorrow, with the exception of one single species of human being, the incurably *mediocre*. The mediocre alone have the prospect of continuing, of having descendants—they are the people of the future, the only survivors. "Be like them! Become mediocre!" will henceforth be the only moral code that still makes sense, that can still find an ear.[2]

Just as the sheep want to discourage greatness, the media tries to elicit our pity and "compassion" for the weak while at the same time discouraging our feeling for the strong.

But a super-man like Mr. Colbert won't have it anymore! No more subversive images of bombed Iraqi hospitals or abused gays! If the hospitals aren't strong enough to keep a stockpile of patriot missiles on hand, and if the gays don't buy some brass knuckles, then we shouldn't feel bad for them!

---

[2] Friedrich Nietzsche, *Beyond Good and Evil* (Oxford University Press, 1998), p. 160.

Why Christianity Is Tougher than All Those Other Religions

Perhaps part of why Nietzsche made his mistake in thinking that Christianity supports the slave morality is because of misunderstood quotes like "turn the other cheek" and "let he who is without sin cast the first stone." But these are just more liberal media lies. If someone hits you, when you hit him back, your cheek turns; a good right hook takes throwing your body weight into it. Obviously, the most important point to take away from that misused quote is "a good super-man hits first." If you didn't bring the war to them, then you deserve to be hit on the other cheek! Hit first; then, hit him again. We can see here, though, how this slave morality has been beaten into us by the media. Shows like "60 Minutes" want us to think that it is a good thing to let people hit you! This is obviously weak thinking and a super-man like Stephen Colbert would never buy such baloney.

The same kind of liberal slave morality perverts the truth of the quote, "let he who is without sin cast the first stone." The message here is obvious. Go to confession, *then* cast the stone! The Bible isn't telling us to be weak and compassionate to sinners. It's telling us *not* to be sinners or else we'll be stoned! And deservedly so. If you're a sinner, you'd better get those sins gone before those stones start flying. The fact that the media tries to cover up is who in that story was without sin. Jesus! I'll bet if we investigated we'd find out that right after the story ends, he let the stones fly. Jesus was no slave! The liberal media tries to keep him down too! Once again, there might be so-called "facts" or "philosophical arguments" brought out to dispute what I am saying here. But, remember, this is truthiness: facts just get in the way.

What Mr. Colbert Has Taught Us (Besides Everything)

Alright. So we've seen that we should have probably have expected that Mr. Colbert's bid for the Presidency would have been cut short by someone or other. Like all super-men, the forces of mediocrity are bent on keeping him down. And we have corrected some of the things that Nietzsche got wrong. Christianity isn't to blame here. The liberal media is. This is surely frustrating to those of us who recognize greatness and wish to see it rewarded as it so rightly deserves to be.

But there's reason to stay hopeful. By definition, the super-man never surrenders in his search for perfection. Neither will our super-man. Mr. Colbert isn't going to let himself get sucked into the perverse world of liberal media bias. He will continue on the straight and narrow path, fighting for America!

Nietzsche states, "The super-man . . . has organized the chaos of his passions, given style to his character, and become creative. Aware of life's terrors, he affirms life without resentment." To philosophers this might mean that the super-man is just a person who doesn't go around blaming others for his failings or crediting others for his successes. But to us proud Colbertites there is no one alive today who better fits that description. Mr. Colbert rebels against the slave morality which is constantly being pushed on him and instead affirms life without resentment. Has he sat back whining because the South Carolina Democratic Executive Council rejected him? No! He continues on, fighting the good fight. Stephen Colbert isn't *just* America. He is Nietzsche's man for the future—the super-man![3]

---

[3] I would like to thank my editor who has seen me through many last-minute drafts. Thanks, Aaron!

What Stephen Colbert Tells Us about Being America

14

Colorblindness and Black Friends in Stephen Colbert's America

AARON ALLEN SCHILLER

Is there a contradiction in Stephen Colbert's attitudes towards race? It probably shouldn't be much of a surprise to find that there is. No one can talk out of both sides of his mouth better than Stephen, the man who debates himself in Formidable Opponent. (I'm using the name "Stephen" to refer to the character of "Stephen Colbert" and the name "Colbert" to refer to the comedian who plays him.)

At the same time, however, the self-proclaimed defender of all things truthy is famous precisely *because* of his relentless self-consistency. Once Stephen has made up his mind (or, rather, his gut) there's no changing it. Not only that, but it's important to Stephen's way of thinking that he has everything figured out. Catching him in a contradiction would show that he hasn't quite thought through the implications of his views.

But careful viewers of the Colbert Report—and especially those who see philosophy in his comedy—might see a tension in Stephen's attitude toward race. Famously, Stephen claims not to *see* race. As he put it to African-American columnist and "friend of the show" Debra Dickerson: "I understand that you're black. I don't see race, but you've told me that you're black, and I believe you," he said, pointing at her cornrows, "because I could never get away with that with my hair."[1]

In fact, Stephen even claims to not see his own race.[2] In another conversation with Dickerson—who, as part of her "critique of

---

[1] Episode 4012, originally aired January 24th, 2008.

[2] My favorite of these lines is: "People tell me that I'm white, and I believe them because I shop at Eddie Bauer" (Episode 2150, originally aired November 20th, 2006).

white self-congratulation" was arguing that Barack Obama is not really "black"—Colbert said,

> I don't see race, okay, because I've moved beyond it—I've developed beyond it. I'm so *not* a racist that I don't see race. People tell me I'm white and I believe them because I think Barack Obama is black.[3]

In the end, I don't think it's possible for someone to be color-blind (what's also called "race-blind") in the way that Stephen claims for himself. Anyone who has the concept of race (or even of the difference between oneself and an "other") is going to see another as different from oneself on such a basis sometimes. (This is a rather controversial thing to say. But as it would take us too far off topic for me to defend this claim, and since it's not central to my point anyway, let's move on.) But then that's part of what makes it a joke; it just doesn't seem possible to "not see race" in the way that Stephen says it is. Let him say it if he wants, we might think; but we know better.

So far so good. No contradiction here, unless there's contradiction in trying to do the impossible.

But Stephen isn't always so colorblind. Quite often when discussing issues of race Stephen will ask Jimmy, the fictional director of *The Colbert Report*, to put up a picture of him with his "black friend," Alan. In the picture, Stephen has his left arm around his black friend, a sign of friendship. But with his right hand, and with a big smile on his face, he's pointing to Alan, as if to say: "See, I've got one! A black friend!" Or at least he did. Ever since Stephen saw footage of Alan at an anti-war rally, Stephen no longer considers Alan his black friend. But he's made a big deal about his nation-wide search for a new black friend to replace Alan.

So where's the contradiction? It's this: Someone who really is colorblind in the strict sense that Stephen claims for himself should-n't be able to even *recognize* someone to be of a different race in the first place,[4] let alone want them as a friend *because* of their race. Stephen risks contradicting himself by saying, on the one hand, that he does not see race but then, on the other hand, being savvy to things about which he should be naive: namely, the poli-

---

[3] Episode 3020, originally aired February 8th, 2007.
[4] To see what it would be like to be colorblind like Stephen, check out the Ishihara Race Test (pp. 259–262) in this volume.

tics of race in America. In short, Stephen's colorblindness seems *inconsistent* with his search for a black friend.

Now, as I said, it shouldn't be all that surprising to find Stephen contradicting himself. But there's an interesting question here: If there's contradiction in these attitudes (his being color-blind in a particularly extreme way and his using race as a way to pick his friends) what does it mean? Is there a flaw in the character Colbert has created, a kind of *discontinuity* in an otherwise carefully crafted character? Did Colbert (the comedian and former philosophy major) break the first rule of character: to make's one character a self-consistent whole? Or does Stephen's inconsistency point to something deeper, some interesting fact about his worldview, or maybe even some truth about race in America today?

As it happens, I think there is something particularly deep going on in Stephen's seemingly contradictory attitudes toward race. I'll try to say what that may be, as well as what it means for race relations in Stephen Colbert's America.

People Tell Me I'm White

Let's start by looking more closely at the two attitudes that I think are contradictory in Stephen's character, as saying precisely how they are contradictory will bring out some interesting features of his thinking. Let's ask two questions: (1) Why does Stephen claim to be colorblind? If it's impossible to be colorblind in Stephen's sense, then he isn't fooling anyone but himself. But if that's the case, then why does he cling so tightly to it? (2) Why does he want a black friend? Why should race matter in who he makes friends with? We'll take the question of colorblindness first.

The idea of a "colorblind" society is often credited to Dr. Martin Luther King Jr., who in his famous "I Have A Dream" speech of 1963 said, "I have a dream that my four little children will one day live in a nation where they will not be judged by the color of their skin but by the content of their character." In this most minimal formulation, to be racially colorblind means not to consider racial markers like skin color when judging another. For example, when considering a candidate for a job, one should only consider those qualities of the candidate that pertain to that his or her ability to perform the job. A colorblind employer is one who ignores race in making hiring decisions.

Now, most of us are not employers in the strict sense. We don't have employees or make hiring decisions. So in that sense we don't have the opportunity to be "colorblind employers" like a shop owner does. But we do have opportunities to be colorblind in other ways. We can be "colorblind jurors," "colorblind colleagues," "colorblind shoppers," "colorblind sports fans," "colorblind friends," "colorblind lovers," and much more. The colorblind society that King envisioned can be defined, roughly, as a society where everyone performs their societal roles—such as juror, shopper, friend, lover—in a colorblind way.

If the way that a colorblind society is understood today is any indication, however, the basic concept isn't as straightforward as it first appears. Consider that, coming up on half a century after King's call for a colorblind society, proponents on both sides of issues in contemporary American racial politics (such as Affirmative Action) try to claim "true colorblindness." Some supporters of Affirmative Action programs claim that the only way a true colorblind society can be achieved is by first "picking up" the African-American population. In his book *I Am America (And So Can You!)*, Stephen quotes "noted beagle-abuser Lyndon Johnson" who likened the situation to a footrace between two runners, one whose legs have been shackled together before the race starts. If, after the unshackled runner had run fifty yards in the time it took the shackled runner to run ten, we were to try and make the race fair, Johnson asks, "Would it not the better part of justice to allow the previously shackled runner to make up for the forty-yard gap, or to start the race all over again?"[5] According to Johnson, King's colorblind society cannot be achieved until all races are on equal footing. This is true even if in making our way to a colorblind society we have to legally formalize policies which are, we might say, *color-sensitive* (that is, the *opposite* of colorblind).

Another contingent believes that supporters of race-based social equity programs, such as Affirmative Action, are advocating precisely that which King was against: using race to make decisions where race should play no role. Even if it were the case that promoting the interests of African-Americans would benefit society as

---

[5] President Johnson made these remarks in a speech inaugurating Executive Order No. 11246, called "Equal Employment Opportunity," which requires that affirmative action be taken by government contractors in their hiring practices.

a whole, they think that we must not succumb to the tendency to judge based on race lest we fail to be colorblind. Just as two wrongs don't make a right, so failing to be colorblind cannot promote colorblindness in the future. Rather, it can only reinforce precisely that which King was against.

Now where does Dr. Stephen T. Colbert, D.F.A., intellectual giant that he is, come down on the issue of Affirmative Action? He seems to be a critic of Affirmative Action programs, but his reasons are, for lack of a better term, kind of dumb. In the chapter on race in his book, Stephen worries that Affirmative Action encourages reverse discrimination, "so-called because it goes in the opposite way of how we naturally discriminate" (*I Am America*, p. 174). We can't have that, right? But he also tries to reduce Affirmative Action policies to absurdity by drawing them to what he thinks is their logical conclusion. "Should Chinese guys," he asks, "get a shot at my wife just because the conditions on the Transcontinental Railroad weren't *ideal*?" Stephen's point seems to be that social equity programs can easily balloon if we try to reimburse everyone for the wrongs done to their race in the past. It's better to put a stop to the whole idea now lest we find ourselves on a rather slippery slope.

In the end, though, I think Stephen's views on this point are not all that principled. Stephen would most likely either take the party line on this issue or let the free market decide, as he's done with global warming ever since Al Gore won the Nobel Peace Prize in 2007. Either way, I don't think we can expect Stephen to have a very deep opinion on the complexities of the issues raised by Affirmative Action. Race is a complex issue that Stephen's black and white thinking is not well suited to.

In fact, this lack of reflection on Stephen's part of the complexities of being colorblind (in the real world, as it were) might explain why his colorblindness is so absurd. He is *so* out of touch with the meaning of King's words that he takes them to mean that one must be blind to race in some crazy literal sense. Only Stephen could engage in the high level of self-deception that would be required to not know what race one is in our contemporary society. The deeper point, though, is that no matter how absurd his version of colorblindness is, Stephen is colorblind not because he understands the in-and-outs of the issues involved, but because *that's what one should do* in this time of sloganeering and political correctness.

Some of My Best Friends Are Black

Why does Stephen want a black friend? Perhaps we should ask: Why not? As Aristotle said, "The antidote for fifty enemies is one friend." No doubt a guy like Stephen could use all the friends he can get. Perhaps Stephen wants a black friend for the same reason that any of us wants any friend: just because it's nice to have friends.

Well, now I'm just playing coy with you. One thing Stephen is most certainly not is hard to read. (His transparency is part of his charm.) Stephen wants a black friend so that he can say racially insensitive things about African-Americans without getting into trouble. *Hey, it's cool. I've got a black friend!* As if that somehow, for some reason, mattered.

Though of course it does. In some circles, there are very strict rules that determine who can say what and when on the basis of one's friendships. Philosophers sometimes call this phenomenon *linguistic license*. The idea is that we sometimes recognize another has having the right to say certain things because they belong to, or are involved in, a certain group—be it through birth, through marriage, friendships, or whatever. We see this all the time. An African-American can say things about members of his or her community that a white person could never say, at least not without daring to offend. A Jewish person can crack jokes about other Jews. A drama geek can make fun of other drama geeks. In cases such as this, we will say that someone has linguistic license that not everyone has, and that they have it in virtue of group involvement.

I bring up linguistic license because I think it gives us a nice way to explain why Stephen's display of his black friend is supposed to matter. (Never mind for the minute if it actually does.) Whenever Stephen puts up a picture of him with his black friend, he is looking for a little extra license to clear the path for, or defend his right to say, something probably more than a little racially insensitive. And there can be little doubt that Stephen, of all people, needs a little extra license when he talks about race. Stubborn ignorance is a defining feature of his character, after all.

To see what I mean, take what he said about Rosa Parks on his show the night of October 25th, 2005. The WØRD of the night was "Overrated." According to Stephen, Rosa Parks is little more than a criminal. All she did was break the law by sitting at the front of the bus. If she and her friends were so upset about the way they were being treated, why didn't they just start their own bus company and let the free market decide which system is better? The best thing Parks did, Stephen goes on, was enrich our vocabulary "by allowing us to call anyone who is the first to do something the Rosa Parks of whatever it is that person did first." For instance, we can use expressions such "Michelle Wie is the Rosa Parks of adorable teenage Asian pro female golfers."[6] Funny though they may be to the it-getters of the Colbert Nation, these words are potentially offensive at any time. But seeing as how Stephen said them the day after Rosa Parks died, he must have brass balls indeed!

Well, that and he knows about linguistic license. It's of course no coincidence that Stephen followed up his controversial comments about Parks by asking Jimmy to put up his picture of him and Alan, saying:

> I was talking about this to a friend of mine last night, Alan. He's a black guy. I gave Alan my take on Rosa Parks and you should have heard the string of expletives he started yelling. [He's] just as mad about this as I am. (Episode 1006)

From Stephen's perspective at least, it's precisely *because* he has a black friend that he can say what even he recognizes is going to be controversial about the Mother of the Civil Rights Movement.

But note something odd here. As Stephen reported (though seemingly with no awareness of the implications) Alan wasn't quite convinced by Stephen's opinions on Rosa Parks. As usual, Stephen has taken what most of us would read as an obvious sign of anger and misinterpreted it as a show of support for him. (This happens a lot during interviews, for example, when the audience applauds something the interviewee says but that Stephen doesn't agree with.) Presumably the string of expletives that came out of Alan's mouth upon hearing Stephen's opinions on Rosa Parks wasn't due to his outrage over how "overrated" she is. Alan couldn't believe what he was hearing!

It's quite an ingenious twist of comedy writing, in fact. Stephen is so oblivious to Alan's feelings—so out of touch with what matters to the African-American community as symbolized by Alan— that he completely misinterprets Alan's protests as support. What

---

[6] Episode 1006, originally aired October 25th, 2005.

this shows us is that Stephen is no honorary member of the black community. His friendship with Alan is a sham. If Stephen's license to say racially insensitive things is based on his friendship with Alan, he's just shown us that his license is invalid.

Stephen's License to Offend

But perhaps we're being too hasty. Perhaps the relevant issue isn't whether or not Stephen is *really* Alan's friend but the mere fact that Stephen is *trying*—in his own self-absorbed way, to be sure—to be his friend. The trying itself, we might think, gives Stephen the license to offer his skewed view of Rosa Parks as overrated.

Maybe this is right. Maybe not. The question is complicated. Linguistic license is tricky precisely because community involvement is so *squishy* (which is a technical term, by the way!). To see what I mean, consider the uniquely American debate about the use of what has been described as "the most hateful word in the English language," a word that many will never say and refer to as the "N-word." Much of the debate is driven by a clash between the existence of a seeming double standard over the use of the N-word and the popularity of that term among African-American performers, at least since Richard Pryor. After an early career that Jabari Asim describes as an "amicable Cosby-esque performer," Pryor drastically changed his comedy act in the late 1960s with monologues such as "Super Nigger," the first track off of his self-titled debut comedy album. In these and other performances for over a decade, Pryor used the N-word in his act as a way to confront his audience's views about race, until, during a 1979 visit to Kenya, he decided to abandon the word.[7]

Many on the long list of performers influenced by Pryor, however, have not taken his lead. Countless comedians, actors, directors, musicians and others have adopted the confrontational use of the N-word so central to Pryor's comedy from those years: Chris Rock, Samuel L. Jackson, Spike Lee, and Tupac Shakur, just to name a few. Not surprisingly, their fans have adopted their use of

---

[7] In his autobiography, *Pryor Convictions: And Other Life Sentences* (Random House, 1995), Pryor recalls saying to his wife during their trip to Kenya, "Jennifer. You know what? There are no niggers here. . . . The people here, they still have their self-respect, their pride." And it was then that he "vowed never to say it again."

that word as well, sometimes without the self-reflective philosophy that might explain *why* they use the N-word. It's partly because of the proliferation of unreflective users of the N-word that there is debate now over how the N-word should be used, if it should be used at all.

In his book *Nigger: The Strange Career of a Troublesome Word* (Pantheon, 2002), Harvard Law School Professor Randall Kennedy takes up this debate and argues against what he calls the "Regulationists" and the "Eradicationists." As Kennedy lays it out, Regulationists believe that the N-word can only be used by a select group of people (though just who belongs to this select group is matter of some debate). For many who hold to this way of thinking, the N-word should be taken back by the African-American community. Only then will the sting be taken out of it. To Eradicationists, however, the N-word is irredeemable and, as such, should be eradicated from the English language.

But why is it irredeemable? And what should we say about the free use of the N-word made by, for example, black entertainers? Noted cultural critic and scholar Jabari Asim takes up just these questions in what amounts to an extended defense of the Eradicationist position: his 2007 book *The N Word: Who Can Say It, Who Shouldn't, and Why* (Houghton Mifflin, 2007). He makes his case through a detailed history of the use of N-word in the service of white racism. The book is difficult, sometimes painful reading. As Asim shows, the N-word has a long and ugly history. It begins with a quote from Abraham Lincoln saying, "I as much as any other man am in favor of having the superior position assigned to the white race"[8] and traces the origins of the white supremacist image of "the nigger" to Thomas Jefferson's *Notes on the State of Virginia*. Asim's view is that once we fully understand the history of the word and the racist ideologies and practices that are crystallized within it, we will see that to use the word is, as it were, to *call forth* that history, whether we realize it or not.

Yet, as Kennedy notes, the history of a term is not obviously at issue when it comes to the elusive logic of offense. When David Howard, the white director of the Office of the Public Advocate in Washington D.C., used the term "niggardly" in a

---

[8] Lincoln said this in his debate with Stephen A. Douglas in Charleston, Illinois, 1858.

closed-door discussion with three of his staff members in 1999, the fact that the word, which means "miserly," has Scandinavian origins and no racial connotations didn't stop him from eventually being forced to resign his post when word of his "misdeed" became an open secret in Washington D.C. To many, the word "niggardly" evokes disgust just in virtue of *sounding* like the N-word; the fact that it has no historical connection to the N-word is beside the point. This just goes to show that how we hear words (perhaps even their very meaning) isn't logical or rational. We can't just decide that something does not offend the ear. The logic of offense, it seems, is personal *and* political, principled *yet* irrational all at the same time.

The less-extreme Regulationists are in favor of what we might think of as a partial ban on the use of The N-word. In some circumstances, it's perfectly acceptable to use it, and in other circumstances it's not. What determines whether or not any particular use is appropriate is a matter of debate. Perhaps only African-Americans should be allowed to say it, on the assumption that one cannot logically be said to be racist against oneself. This seems to be the way Chris Rock thinks about it. As Randall Kennedy points out, Rock, who is not alone in doing so, holds to a strict double standard when it comes to the use of the N-word:

> even blacks who use *nigger* themselves adamantly insist that it is wrong for whites to do so. On the album containing his "I hate niggers" skit, for example, Chris Rock . . . presents a sketch in which a white man approaches him after a performance and appreciatively repeats some of what Rock has just said onstage. The next sound heard is that of the white man being punched. Rock's message is clear: white people cannot rightly say about blacks some of the things that blacks themselves say about blacks. (*Nigger*, p. 100)

In the skit, Rock "punches" his white fan, much to the delight of his audience, even though the fan is coming to Rock, one assumes, in the highest respect and with the best possible intentions. He's a fan! But that doesn't matter to Rock. No matter what the intentions of the white fan, the use of the N-word is always off-limits to him, presumably because of the color of skin alone.

It's in response to episodes such as these that Kennedy asks the question,

Can a relationship between a black person and a white one be such that the white person should properly feel authorized, at least within the confines of that relationship, to use the N-word? For me the answer is yes. (*Nigger*, p. 42)

According to Kennedy, if the white person has shown himself to not be racist, and perhaps if no other word will communicate the idea that the white person is trying to get across, then, yes, it would be okay for a white person to use the N-word in that situation ("within the confines of that relationship").

Put in the terms of linguistic license, Kennedy is clearly against Eradicationisism which says that no one ever has linguistic license to use the N-word. And he thinks that Regulationism, which issues linguistic license based on skin-color (or other racial markers), is just arbitrary. For him, what matters is the *intention* of the words as spoken in a particular situation. The white person who has cultivated a relationship with a black person and who cannot express himself in any other way than to use the N-word may, since he or she has shown themselves to have good intentions in using it. If this is an accurate characterization of his position, let's call Kennedy an "Intentionalist." An Intentionalist is one for whom the intentions of the speaker (for good or for ill) matter in determining if a particular use of the N-word is appropriate in some situation. If a speaker *intends* to communicate something in a wholly non-racist manner, and if that intention is backed-up by the person's personality, as well as clear to the audience that would normally have right to be offended, then and only then could such uses be permissible. At this point, the simple picture of linguistic license with which we started has become pretty complicated.

All that said, let's get back to Stephen Colbert. Stephen, it seems right to say, wants a black friend to pad his anti-racist credentials, to show that he's part of the community. No one with a black friend could really be racist, right? That's the point of him putting up the picture of him with his black friend.

But then what are we to say about the fact that Stephen no longer has a black friend? (He ended it with Alan, after all.) If his linguistic license to offend were based on that he'd be out of luck. But Stephen is savvy enough to recognize that it isn't really the having of the black friend that matters. It's that he be *seen by others* to have only good intentions in talking about racially sensitive issues. Now, if a white person is truly open to having a black friend but does not have a black friend—perhaps because her circle of acquaintances is limited to an undiversified workplace—this might not even be enough to provide her linguistic license enough to ask for Kennedy's book (*Nigger: The Strange Career of a Troublesome Word*) by name at a Barnes and Noble. She simply wouldn't get a chance to prove her good intentions within the confines of whatever limited relationships she has with the employees and other customers when she went to buy the book. However Stephen's thought seems to be that no one could fault him if were to make it absolutely clear (through the holding of a well-publicized national search, no less!) that he wanted a black friend. For all his ignorance and insensitivity in other areas, Stephen knows that good intentions matter when it comes to race relations in America today.

Claiming Rights, Shirking Responsibilities

Now that we've tried to say in more detail why Stephen would want to both be colorblind (in his own impossible manner) and yet actively search for a black friend, let's get back to the question of what this tension means.

As I see it, Stephen is trying to game the system by claiming rights of linguistic license while at the same time shirking the responsibilities that come with such rights. Stephen takes himself to have the right to say potentially offensive things on the basis of a linguistic license he earns by actively seeking a black friend. But he dodges all calls to act responsibly when it comes to issues of race to the extent that he claims to be colorblind. Let me explain.

What do we mean when we talk about rights and responsibilities in the context of race relations in America? We've already talked about rights in the context of linguistic license, so that should be easy to state. The rights in question here concern the ability to tackle racially charged issues and risk saying racially insensitive things in the process. As we saw, such rights are sometimes conferred on one's community memberships. To someone like Chris Rock, only another African-American can utter the N-word, no matter how many black friends he or she has. A more liberal position has it that community involvement through one's friendships is enough to license certain kinds of talk. If Stephen in fact does have linguistic license to risk saying racially insensitive things, it doesn't seem that his right to do so is based on either of these things.

Stephen is clearly not African-American (even if he doesn't see race) and he wouldn't be searching for a black friend if he already had one. To Stephen's way of thinking, at least, his linguistic license to tackle racially charged subjects is issued on the basis of his mere *wanting* a black friend. He publicizes his search for a new black friend so that he can advertise his desire to have a black friend, not because, like Aristotle thought, he thinks having friends is in itself valuable.

But here's the problem with the rights that Stephen's license confers. Not only does Stephen again and again display that he's insensitive to the issues that matter to African-Americans (as he proved in his discussion with Alan over Rosa Parks being over-rated), it seems that he claims to be colorblind precisely so that he doesn't have to pay any attention to such issues!

Think of this way. As Spider-Man's Uncle Ben once said, "With great power comes great responsibility."[9] Having linguistic license to say racially charged things is a great power. What great responsibilities come with that power? This is a difficult and complex question. But I would suggest that a necessary element of such responsibilities must be a deep and abiding interest in the issues that matter to the potentially offended group. Though it would take an argument to show that these attitudes are *required* for, for instance, the issuing of a linguistic license to a white person to use the N-word, at least one writer (Randall Kennedy) seems to be of the same opinion. (Indeed, it's quite possible that *all* currently held Intentionalist views come down to this.) Either way, I think that these are the attitudes that being colorblind in Colbert's impossible sense rules out. By treating Alan as he did, Stephen proved that he is out of touch with African-Americans. But if one were to suggest that Stephen needs to change his ways, he would just turn it around on them. He would simply claim that he is "so not a racist" that he can't even fathom what the problem is.

This was essentially Stephen's response to Hurricane Katrina. Consider the conversation that Stephen had with noted African-

---

[9] From *Spider-Man* (2002). Peter Parker's Uncle Ben says these somewhat prophetic words to him early in the picture. But they've taken on a much deeper meaning by the end when Spider-Man decides that he must leave Mary Jane Watson and become a vigilante.

[10] Episode 2022, originally aired February 22nd, 2006.

America scholar and social critic Michael Eric Dyson.[10] Dyson, who was on the show promoting his book *Come Hell or High Water: Hurricane Katrina and the Color of Disaster* (Basic Civitas Books, 2006), was arguing that Hurricane Katrina was, in a sense, an "unnatural disaster" in that African-Americans bore a disproportionate burden of the pain and destruction of the otherwise natural disaster. But Stephen couldn't make sense of this idea. His response was to ask how New Orleans is doing, and in particular if Bourbon Street is "still there." When Dyson says that it is, Stephen replies, "So what's the problem?" Stephen's colorblindness causes him to overlook the racial element of Hurricane Katrina, something Dyson would not have been surprised by. In a later interview with Stephen, Dyson has this to say about colorblindness: "I don't want to be colorblind. . . . I don't want race to be something that I overlook."[11]

If this is what being colorblind really amounts to (at least as practiced by Stephen and others like him), then it seems fair to say that Stephen wants to have his cake and to eat it too. With the power to say racially charged things comes the responsibility to be sensitive to the complexities of racial identity. But it's this complexity that Stephen, hiding behind his colorblindness, refuses to understand.

Now, let me make perfectly clear what I hope is already obvious. I am not saying that Colbert the comedian is insensitive to racial issues. Fans of his show (along with all the other work he's done) know that Colbert displays a great deal of sensitivity to issues of race. Colbert regularly treats racial issues with the complexity that they deserve. What's so impressive is that he successfully treats these complex issues by way of a character (Stephen) who himself treats them as simple. It's in showing us how poorly the complexities of race can be grasped that Colbert displays how complex they really are.

Truthiness and the Denial of Responsibility

To wrap things up, let me make one general observation about how Colbert's treatment of race in America relates to his most characteristic idea: truthiness.

---

[11] Episode 3034, originally aired March 13th, 2007.

We shouldn't see Colbert's character Stephen as claiming rights and shirking responsibilities, when it comes to race relations, by accident. This general pattern runs through much of Colbert's comedy in the form of Stephen's commitment to truthiness. Asserting that there is no truth beyond truthiness, no matter of fact beyond what *feels* like fact, is the ultimate expression of claiming rights while shirking responsibilities. Why? Because truthiness justifies running roughshod over the complexities of the real world. (Go ahead and ignore that which doesn't agree with you. It's all just truthiness anyway!) Yet at the same time, it muddies our understanding of rights. It seems arbitrary that we should confer rights on those that take the time to try and understand complex situations like when and why someone else is liable to be offended by something that we say. (Again: it's all just truthiness anyway.)

In the closing pages of his book, Randall Kennedy says that though racial relations are complex, we should not allow individuals to use the "rhetoric of complexity" to cover the misconduct of racists (*Nigger*, p. 138). Just because it's not clear whether or not David Howard's use of the term "niggardly" is *really racist* does not mean there aren't other uses that clearly are. If the way I've characterized truthiness in the last paragraph is correct, truthiness is a *crystallization* of the rhetoric of complexity.

So here's the lesson. Politicians, pundits, and powerbrokers don't go around talking about truthiness. They don't go around referring to their guts. But they're well-versed in the rhetoric of complexity and in how to use it to deny responsibility. "Global climate change, affordable health care, social justice for all peoples, these are important issues," they'll say. "But they are complex. *That's* why we see so little progress being made on them!" And yet, somehow, the status quo on these issues always seems to favor the rich and powerful. Those who have figured out how to game the system are always telling the rest of us how complicated and ungameable the system is.

But as I think our discussion of Stephen Colbert's attitudes toward race show, even if the issues are complex—perhaps even irresolvable—certain attitudes and actions are clearly better than others to the extent that they reflect an honest effort to understand the complexities. If truthiness is the grasping at simplicity in the face of complexity, then we should reject it as incompatible with our responsibilities as rational human beings. This is true not only in our public officials but in ourselves as well. Only if we keep our eyes open to the complexity of the issues facing us can we begin to hope to deal with them. Such, anyway, is the philosophy of Stephen Colbert.[12]

---

[12] Many thanks to everyone who read earlier versions of this chapter, including the UC San Diego Undergraduate Philosophy Club, Nina Brewer-Davis, John Jacobson, Larry Schiller, Dan Rosenberg, and Denise Schiller.

15

The Wealth of Colbert Nations

KURT SMITH

Stephen Colbert has become America's favorite right-wing enthusiast and egomaniacal talk-show host. Fanatical follower of the capitalist prophet Milton Freidman, Stephen holds the free market to be sacrosanct. "The market is a dangerous and destructive God," he says.

On a slightly different rendering, Stephen conceives participation in the free market as being akin to something like a soul's participation in the Beatific Vision, depicted by Dante in his *Paradisio*. Looked at this way, since privatization is what makes one a participant in the holy marketplace, those who do not participate in the "private sector" are not in communion with the one true God. The aim of the free market zealot, then, is to convert all comers by fire if need be, and to transform them into participants of the sacred private sector.

Healthcare was the zealot's most recent convert, almost burned beyond recognition by the priests of the free market who before setting it aflame accused it of being an instrument of socialism. Education has more than once been scrutinized by the inquisition of the far right and now finds itself tied to the stake. In what follows, I want to challenge the view that tells us that not only must higher education answer to the priests of the free market, but must be converted (privatized) in order to be a participant among the holy elect.

Are Stephen and his fellow worshippers of the free-market right? Should colleges and universities be geared as businesses, their ultimate or primary aim being neither to teach the next generation nor to produce new knowledge, but to generate profits for shareholders? Borrowing from a certain analysis offered by Socrates, I argue that privatizing colleges and universities, throwing them into the arena of free-market capitalism, and thus turning them into for-profit corporations, dramatically alters their primary aim. This in turn alters their very nature.

As Socrates, Plato, Aristotle, and other ancient Greek philosophers would tell you, altering the nature of a thing is as good as destroying it. So, by altering the natures of our colleges and universities we destroy them. This will be my main argument against Stephen (and the far-right). Along the way, I critically poke here and there at Stephen's view of the free market, showing how it not only looks to be internally inconsistent in places, but is the source of his (mis)understanding of the nature of knowledge and, more importantly, the nature of higher education

There are two Stephen Colberts. First is the real guy: Mr. Colbert the entertainer—the guy who went to college, who is married, who pays taxes, and so on. Second is the *persona* we see nightly on *The Colbert Report*—the egomaniacal talk show host I refer to in the previous paragraph. Mr. Colbert satirizes the political right, which I think is his critique of the right; Stephen, as I shall refer to him, the second Colbert, *embodies* the political right. He is the satirical vehicle through which Mr. Colbert brings his audience to see the extremism of the political right. What follows focuses on Stephen—the Stephen that embodies the right.

The Marketplace: Free or Freest?

It's inevitable that at some point in a heated conversation with Stephen, he will invoke the free market. Since his view of the free market is central to his worldview, it will be helpful in getting some sense of it before dealing with his view on higher education. "The free market," Stephen says, "is not just some economic theory we can abandon when things get rough—it requires *faith*." The connection to the religious concept of faith is not an accident. In a segment called "The WØRD," Stephen tells us that "The market is all around us . . . the market guides us with an invisible hand . . . [and] if we have faith in it, the free market is the answer to all our problems, but if we doubt it, it will withhold its precious gifts." In a debate with himself (in a segment called "Formidable Opponent"), he tells himself that "The free market can do anything—it can self regulate; it can self correct; it tiptoes into nurseries at night and puts dreams into the minds of sleeping children." The recent Wall Street bailout is urgently needed, he says. Why? As he matter-of-factly puts it, if we don't act, "God will die."

A quick example of the central role that the market plays for Stephen comes to light in his talking about global warming during season two of *The Colbert Report*. Stephen admits, "I'm no fan of science," adding, "gravity . . . *just* a theory." In the exchange with his guest, Stephen was quick to note, "President Bush refuses to say whether global warming exists until all the science is in . . . is *all* the science in, Sir?" Yet, by mid-third season, Stephen professes that global warming is real. Why? Because Al Gore's movie, *An Inconvenient Truth*, made some scratch at the box office. As Stephen put it, "The market has spoken." So, science wasn't enough to persuade Stephen of the reality of global warming, but the market was.

In attributing to the free market this kind of power, Stephen is simply expressing the views of certain economists, politicians, entrepreneurs, big business and Wall Street corporate types, and even those who play such on TV (like "the Donald"), who have from time immemorial appealed to the free market as a cure to all that ails the Western world. Well, not from time immemorial, but certainly since the eighteenth century, following in the wake of one Adam Smith (no relation, I think). Smith wrote the famous *The Wealth of Nations*[1] (published in 1776), which was a reaction to mercantilism, a set of policies enforced by the British government that advocated the hoarding of gold bullion. Mercantilism held that the hoarding was necessary to do business. Hoarding (or keeping the wealth in England) was guaranteed in part by attaching high tariffs and taxes to foreign products. This made it costly for the British consumer to purchase them, and at the same time not so costly to purchase British-made products, thus keeping the gold *in* the country.

Smith argued that one simply didn't need all that bullion clogging up the system just to do business (there's a constipation joke in here somewhere, but I'll ignore the temptation to find it). If the British government along with all those others that subscribed to such policies would do away with tariffs and taxes, and would establish a level playing field for competition, things would be

---

[1] Adam Smith, *The Wealth of Nations* (Prometheus, 1991).

great. By paying attention to the needs, demands, and wants of consumers, suppliers could produce and then provide those products that best fulfilled those needs, demands, and wants. Simple. Now with a variety of products available, consumers would choose among them—the ones best fulfilling their needs, demands, and wants rising to the top. Charge too much for those products, and consumers will buy their less expensive alternatives. So, seller (supplier) and consumer (demander) play equally important roles in the "Supply and Demand" equation.

Focusing on the exchanges between suppliers and demanders, one definition of the "free market" arises:

> *The market in which anyone is allowed to participate, both with respect to selling and to buying, is a free market.*

If all comers are welcome (whether buyer or seller), and none are excluded, then the market is free. Allowing all comers, it is believed, promotes an essential element of the free market, namely, competition. Consumers serve as ultimate arbiters of success, choosing to buy from those suppliers who supply what consumers need, demand, or want. Simple.

Milton Friedman roots his economic theory—a theory that would have a great impact on Ronald Reagan—in *The Wealth of Nations*. Friedman's theory emphasizes Smith's metaphor of the invisible hand.[2] According to this conception, the market if left to its own devices would be self-regulating and self-correcting. This, as we have seen, is exactly what Stephen thinks. In Book IV, Chapter 2, of *Wealth of Nations*, Smith sets up his hypothetical marketplace by postulating actors who act with the aim of benefiting themselves. So, in Smith's ideal market, folks will act out of self-interest. Now, it is frequently the case, he says, that even though an individual acts out of self-interest, his or her actions will result in benefiting society. Why does Smith worry about such a thing? One answer, I think, is that he was aware of Thomas Hobbes's *Leviathan*, a work that showed how a society or collective might be built out of individuals—atomic elements, so to speak, that act out of self-interest.

Smith argues that in order to build a collective (or, better put, a unified whole) out of such individual elements, he must explain

---

[2] Milton Friedman, *Capitalism and Freedom* (Chicago University Press, 1982).

how the "acting out of self-interest" thing will nevertheless lead to benefiting the collective. This is tricky. As is now well known, a rather difficult paradox arises. The paradox, as Hobbes raises it, tells us that if folks within the context of a collective act in their self-interest, not only would they not bring about what is good for the collective, but each would not bring about what is good for him or herself. Simply put: in acting in their self-interest they would not be acting in their self-interest. Scholars have come to call this paradox "the prisoner's dilemma."

Brian Skyrms, in his *Evolution of the Social Contract*, notes that around the time of Smith certain physicians and natural philosophers were aware of a very strange fact.[3] Records kept by royal armies showed that when men, for example, were killed in large numbers—say, during wartime—the subsequent ratio of male to female babies born would strangely alter. In such cases, the number of male babies would increase, and would remain increased until it looked like the number born would replace the number of males killed during wartime. The phenomenon occurs in non-human animal populations, too.

Weird, right? What I'm thinking is that in addition to a worry over Hobbes's paradox, Smith was aware of this strange biological phenomenon, where the only explanation he could muster at the time of writing *The Wealth Of Nations* was that invisible hand. Though individuals boinked out of self-interest (it's just plain fun), the invisible hand was responsible for transforming the boinking into a good for the collective: the number of males lost in war were replaced by the increase in male babies born. The invisible hand works in translating those "exchanges" between individuals made out of self-interest and those exchanges somehow working to benefit the collective. One thing is clear: we should tell those doing the exchanging to get a room—all this exchanging in the marketplace cannot be good for the kids.

For Smith, the good of the collective is understood in terms of economics—the *wealth* of a nation is its good. The trouble with Smith's solution to Hobbes's puzzle (or even that puzzle about an increase in male babies), of course, is that it is not really a solution at all, but is a proxy for one. Nothing is explained by introducing

---

[3] Brian Skyrms, *Evolution of the Social Contract* (Cambridge University Press, 1996).

the invisible hand. In fact, it reminds me of an episode of *South Park* in which gnomes are stealing the underwear of the boys. The boys follow the gnomes to an enchanted gnome city (somewhere in the woods) and ask a gnome why they are stealing their underwear. The gnome is a businessman, and presents the gnome-business plan: Step One: get underwear, Step Three: make profit. The boys ask for Step Two. The gnome draws a blank and asks the Milton Friedman of the bunch. Milty the gnome also draws a blank. There simply is no Step Two, and so *how* they are to get from collecting underwear to making profit is a mystery. Smith's invisible hand is like the gnomes's mysterious Step Two.

The absence of regulation is what Friedman emphasizes when telling Smith's story. You simply do not need governmental regulation when you've got that invisible hand doing all the work. Here is where another (slightly different) definition of the "free market" arises:

> *The market in which a participant is not bound by regulation is a free market.*

This is different from the first definition insofar as it does not have anything to say about who gets to participate in the marketplace. According to this second definition, the market is free in the sense that trade between participants (assuming we have already settled *who* gets to participate) is not limited by any restrictive laws. Even so, economists look at the *completely* unregulated market as only an ideal, and recognize that a market can be said to be "free" even if some regulation limits it. The fewer the regulations, they say, the freer the market. Competition is fostered in a market that is limited by as few regulations as possible. Increase regulation, and suppress competition. Regulation, say these free market worshippers, keeps sellers from taking risks—it keeps them from being "innovative." How so? It imposes punitive consequences that companies understandably would rather avoid (like having to pay steep fines). So, keep regulation down (or, ideally, completely deregulate) and foster innovative competition.

Using Stephen's way of measuring the success of President Bush's administration ("great or greatest"), we can say of the market that it is free or freest, where "free" denotes a market with some degree of regulation. Consequently, some instances of the market will be "freer" than others. As I said, the freest (or most free) market is ideal, with no regulations. It is the Platonic form of the marketplace, if you will. So, putting this now in philosophical rigor, where the freest market is M_0, market M_1 is freer than market M_2 just in case M_1 is closer to M_0 than is M_2. In other words, M_1 is freer than M_2 just in case M_1 sports fewer restrictive regulations than M_2. I'll try to keep from putting things this way from here on out, but some rigor is necessary in making all this as clear as possible.

In adopting Friedman's view of the free market, Reagan nevertheless imposed some of the most restrictive taxes and tariffs on non-U.S. companies. In fact, according to Noam Chomsky, Reagan imposed more restrictions on foreign competition than all administrations before him combined. This was not only a return to a form of mercantilism, which Smith's theory argued *against*, but as Chomsky rightly points out, Reagan's economic policy was an all out assault on the free-trade principle.[4]

Reagan also adopted the view that suppliers were more important in the "Supply and Demand" equation than consumers (who constitute the demand side). His reasoning, it seems, is connected to the assumption that there would be no consumers if there were no suppliers, in the sense that if not for the supplier the consumer (an employee of the supplier) would not have any money to buy things. In other words, the supplier is seen as the one who gives to the employee the very money that the employee (when acting as consumer) will return to the supplier once the product being sold is bought (a product which the consumer in fact made when acting as employee). Valuing the supplier over the consumer (demander) in this way gave rise to an economic model known as *supply-side economics*. According to this model, since suppliers play the most important role in the economy, the government must do everything within its power to foster and to protect them—especially from those pesky consumers. The idea is not only to provide substantial tax relief to suppliers (corporations), but to provide subsidies that assist them in generating capital, and to secure legislation that restricts consumers from suing suppliers.

As we all know, this form of "capitalism" sports another name, "trickle-down economics," which holds that as suppliers accumulate more wealth (in part because the system gives advantages to

---

[4] Noam Chomsky, *Profit Over People* (Seven Stories, 1999), p. 69.

them) that wealth will trickle down to consumers, who occupy the lowest rung of the economic ladder. This is brought about, in part, by way of those suppliers in their providing more jobs (and presumably higher wages), but also by way of suppliers in their offering products at the lowest possible prices (and so, presumably, this allows the consumer more purchasing power).

The reader may suspect that if the above is Stephen's view, which values suppliers over demanders, the view looks to stray from the free market as defined above (or, certainly from the way in which Smith envisioned it). Another potential problem arises, I think, in Stephen's not only giving preference to suppliers over demanders, but in giving them preference over the free market itself. To Maria Bartiromo, for example, he says, "I believe in the free market except when it might hurt a corporation." Given his identification of the free market to God Almighty, valuing suppliers over the market is like valuing those souls constituting the hierarchy of the Beatific Vision over that at which they are directed (God). So, Stephen's view is really a religion that worships corporations, not the free market *per se*. If Stephen's view is representative of that held by the Bush administration, this would explain, I think, the strategy of Treasury Secretary Hank Paulson to save certain corporations from the destructive forces of the market—to save them from capitalism—that have given birth to the current financial crisis.

Okay, so this is the nutshell version of Stephen's view of free-market capitalism. I now turn to taking a quick look at how it has (mis)informed his view of the nature of knowledge, and more importantly, the nature of higher education.

The Academy: Left or Leftest?

"You can't put a price on knowledge," Stephen says, "but the *market* can!" Borrowing from John Milton, Stephen and the far-right declare that college and university classrooms should be "marketplaces of ideas." Here, "ideas" are analogues to "products," and those selling the ideas are analogues to producers (or suppliers). Students—those buying the ideas—are the consumers. The view is that a free market of ideas is one in which ideas are offered to students, who are then encouraged to purchase those that best suit them. Regulation either keeps certain ideas out, or hinders competition among those who act as suppliers.

Since NO ideas should be kept out of our marketplace, professors must offer to students whatever is available. So, the idea of creationism, for example, should be offered alongside the idea of evolution. If the idea that the holocaust never happened best suits students, it should be offered and they should be encouraged to buy it. According to scholars such as Stanley Fish, to advocate for one idea over another is to indoctrinate. So, when professors teach that the holocaust did happen, and refuse to entertain the viewpoint that it didn't, they are indoctrinating students. Not only must they teach both sides, but according to Fish, they must remain neutral—professors cannot advocate for one view over another. Of course, if Fish advocates in his classroom for his view of neutrality, which I'm sure he does, I wonder whether he considers himself an indoctrinator? But, I digress. Let's get back to Stephen.

Those of you who watch carefully will notice that Stephen has been slowly introducing the idea of making reality from what can only be called "believing in large numbers by brute force." We just *will* or *believe* reality into existence, or something to that effect. What's real is what we say is real. What's true is what we say is true. This is supply-side ontology and supply-side epistemology. "I'm no fan of reality," Stephen tells us, "it has a liberal bias." And, he is also no fan of encyclopedias. "Who is *Britannica* to tell me that George Washington had slaves?" he asks. "If I want to say he didn't, that's my right! And thanks to Wikipedia (now violently typing on his laptop), it's also a fact."

Supply the facts that you want to be facts, and thems is the facts! Consumers of facts, then, are irrelevant, and one needn't care about them (consumers, I mean). They simply will buy what's made available by those in a position to supply the facts. This, I think, mimics the irrelevance associated with consumers in the free market model laid out a bit earlier. What licenses someone to do business in Wikiality, as Stephen calls it, is their having access to a computer and a connection to the internet (there is a Ted Stevens or John McCain joke in here somewhere, but I'll let it go).

Stephen, in the typical far-right attempt at making all things far-right appear patriotic or pro-American, casts the construction of Wikiality as a democratic process. The facts that win out are those that the majority of suppliers supply. If the majority of people say that the holocaust never happened, then that is the case. To not accept this fact would be to *hate* democracy, he says. Stephen argues:

We should apply these principles to all information. All we have to do is convince the majority of people that some factoid is true. . . . What we're doing [he includes the Bush administration and the Wikipedia community of users here] is bringing democracy to knowledge. Now, the "blame ignorance first crowd" is going to say that something is either true or it isn't, and it doesn't matter how many people agree. . . . See, if you go against what the majority of people perceive to be reality, *you're* the one who's crazy. Nation, it's time we used the power of our numbers for a real internet revolution. We're going to stampede across the web like that giant horde of elephants in Africa. In fact, that's where we can start. Find the page on elephants on Wikipedia and create an entry that says the number of elephants has tripled in the last six months. . . . Together we can create a reality that we can all agree on—[namely] the reality we just agreed on.

Even so, Wikiality is not really democratic. It, like I say above, is actually an exchange of factoids resembling supply-side economics. The facts are determined by the *suppliers* of fact, where the notion of an expert is repugnant—Why? Because recognition of expertise, criteria for truth, standards for determining when one speaks falsely, and so on, would all require regulations! And, our free-market will have none of that (or, at any rate, we will want as few restrictions as possible). Ideally, "any user can change any entry [on a Wikipedia site]," he says, "and if enough other users agree with them, it becomes true!" Just think, he ponders, "If only the entire body of human knowledge worked this way." It is a deregulated free market of ideas.

What's more, it seems pretty clear that Stephen, in casting knowledge (sold piecemeal in the form of ideas) as a commodity, ultimately sees those supplying it as being bound to whatever restrictions (as few as those may be) found in the marketplace. Whatever the suppliers in the marketplace think is valuable is valuable. Consumers of ideas are simply asked to buy whatever ideas best suit them. The trouble, as Stephen sees it, is that currently the suppliers of ideas, those pesky professors, are biased—they are "liberals" and "socialists," both being downright un-American. They only offer ideas of the left (this is akin to the sort of thing claimed by David Horowitz, Anne Neal, and others of the far-right, in their campaign to legislate an *Academic Bill of Rights*). As Stephen says at the opening of his chapter on higher education in *I Am America (And So Can You!)*:

> If there's a bigger contributor to left-wing elitist brainwashing than colleges and universities, I'd like to see it. There's an old saying, "A little knowledge is a dangerous thing." Which means a *lot* of knowledge must be a *really* dangerous thing. (p. 119)

Every idea should be offered in our marketplace, he says. And, this is not happening with those lefties controlling which ideas are made available. No doubt, if a physicist could pull it off, they would tell unsuspecting students that electrons spin only one-half to the left—bastard socialists! To fix this, Stephen says, we need to convert higher education and its institutions that trade in ideas to the private sector, to the holy of holies. Let the same people who control the marketplace (the suppliers) control education—after all, the sole reason for higher education, Stephen thinks, is to train people for jobs. Education must serve the needs of corporations.

Stephen reported on an article in the *New York Times*, an article revealing that the State University of New York was batting around the idea of charging tuition based upon a student's declared major. The higher the cost of administering a program, the higher the student's tuition. According to the article, one reason that business programs, engineering programs, and so on, cost more is because of the high salaries associated with faculty teaching in these fields, and the high costs of technology. By contrast, students majoring in philosophy or art history are charged less in the way of tuition, since the cost of running those programs is relatively low. In light of the *real* marketplace, Stephen takes this to clearly show that business, marketing, and chemical engineering, are more *valuable* than philosophy, art history, and poetry.

As it stands, in the hands of those lefties, universities charge the same amount in tuition to both the student of poetry and the student of engineering, who designs weapons that repel poets. Is higher education a hotbed of socialism, or what? Stephen suggests that universities ought to "arrange all fields of knowledge in a three-tiered pricing system: marketable, non-marketable, and can't-you-see-this-is-killing-your-parents?" Let tuition costs be based on this tripartite division of knowledge.

Taking things a bit further, and trying to make the classroom look more like a for-profit business, Stephen argues that higher education should attach prices to individual facts. Desks could be equipped with credit-card-swipers. As a professor provides a fact, students swipe their credit cards. Of course, since there is no expert here, the idea is that anyone could conceivably provide the facts to students. No need to hire fancy Ph.D. types to do such menial work. On this view, knowledge, though cast as a commodity, is nothing more than lists of facts. To capitalize on this product line, Stephen even envisions that facts be assigned different prices: charge one price for showing how to start a dangerous chemical reaction, he says, and charge an even higher price for showing how to end it. Of course, none of this is possible unless we privatize higher education. We simply have to make it conform to the marketplace, and the only way to do that is privatization.

So, how does higher education get privatized? Here's how. In *Universities and Corporate Universities*, Peter Jarvis notes that beginning in the 1980s:

> [The] neoliberal monetarist government [of the U.K., decreased] the funding levels of the universities so that they had to become more competitive. This has resulted in many of the traditional universities [in the U.K.] assuming a more corporate form and functioning more like businesses. (Stylus, 2001, p. 96)

Jarvis cites Aronovitz, who locates the decreased funding of universities in the U.S. at the end of the Cold War, under Reagan, which aligns time-wise with the assault of the U.K. universities, under Thatcher. The idea is to first get the government to reduce funding. Once funding is cut low enough (or it's simply non-existent), privatization is all but official—that's assuming that the institution has survived the transition. It's important to understand that "for public colleges and universities, privatization involves becoming more like for-profit corporations."[5] That is, in not funding public education (which turns out to be the same as privatizing education) corporatization is inevitable. Jarvis goes further to point out that in addition to his and to Aronovitz's assessments of universities becoming more corporate-like, some newer universities in the U.K. have in fact been *founded* by corporations. Huh? You heard me. As Jarvis notes: "The churches and then the states and civic authorities founded the universities, and *now* it is the corporations" (p. vii, my italics), where students are no longer students,

---

[5] Douglas Priest and Edward P. St. John, eds., *Privatization and Public Universities* (Indiana University Press, 2006), p. 2.

but are cast as "consumers," "clientele," or "captive markets." The most famous college accredited university in the U.S. founded by a corporation (McDonalds) thus far is Hamburger U. Top that, England!

U.S. colleges and universities, then, have (starting under the Reagan administration) become increasingly corporate-like. Marketers and advertising executives are hired to establish "brands" to increase marketing success with the aim of reaching more potential consumers—that is, potential students and their families. According to Slaughter and Rhoades, in a recent book titled (of all things), *Academic Capitalism and the New Economy*, "By 1995, university trademarks were generating billions in external revenues." In these authors' view, the university isn't *really* wanting to become privatized, rather it simply wants to *act* like it has been privatized while remaining not-for-profit. Here's how to do it:

> Academic capitalism does not involve "privatization"; rather it entails a redefinition of public space and of appropriating activity in that space. . . . These new configurations and boundaries change our conception of what "public" means. (2004, p. 306)

So, how does one act like one is in the private sector while one is *really* in the public sector? Easy. You redefine what it means to be public. Simply redefine "public" to mean the same as "private" and—*voilà!*

Look at how the corporatizing of colleges and universities is cast by Slaughter and Rhoades:

> The theory of academic capitalism moves beyond thinking of the student as consumer to considering the institution as marketer. . . . Colleges and universities [should] compete vigorously to market their institutions to high-ability students able to assume high debt loads. . . . Student consumers choose [colleges and universities, and] choose majors linked to the new economy, such as business, communications, media arts. Once students have enrolled, their status shifts from consumers to captive markets, and colleges and universities offer them goods bearing the institutions' trademarked symbols, images, and names at university profit centers . . . [What's more] colleges and universities also regard their student bodies as negotiable, to be traded with corporations for external resources through all-sports contracts, test bed contracts, single product contracts, and direct marketing contracts. (pp. 1–2)

Luring consumers able to "assume high debt loads" means that they are luring folks willing to go into serious long-term debt by taking out some major-league loans. Education, then, becomes an avenue by way of which consumers become indebted to corporate lenders. You see, according to the authors of the above business-speak, the corporate environment takes the *aim* of higher education to be that of making money. One way to do that is to get people to take out loans. But don't these loans usually sport pretty low interest rates? Such loans wouldn't be very *profitable* to service. So, in addition to instituting those profit centers, and to trading students (like so much cattle) for corporate contracts, the capitalist advises that we stop lending money to people for little or no profit.

As an example of how higher education looks when mimicking big business, take a look at PHEAA (Pennsylvania Higher Education Assistance Agency).[6] PHEAA is a state agency responsible for providing and servicing loans to Pennsylvania residents headed for college. PHEAA just pulled from its shelves the providing and servicing of federal student loans. Why? According to James Preston, acting president of PHEAA, "Right now, it's not at all profitable to finance" federal loan students. PHEAA acts as though it is a privatized provider and servicer of student loans. It doesn't take its primary aim to be that of helping students afford college, but rather of making a profit off of students, to maximize profits for its shareholders (even though in being a public agency there are none!). His predecessor, Dick Willey (I'm not kidding), received over $400,000 in 2007, which included a bonus of over $180,000 that he gave to himself just before retiring. He also handed out over seven million dollars in bonuses to top PHEAA executives. Willey retired in August, and a month later Preston told Pennsylvania students that PHEAA was simply too strapped to provide federal loans to them. The bonuses given to executives would have put over 1,700 students through college. Here's just one more invisible hand job that doesn't have a happy ending.

The corporate model has turned university presidents into corporate CEOs. They're paid the highest salaries, just like in corporations. Why? Well, I'm not sure, but it has something to do with how salaries are structured in the "real world." Presidents and CEOs *have*

---

[6] See "PHEAA Temporarily Suspends Federal Student Loans," *Chronicle of Higher Education* (February 26th, 2008), http://chronicle.com/news/article/4040/pheaa-temporarily-suspends-federal-student-loans

to make more money than those they manage. It's just a matter of logic they will tell you. Here's how Dominic Basulto explains it:

> [T]here's strong evidence that, far from being paid too much, many CEOs are paid too little. Not only do the top managers of multibillion-dollar corporations earn less than basketball players (LeBron James of the Cleveland Cavaliers makes $26 million), they are also outpaced in compensation by financial impresarios at hedge funds, private equity firms, and investment banks. Should we care? Yes. If other positions pay far more, then the best and the brightest minds will be drawn away from running major businesses to pursuits that may not be as socially useful—if not to the basketball court, then to money management.[7]

Basulto schools us on how "real world" business works. According to him, had Yahoo refused to pay Terry Semel $230.6 million, or had AIC/Inter-ActiveCorp refused to pay Barry Diller $156.2 million, both would have said "Screw CEOing!" and instead would have headed straight to the NBA! LeBron James is lucky that corporations pay CEOs what they do, for had they not, the Cavaliers small forward position would no doubt be occupied by the likes of Semel, Diller, or even Sumner Redstone, Stephen's old boss. (I was going to include Enron CEO Kenneth Lay, but he's dead, and probably playing for Hell's Basketball Association, the HBA.)

Okay, we now see how Stephen thinks of higher education—it should be a supplier of ideas, where ideas are a kind of commodity, and where colleges and universities are structured just like for-profit organizations. This, as we will see, entails that their primary aim will be to generate and to maximize profit. So, what's wrong with this picture? Plenty, if Socrates is right.

Why Socrates Thinks Stephen Is Wrong

In Plato's *Republic*, Socrates argues that an action is made intelligible by way of its aim or end—that is, an action is made intelligible by whatever it aims at bringing about.[8] Socrates reiterates in the *Phaedo* that understanding human action requires understanding

---

[7] Dominic Basulto, "Why Do We Underpay Our Best CEOs?," *The American* (December 5th, 2006), http://www.american.com/archive/2006/december/under-paid-ceos.

[8] Plato, *The Republic* (Hackett, 1992).

the aims or ends of actions.[9] He recalls that as a young man he had
heard that Anaxagoras had developed a novel approach to explaining human action. But, when he read Anaxagoras's book he was
greatly disappointed. Socrates tells us how Anaxagoras would
explain why he [Socrates] sits:

> [I]n trying to give the causes of the particular thing I do, [the sort of
> account that Anaxagoras gives would] say first that I am now sitting here
> because my body is composed of bones and sinews, and the bones are
> hard and have joints which divide them and the sinews can be con-
> tracted and relaxed and, with the flesh and the skin which contains them
> all, are laid about the bones; and so, as the bones are hung loose in their
> ligaments, the sinews, by relaxing and contracting, make me able to
> bend my limbs now, and that is the cause of my sitting here with my
> legs bent . . . [But in explaining my sitting in this way, Anaxagoras fails]
> to mention the real causes, which are, that the Athenians decided that it
> was best to condemn me, and therefore I have decided that it was best
> for me to sit here and that it is right for me to stay and undergo what-
> ever penalty they order. (Plato, *Phaedo*, lines 98c–98e)

The idea, I think, is that an anatomical description, as informative as
it may be, does not make intelligible what Socrates is *doing* (namely,
sitting). Rather, what makes what he is doing intelligible is knowing
that he is tired, for example, or awaiting execution. Knowing *why* he
sits makes what he does intelligible. The aim of his action, then, is
what the action is for; it is that for the sake of which he acts.

Now, let's return to the *Republic*. Here is a good analogy that
will help me make my case down the road. Socrates asks: "Is the
physician, taken in that strict sense of which you are speaking, a
healer of the sick or a maker of money? And remember that I am
now speaking of the *true* physician" (*The Republic*, 341c).
Thrasymachus, his interlocutor, rightly replies that one who *truly*
practices medicine is "a healer of the sick." The idea is that when
a physician is practicing medicine there is something specific that
the physician is trying to bring about. Since the practice of medicine is aimed at bringing about health in the patient, someone
engaged in bringing about anything else would not be practicing
medicine, but would be engaged in doing something else. To be
sure, a physician who aimed at bringing about a good in the

---

[9] Plato. *Phaedo*, Loeb Classical Library (Harvard University Press, 1982), pp.
339–341.

patient, but instead brought about harm, could still be said to be practicing medicine, only badly. But, if he or she were trying to bring about harm in the patient, the physician is not practicing medicine badly, but is doing something else.

Socrates contrasts the practice of medicine in the above passage to the practice of money making. They are NOT the same thing. When the physician is practicing medicine, the aim is to bring about health in the *patient* (this is the good that the physician is aiming at bringing about) whereas when practicing money-making the physician's aim is to bring about an increase in wealth for him or herself. In other words, it is to bring about a good in the *physician*, not in the patient. So, in aiming to bring about a good in him or herself, the physician is not simply practicing medicine badly, but rather is NOT practicing medicine at all. What he or she is doing is making money—which in fact can be done independently of practicing medicine, and shows that the two—practicing medicine and making money—are not the same.

Socrates again emphasizes the difference:

> [N]o physician, in so far as he is a physician, considers his own good in what he prescribes, but the good of his patient; for the true physician is also a ruler having the human body as a subject, and is not a mere money-maker . . . (*Republic*, line 342d)

Here, Socrates again emphasizes that the aim or end of medicine is to bring about a good in the patient (health), whereas the aim or end of money-making would be to bring about a good in the physician (wealth). And, if the physician were aiming at bringing about such a good for him or herself, that is, if he or she were acting so as to make a buck, he or she would not be a *true* physician, as Socrates puts it, (that is, someone actually practicing medicine), but would be a mere money-maker.

As Bill Willers notes:

> The corporate aim is to increase profit, and any competing or interfering value is to be neutralized. As movement up through corporate ranks takes place, individuals with qualms or values that hinder profiteering are selected against.[10]

---

[10] Bill Willers, "Darwin and Friedman in the Corporate World," *Dissident Voice* (July 9th, 2007), http://www.dissidentvoice.org/2007/07/darwin-and-friedman-in-the-corporate-world.

So, any competing value, like performing expensive medical tests or procedures to benefit *patients*, will be "selected against" by higher-ups in the corporation (if these compete with the aim of making profit), and consequently neutralized. Willers continues:

> Profiteering is so established as the primary function of the corporation that the corporate world's foremost sage and theorist, the late free-market economist Milton Friedman, declared that any corporate management failing to function so as to maximize profit should be sued by shareholders.

When the *primary* aim of corporate healthcare, for example, is the making of profit, the aim is to benefit shareholders, not patients. In light of Willers's remarks, Socrates seems able to make the following sort of argument: Corporate healthcare is a practitioner of medicine only if the primary aim of corporate healthcare is to benefit patients. But, the primary aim of corporate healthcare is not to benefit patients (rather, it is to benefit shareholders). Therefore, Corporate healthcare is NOT a practitioner of medicine (rather, it is a practitioner of money-making).

Now, why can't corporate healthcare do both—benefit both patients *and* shareholders? Well, it presumably does. But, if the *primary* aim is what defines an action, and the primary aim of corporate healthcare is to make profit for shareholders, then its activity is NOT to be understood as the practice of medicine, but rather is to be understood as the practice of profiteering. As Willers's analysis suggests, if benefiting patients ever comes into conflict with corporate healthcare's primary aim, then it will "select against" the patient in favor of benefiting the shareholder. The nature or aim of corporate healthcare, then, is not the bringing about of *health* in the patient, but rather is the bringing about of *wealth* in the shareholder. These are two entirely different actions, and one would be deeply confused in thinking that corporate healthcare, understood in terms of its primary aim, is a practitioner of medicine.

In the *Republic*, Socrates argues that both the republic, which is the ideal city-state he is constructing, and the tyrannical state, which is a city-state furthest removed from the republic, nevertheless have the same political structure—Rulers oversee Soldiers, who in turn oversee the Artisans. Four virtues are located with respect to this model. Wisdom is attributed to the Rulers, courage is attributed to the Soldiers, moderation is expressed when the three classes of functionary (Ruler, Soldier, Artisan) agree that this hierarchy of authority is best, and justice is expressed when each class does its work without meddling in the work of the others. So, given that the republic and tyrannical state have identical structures, why are they so different? The answer to this question is important, for it can point the way towards an answer to the question about how practicing medicine and money making are different, even though both appear to be exercised by the same agent at the same time. In other words, the act of practicing medicine seems to be the very same act the physician is engaged in when making money. There appears to be only one act, but two very different takes on what the action may mean.

Socrates's answer seems to be that given the act of ruling is aimed at bringing about a good in those ruled,[11] and the tyrant acts so as to bring about a good in himself (the ruler) and not in those ruled, the tyrant isn't really ruling. Rather, he's doing something else. In fact, he's acting in a way that runs counter to what he takes himself to be after. That is, he takes himself to be establishing a good for himself, but in fact has made it such that "he's full of fear, convulsions, and pains throughout his life" (*The Republic*, 579e), since in being a tyrant he is hated by those over whom he rules and as a consequence his life is always in jeopardy. Presumably the most powerful man, ironically he lives the life of a prisoner (*The Republic*, 579b). Thinking now about the physician, if she practices money-making, she acts so as to bring about a good in herself, not in the patient on whom she practices. This is not practicing medicine badly, but as I said earlier, and in line with what Socrates says about the tyrant who in acting isn't ruling, it isn't practicing medicine at all. Let's apply this now to higher education.

Thinking of the professor along the lines of physician, and the student along the lines of patient, the primary aim of teaching is to bring about some good (knowledge, for example) in the student. In privatizing higher education, which forces colleges and universities to corporatize (they turn into corporations), the primary aim of the institution shifts. As we know, the primary aim of the corporation is to make money for its shareholders. The

---

[11] *The Republic*, Book I, lines 346a–347d.

good of students will be neutralized by higher-ups in the corporation, if that good ever comes into conflict with profiteering. Making a profit will be the ultimate aim. Consequently, if Socrates is right, corporatizing higher education will transform the nature of higher education—the institution will no longer primarily aim at benefiting students, but will primarily aim at benefiting shareholders.

By trying to get colleges and universities to mimic big business, the transformation would destroy higher education understood as an institution whose primary aim is to educate. How so? In aiming to make money, a teacher isn't practicing teaching. And so, if we privatize (and hence corporatize) higher education, higher education as we know it does NOT survive the transformation into the holy marketplace. Stephen's position, recall, thinks that privatizing higher education will simply make it more cost efficient (to taxpayers anyway), bringing with it the benefits of free market competition. But, if my argument is right, there simply is nothing left of higher education (at least nothing that we would identify as such) post-privatization.

I'm Done: But The Editor Expects Some Sort of Fancy Conclusion

Although Stephen the right-wing crazy attended Dartmouth, Mr. Colbert, the Emmy and Peabody Award winning satirist, went to Hampden-Sydney, transferring to Northwestern's School of Communication. I'm not sure whether he graduated before moving on to Chicago's famous Second City comedy troupe, but since then he has been granted an honorary doctorate in fine arts from Knox College in 2006, and was made an honorary member of the class of 2008, Princeton, having delivered their "Class Day" speech. So, whether Stephen or Mr. Colbert, the guy is no stranger to higher education. Taking Stephen's position to its logical end (which is the satire here), Mr. Colbert shows us the bankruptcy of the extreme ideology of the far right, a view that is in fact anti-intellectual and anti-educational (for a quick example of one who represents the view, look at Governor Sarah Palin). Mr. Colbert, in continuing to show the country this ugly side of right-wing political ideology, does a great service for American higher education.

Thanks, Mr. Colbert! As for Stephen's urging of supply-side epistemology, the privatizing of higher education, the making of profit over service to the public good—that is, Stephen's vision of unceasing happy endings of those Reaganite free-market invisible handjobs . . . thanks, but no thanks. But if you must persist, Stephen, might I suggest Senator Larry Craig or former House member Mark Foley. No doubt, they would be in the market for such a promising vision.

16

Freedom Isn't Free, but Freem Is

MICHAEL F. PATTON, JR. and
SAMANTHA WEBB

> It is easy to take liberty for granted, when you have never had it taken from you.
>
> —Dick Cheney

> You have freedom when you're easy in your harness.
>
> —Robert Frost

The Colbert Report's opening sequence of scrolling words intended to define the host's outstanding qualities has been a distinctive feature of the show since it premiered. On January 9th, 2007,[1] the opening sequence flashed a made-up word that subsequently came to define the post-9/11 American moment: freem.

As Colbert reportedly explained it to an audience member, freem means "freedom without the do."[2] What makes this definition so rich is the way it turns on its head the traditional American rhetoric of freedom—that it's something Americans must vigilantly guard, continually fight for and, more recently, actively spread around the world. Accordingly, the logic of freem suggests that no one needs to *do* anything to preserve freedom. It celebrates inactivity, particularly as it defines television viewers who (in the ironic

---

[1] The date is confirmed by *Wikiliaty: The Truthiness Encyclopedia.* http://www.wikiality.com/Freem.

[2] Other definitions abound—*Wikiliaty* lists two others—but the blogosphere seems to settle for that one, as it was relayed by blogger "radvivi," who claims to have been at the taping when Colbert answered a question from the audience about what freem meant.

imaginary of the show) cheered on the Bush Administration as they took the country to war with Afghanistan and Iraq, as they chipped away at civil liberties, and as they eroded U.S. standing in the world.

But there's more to freem than this self-reflexive commentary on armchair generals and pundits, of whom the Colbert Nation is the parodic embodiment. In rejecting *doing* as essential to the preservation of freedom, freem encapsulates President Bush's call to action after 9/11: "go shopping." That call, obviously designed to protect segments of the economy and echoed by other world leaders, reflected a conception of the consumer as patriotic actor. *The Colbert Report*'s freem discloses the near total appropriation of the American rhetoric of freedom by American consumerism, in which consuming everything from goods and services to a television program is identical to acting.

But Colbert goes further than perhaps even George W. Bush would have dared. Although freem didn't debut until 2007, the first episode of *The Colbert Report* laid the groundwork for the word's logic. Colbert dedicated the show to his viewers, "the heroes," clearly invoking all of the post-9/11 resonance of the term. He declared that "the heroes" can make a difference in the world by watching his show. In doing so, Colbert turned that most passive of activities, watching TV, into an act of patriotism akin to the work performed by firefighters, policemen, Ground Zero crews, and U.S. military personnel. And he did so simply by calling it one. Truthiness indeed!

In what follows, we'll unpack the logic of freem in terms of its implications for American consumer practices of all kinds in the post-9/11 cultural moment. We'll also raise questions about whether *The Colbert Report* implicitly offers a sustained critique of the kind of mindless yet rampant consumerism that menaces our planet, or whether, as a television show owned by a giant media conglomerate, it participates in the perpetuation of a freem consuming public, albeit one that plays along with its own freeming.

Consumer actions and protests have been a time-honored tradition since the Boston Tea Party. Patriotic consumption has been a hallmark of the American auto industry ("See the U.S.A. in your Chevrolet"), as well as the union movement ("Look for the union label"). Twentieth-century economics posits consumers as empowered actors whose buying habits have a meaningful and measurable impact on the economy. But being a consumer has also carried connotations of inactivity, parasitism and lack of agency. No less a personage than Adam Smith expressed ambivalence about profuse consumption, and took it as axiomatic that humankind was hardwired for frugality because of the innate desire to "better one's own condition."[3] "Freedom without the do" actually hearkens back to—and even celebrates—these old stigmas about consumer profusion and passivity, particularly associated with the consumption of mass culture like novels and popular entertainment, whose anxiety-provoking properties arguably have been transferred in our time to television shows, video games, iPods and a host of disposable, ephemeral products that constantly need recharging, upgrading or replacing. While patriotic consumption offers the illusion of freedom and agency, freem exposes that illusion for what it is by celebrating consumers who'd rather do nothing and get credit for it. *Doing nothing* for freedom is exactly what we consumers want to do.

Keeping America Freem

Okay, so freedom isn't free but freem is. But how does that square with the universal truth that there's no such thing as a free lunch? Easily, once you realize that the lunch, too, is not free but freem. Here's how it works:

We, as patriotic Americans, have not slowed down our spending one bit. If anything, we are taking our economic stimulus checks and spending them to keep the dreaded recession at bay. The trick is that we don't notice this spending much, because we're all always buying something. The protectors of our freem merely have to direct our spending towards the right ends to keep America freem. How do they do this? By controlling the marketplace.

I know we all get told we live in a free market, but hey, we were told that Saddam had a nuke zeroed in on each our hometowns, too. The market *is* free to the extent that there is no overt control over what gets designed, produced and sold, but the access to the market and to advertising is limited to those capable of meeting the rules set by the media outlets. Advertising plays a tremendous role in shaping our desires which are then responded to by the market. If you don't believe it, just think back to the day not

---

[3] See *The Wealth of Nations: Books 1–3* (Penguin, 2000), pp. 438–442.

too long ago when we neither had nor had to have iPods. But the access to advertising is limited to those capable of meeting the rules set by the media outlets. As we will see, this means only the wealthiest corporations can advertise, and they predictably shape our desires so that we want what they can most profitably produce and sell.

Thanks to the tireless work of the FCC in overturning long-standing protections barring single companies from owning large shares of the media in this country, the major media are currently owned by six companies: Viacom-CBS-MTV, Murdoch-FoxTV-HarperCollins-WeeklyStandard-NewYorkPost-LondonTimes-DirecTV, G.E.-NBC-Universal-Vivendi, Time-Warner-CNN-AOL, Disney-ABC-ESPN, and Comcast. These companies are constantly circling each other and looking for mergers that would be profitable. No less liberal a person than long-time *New York Times* columnist William Safire has predicted that before too long, the number will be at three or possibly two companies in charge of essentially all media in the freem world.

Now it doesn't take a conspiracy theorist to see that these publicly-traded corporations and their owners have an overwhelming interest in seeing the stock market stay healthy and continue to grow. The best way to do this is to stimulate one of two types of economic activity, or both: consumer spending and industrial performance. What single stone could kill both these birds at once? Perhaps the stone of the Iraq war, cast this time from Goliath's sling at tiny David, accompanied by the new message that buying is being patriotic and supportive of our troops. If the war starts to go badly or to sap the public's will, all the freem machine need do is to mobilize the media both to give us more shiny objects to spend our money on and to parade pentagon shills on "news" shows telling us that all is well. If oil prices spike, just flood the airwaves with calls for more drilling inside US borders and ads for hybrid cars, along with "news" reports about the imminent hydrogen car and the like.

Spending still not at a high enough level? Deliver tax cuts and stimulate the housing market by failing to vet applicants for income or assets and by lowering interest rates. Combine this proposed tax break with the drumbeat claim that it is our money and we, not the government, should decide how to spend it, and we have the perfect storm to create freem citizens in a freem America. We end up with frightened citizens desperate to make things better being told

that what they already wanted to do is the most helpful and patriotic course of action. If things still continue to deteriorate, issue the
previously mentioned tax rebate and tell people to go spend it to
shore up the economy on which they all depend. All of this is supposed to keep the Dow up so that the corporations that own the
media, make the goods and fight the wars keep posting record
profits, come what may for the consuming class and their debt
loads.

In this way, the mighty freem cycle is complete; we can make
the world safe for democracy as we let freem ring.

After that admittedly breathless rant, a sort of weak homage to
Dr. Colbert, let's slow down and examine these issues a bit more
carefully.

Find the Cost of Freemdom . . .

As it turns out, freem might have a higher cost to our society than
freedom. From the set decor to the graphics and honoraria for
guests, the Colbert Report cannot be cheap to produce. Even the
extent to which the producers go to get the interviews is impressive and expensive. In one particularly egregious instance, Colbert
interviewed a NASA astronaut aboard the International Space
Station (or ISS) on Thursday, May 8th during which, among other
things, a *Wriststrong* bracelet was sent spinning in the zero-gravity
environment before its wearer promised to flick it towards God
during his next spacewalk.

Now fun is fun, but there were literally billions of tax-payer dollars invested in the space program in general and the ISS in particular. While preaching his doctrine of freem, Colbert is using the
work-products of the very military-industrial complex that is telling
us that freedom *is* free. This is the same bunch that refuses to do
anything to clean up our messes other than cut taxes and push their
plans for discovering new fuel sources and "protecting"[4] our existing ones. Despite the foreground of the ISS and all the tech toys at
NASA, the entire message of the freemers is delivered via infra-

---

[4] We put the word in scare quotes because the Bush administration recently
agreed to supply Saudi Arabia with enriched uranium in return for increased military presence in the country to guard the oil supply and an agreement to step up
oil production. At least the Saudis, unlike Saddam, had nothing to do with 9/11.
Oh, wait . . .

structure that for which taxpayers have footed the bill. The radio, television and satellite infrastructure, not to mention the road-and-bridge traditional infrastructure, didn't just happen—we and previous generations paid for it with our tax dollars. But now that consumer and national debt is reaching the point that people are losing their cars and houses, the Lords of Freem must choose between continuing to use tax dollars for their traditional purpose, the public good (maybe even health care?) and giving them back to the citizens to spend on the gewgaws advertised by the media juggernaut. Guess which one they're choosing so far.

In *The President of Good and Evil*, Peter Singer investigates the constant Republican and Libertarian cry of "It's your money" and comes to the conclusion that the percentage of a person's income that is due to the existence of social capital (such as existing infrastructure and technology) is as high as ninety percent. This means that we could reasonably tax income at a ninety-percent rate if we wanted to give the money back to those who are actually its real owners.[5]

And yet more and more people believe that we should pay virtually no taxes at all. Capital "L" libertarianism, as well as its milder forms, is gaining credibility in the political marketplace because it somehow seems reasonable to people that the government is there only to protect our property from internal and external threats. Certainly ours is one of the first generations that could even countenance such a thought without blushing. During the building of the roads, the air and rail transportation systems, the power grid, the cities and the telecommunications networks it was obvious that government had the crucial role in the projects on which our society as we know it depends. Now that we have the temporary illusion that these projects are completed, it is possible to suggest to a gullible and debt-ridden public that they should keep more of "their" money to spend on themselves (and to keep the economy humming). But this ignores the need for upkeep and expansion, which are becoming especially acute as demand and usage grow. The corporate need for growth, however, needs money in the consumers' hands instead of in the hands of the highway maintenance department, and so the freem clarion call is sounded from every media outlet.

---

[5] Peter Singer, *The President of Good and Evil* (Dutton, 2004), pp. 16–17.

. . . And the Truth Shall Set You Freem?

The freemers in the government sit idly by while the gospel of prosperity they preach leads to skyrocketing oil prices, the sub-prime (and more) mortgage lending crisis and an overall depleted economy, all the while getting amens from their corner in the form of promised technological relief. This promised relief comes not from any lowering of demand for energy from the public—that would put the "do" back into freem—but with illusory clean-coal technology, biofuels and increased investment in nuclear power. Never mind the fact that each of these proposals further concentrates wealth in the hands of the wealthy. Give us tax cuts and we're happy, even while food and gas prices continue to rise, basic governmental services are slashed, and the public infrastructure collapses faster than a Minneapolis interstate bridge.

And this market worship eventually calls its own shots. When Stephen Colbert says "Global warming is real because Al Gore's movie made money—the market has spoken," it is not really a joke. Every large corporation is busy hiring PR firms and executives to shape the green policies that are currently being adopted. So long as there's a market for taking global warming seriously, the corporations will try to appear to do so. The nature of markets abhors a vacuum created by unmet demand and quickly provides product to fill it. At the moment, the demand is met with commercials about the viability of biofuels, the plausibility of the hybrid or hydrogen fuel cell car and the allegation that there is a clean way to burn coal to make electricity. As these claims are more completely put to the test and found wanting, either another shiny object will become the apple of the buying public's eye (maybe a holographic iPod?) or some replacement product bearing the appearance of greenness will be trotted out.

Could demand for real greenness be met, if it were to surface in a sustained way? Not likely. What is needed is a dramatic adjustment of our level of consumption. Peter Singer, in *How Are We to Live?*, points out that consumption is rising at a disastrous and amazing rate:

> The global economy now produces as much in seventeen days as the economy of our grandparents, around the turn of the century, produced in a year. We assume the expansion can go on without limit, but the economy we have built depends on using up our inheritance. Since the middle of the [last] century the world has doubled its per

capita use of energy, steel copper and wood. Consumption of meat has doubled in the same period and car ownership has quadrupled . . . Since 1940, Americans alone have used up as large a share of the earth's mineral resources as did everyone before them put together.[6]

Furthermore, we have made the lifestyle we currently have so appealing to the rest of the world that they want to join us at the feast. The Chinese government hopes to have a car in every family's garage by 2050, and almost all other countries hope to catch up to the US in material standard of living. At least, unlike us, most of them are willing to sign the Kyoto Protocol. That's too close to putting the "do" back into freem. E.O. Wilson has calculated[7] that for all currently living people to have the median US material standard of living, we would have to have four extra Earths' worth of *raw materials*. This says nothing of the energy needed to pull off this feat but, as Wilson realizes, that point is moot. We have to choose between serious, permanent inequality at the level we now find it or else have less material wealth per person in this country (and in other parts of the West). Furthermore, even if we were to freeze world population and material well-being at current levels, we in the West would still run through the remaining raw materials at an unacceptably brisk pace.

Yet buying greener products such as more fuel efficient cars is just another way of having this unsustainable amount of stuff—we are still aiming at the lots-of-material-goods-per-person ideal, and this is not an ideal that can be met globally.

Idealistically, even assuming we could shake off the ideology of freem and consume less, there's just no profit in it for the corporations that feed on freem. You cannot keep the stock market healthy if there's no one buying stuff, and you can't keep the assembly lines staffed and running when people have started to do with less, to recycle and to value things other than the latest toy.

Born Freem?

So how ingrained is freem? Osama bin Laden has often been reported as holding the view that Americans, since Vietnam, lack the stomach for a protracted war with a large body count. This sup-

---

[6] Peter Singer, *How Are We to Live?* (Prometheus, 1995), p. 42.
[7] Edward O. Wilson, *The Future of Life* (Knopf, 2003).

posed squeamishness of the US population is what Republican pundits like O'Reilly accuse the Democrats of courting and exploiting. We're constantly told that we must buck up and not let the terrorists win simply because we refuse to let the body count climb as the calendar pages flip by. It seems to us that, for now, freemdom has become a strand of our national DNA. It is not a long, expensive and casualty-filled war that we can't abide. Rather, we cannot stomach an economy in which we cannot fill up on the latest combo platter at TGI Friday's.

As long as iPods continue to evolve, new cars come with subsidized gas and WalMart supplies us with ten-dollar shirts that we can buy with our cut and rebated taxes, we're good. As long as the news is full of stories about there being no recession, the recovering stock market, the success of the surge and how technology is about to give us a new miracle fuel that will defeat the terrorists and let us get our SUVs back (basically, as long as we can live as we are told we want to live without *doing* anything), we'll put up with anything else—even staying in Iraq for another hundred years. And as long as the stock market stays good, the overlords of freem are as happy as clams at high tide and we seem never to tire of being congratulated for helping in the fight. It seems that as long as the control of media remains in the hands of those who profit from citizens dutifully buying things, we are born into a mind-set of freem from which escape seems unlikely. Try to imagine how long you could go without the internet, television, newspapers, or electricity. Despite the fact that most people in the history of the world have lived and died happily without any of these things, it is a symptom of our immersion in the culture of freem that we can scarcely put ourselves in their shoes even for a short while.

Doing Nothing Is Still Doing Something

Absorbing and parodying these realities, *The Colbert Report* renders the consumer of the show active in his or her passivity. Modern theories of media consumption tends to fall along two broad lines: those who view mass media as a sort of "narcotic" that eliminates agency on the part of viewers, and those who see it as offering opportunities for critique and consequently for resisting the encoded message. It seems clear that *The Colbert Report* blurs these two theoretical lines. On one hand, Colbert plays up his role as a culture warrior-pundit whose every word on any subject is received as gospel; on the other, his viewers actively play the role of passively gobbling down what he's selling. Faux-apologist for narrowly-defined American values that he is, Colbert celebrates that audience torpidity. What's striking—and potentially new—about *The Colbert Report* is that the audience is in on the joke, performing the part of the torpid audience.

As a stance toward viewing audiences, therefore, freem can be thought of as both a revisionist take on early capitalist representations of profuse consumption, and a radical encapsulation of the current phase in the history of American media consumption, wherein our self-conception as consumers has given us the illusion of being free at the very moment when we are most bombarded with consumerist ideologies. Such a state was described by sociologist Jean Baudrillard (1929–2007) in his early work, *The Consumer Society*. In the early 1970s, long before cable and the twenty-four hour news cycle, he observed how mass media's distillation of world events essentially placed those events in the category of consumable goods. Baudrillard writes:

> This careful balance between the discourse of 'news' [*information*] and the discourse of 'consumption,' to the exclusive emotional advantage of the latter, tends to assign advertising a background function, to allot it the role of providing a repetitious, and therefore reassuring, backdrop of signs against which the vicissitudes of the world are registered through an intermediary. Those vicissitudes, neutralized by editing, are then ripe, themselves, for simultaneous consumption.[8]

In this account, mass media offers a picture of world events in bite-sized ("ripe") pieces that the viewer knows will eventually be followed by advertising. Thus, we're called on to consume news in the same way we're called on to consume the breakfast cereal or cars or (increasingly) pharmaceutical drugs whose commercials sponsor the broadcasts.

Baudrillard's reading is uncannily prescient, especially if we consider that, nowadays, the news personality is part of the package we are consuming, from Anderson Cooper and Keith Olbermann to Sean Hannity and Bill O'Reilly. Visit *The O'Reilly Factor*'s webpage, and you will be offered the opportunity to buy t-shirts, fleece and outerware, coffee mugs, or signed copies of

---

[8] *Consumer Society: Myths and Structure* (London: Sage, 1998), pp. 121–22.

O'Reilly's latest book. Not all media websites so blatantly seek to sell specialty products, but they all contain advertising of one sort or another.

The simultaneously empowering and enfeebling logic of freem extends to the ways in which Colbert co-opts the Colbert Nation for meaningless acts of protest and activism. For a brief period, the online, reader-produced encyclopedia *Wikipedia* contained the untrue fact that African elephants were not endangered. Colbert had called on the Colbert Nation to change unpleasant reality by changing the elephant population estimate to take the species off the endangered list. Colbert also had an impact on a Hungarian bridge-naming contest. By urging his fans to vote for him, Colbert actually won the contest, only to find out from the Hungarian ambassador to the U.S, good-naturedly playing along, that the winner of the contest had to be a Hungarian citizen.

When the real Stephen Colbert suffered a broken wrist (he tripped while running around the set during the audience warm-up), the fake Stephen Colbert peddled red plastic *WristStrong* bracelets to raise awareness of "wrist health." Occupying a liminal position between parody of activist awareness campaigns and actual corporate product, the *WristStrong* bracelet simultaneously signified ironic awareness of the vapidity of the issue, and blind acquiescence to corporate manipulation. [9] Colbert raised the kitsch value of the bracelets by solemnly insisting on the importance of wrist health awareness, and the audience gleefully played along. Postings on the Colbert Nation website praised Colbert for his courage in bringing awareness to the "issue":

> I just suffered a recent wrist injury and I couldn't do anything. I was so careless about my wrist I just broke it because I didn't take any precautions. But now, with the wrist strong bracelet (when I get one) I can always remember to keep that wrist strong. And if I forget how to spell wrist, strong, or wriststrong . . . BOOM, it's right there.[10]

In what is perhaps his most redundant gesture, in a December 2007 episode, Colbert gave his audience a present by giving himself a

---

[9] Proceeds from the sale of *WristStrong* bracelets were donated to Veterans' organizations.

[10] Scott Classified, posting on *Colbert Nation*, August 9th, 2007. ColbertNation.com. Accessed May 10th, 2008.

present. In a later episode, he called on The Colbert Nation to sacrifice the concept of sacrifice. The more passively receptive the viewer is to Colbert's message, the more patriotically freem "the heroes" are presumed to be. That supposed receptivity to the *Colbert* message is performed repeatedly when Colbert works up the audience to cheer his most outrageous statements or to boo guests who don't submit to a Colbert "nailing."

Always at the center of his own universe, the persona Colbert absorbs the media discourse of the moment and marshals it for real action on the part of his fans in ways of which other media personalities can only dream. He takes literally the self-important claims of figures like Bill O'Reilly—who actually claimed that his viewers' boycott of France caused palpable damage to that country's economy, and later threatened a boycott of Canada—and calls on his audience to do likewise.

The fact that a Colbert Nation action isn't really important or meaningful or transformative isn't the point. The point is that fans will do anything Colbert tells them to do, often in extremely creative ways, as we've seen in the Green Screen Challenges to stage Stephen fighting with a light saber, or to pose Presidential candidate John McCain in more interesting settings. Freem allows Colbert to do this by blurring the distinction between doing something and doing nothing. In the end, the projected audience of the show— the real people who construct themselves as part of the faux Colbert Nation, the real fake "heroes"—ironically imbibe Colbert's brand of heroicized freem ideology.

Who Watches the Watchers?

One question still remains: when fans of the show post on the Colbert Nation website extolling the importance of the *WristStrong* bracelet, when the studio audience ironically cheers Stephen Colbert's outrageous political positions, when they change *Wikipedia* entries at his behest, are they resisting the narcotic of a freem media or swallowing it wholesale? At what point does the parodic audience of a parodic television show cross the line and become simply another set of consumers of Viacom's "product"? And the line has recently gotten even fuzzier. When Colbert insulted Canton, Georgia, on July 21st, 2008 by referring to it as "that crappy Canton" instead of the good Canton in Ohio, the responses of local officials were covered in the *Atlanta Journal-*

Constitution. When Colbert "apologized" by calling another Canton in Kansas an even worse series of names on July 30th, and in the aftermath of that went after Canton, South Dakota, on August 5th, CNN didn't wait. Before there was any local reaction or media coverage, on August 6th CNN sent a news crew to ask residents for their reaction to a slight they didn't know they'd suffered. When Colbert and his nation end up as news stories for a world-renowned news organization, that's not just a slow news day, that's the emperor's new clothes becoming the latest fashion trend.

Those of us who watch Colbert might well worry that we have fallen for the siren song of freem as well. It's incredibly fun to laugh with and at Colbert's persona and the positions he takes—after all, he's a satirical genius. But there's a sense in which he's turning even angry critics of the current trajectory of the US's internal and international policies into freemdom-lovers. We watch *The Colbert Report* and feel vindicated about our judgment of the clueless guests he nails. We talk with one another about how outrageous it is that Bill O (Papa Bear) can say those things in earnest and be taken seriously.

And most of us do nothing else. We seemingly congratulate ourselves and the other members of the Colbert Nation for being smart enough to "get it" and that's about all. We may buy the occasional book or wear a *WristStrong* bracelet, but we're not leading marches or rallies. Even to the extent that we change our behavior to be greener, for example, we only do it when that consummate mouthpiece of the corporate agenda, the TV, tells us to do so. It's only when the powerful corporations decide that a topic is mainstream enough to be on TV that we hear about it. And that means we hear about these topics only when they've become profitable for the dominant corporations.

But we should always remember that freem is a powerful concept because it's so comfortable and soothing. By its nature it bestows upon those who believe in it a confirmation of the status quo and a huge boost to one's self-confidence. The *Report*'s consistent editorial stance is that things are fine as they stand. At a recent pre-graduation ceremony, Dr. Colbert recently implored the graduates at Princeton not to go out and change the world simply because they had been educated to the point of being able to do so. He urged them to leave it the same as it is, since he and many others like it that way, and he promised that they would grow to like it, too. As long as you're on the side that's winning (even if only by a little and for a short while), freem is more than just a state of mind. It is your whole world. Keep buying those *WristStrong* bracelets and O'Reilly fleeces, keep providing Viacom with a good audience share. Keep doing all of this because, as all freemdom lovers everywhere know, consuming TV programs is the most patriotic act of all.[11]

---

[11] The authors gratefully acknowledge the generous help of Aaron A. Schiller on earlier versions of this paper.

Stephen Is Race-blind (And So Can You!)

JOHN JACOBSON and JEFFREY GAUTHIER

This is a test. Look closely at the following images. Your responses will determine whether you, like Stephen, are truly race-blind.

FIGURE 1: Stimulus A

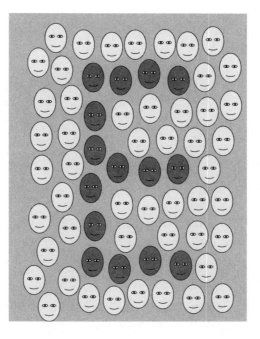

FIGURE 2: How Stephen Sees Stimulus A

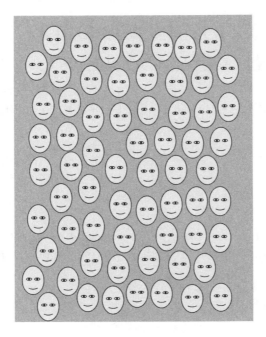

FIGURE 3: Stimulus B

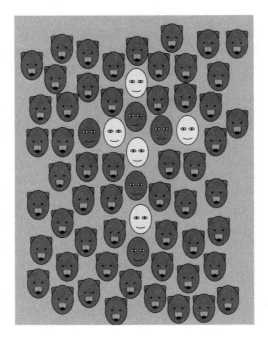

FIGURE 4: How Stephen Sees Stimulus B

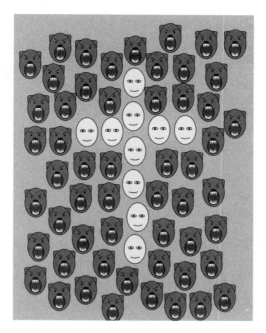

Here's How to Evaluate Your Results

Figure 1. If you're oblivious to the big 'E', you may suffer from Colbertian Race Blindness. For Colbert, blacks and whites look the same. If you see the big 'E', but want to know how the race-blind would see *Figure 1*, then look at *Figure 2*.

Of course Colbert could be faking, just putting us on, and pretending he cannot see the big letter. So, the race-blindness test battery includes stimuli such as *Figure 3* in which normals see just bears and people who are race-blind can see a super-imposed figure; in this instance a lowercase letter 't' (*Figure 4*).

As far as we know, race-blindness only afflicts whites, and is associated with, among other things, the confounding of racial equality with racial indifference, the belief that Chinese and Japanese are the same, and, in the worst cases, schizoid identity disorder (witness Colbert's "People tell me I'm white, and I believe them because police call me 'sir.'"[1]).

---

[1] Episode 3016, originally aired February 1st, 2007.

To truly generate empathy for the race-blind and see the world from their eyes, it's useful to understand their view of the Civil Rights Movement (1954–1968). According to the race-blind, Civil Rights philosophy discovered that whites and blacks are the same, with the same histories, the same developmental environments, and perfectly identical cultures. And when the race-blind imagine Dr. King's vision of a colorblind society, all people are one color: white.[2]

---

[2] Episode 5012, originally aired January 22nd, 2009. "Why not have everybody just be white? And then there's no racism. . . . Why not dream, as I believe Dr. King did, that one day *everyone* would be the same color?"

Citizens of the Colbert Nation

DAVID DETMER is a Professor of Philosophy at Purdue University Calumet. He's the author of three books: *Sartre Explained* (2008), *Challenging Postmodernism: Philosophy and the Politics of Truth* (2003), and *Freedom as a Value* (1988), as well as essays on a wide variety of philosophical topics. In all of his writings he relentlessly attacks those who make grand philosophical claims without backing them up with facts, evidence, and carefully constructed rational arguments. The reason he opposes this practice so strongly is that he just knows, in his gut, that it's wrong.

BRAD FRAZIER is Associate Professor of Philosophy and Religion at Wells College in Aurora, New York. He recently published *Rorty and Kierkegaard on Irony and Moral Commitment: Philosophical and Theological Connections* (2006). He also has published essays in *Philosophy and Social Criticism*, *Journal of Religious Ethics*, *International Philosophical Quarterly*, *History of Philosophy Quarterly*, and *The Daily Show and Philosophy*. He resides in Aurora with his spouse, Dianne, and three children, Timothy, Jonathan, and Anna, where he awaits the second coming of the God-Machine.

JEFFREY GAUTHIER earned a BS from the Midwest's most famed bastion of liberalism, the University of Chicago, and a PhD from the University of California at San Diego's Neurosciences program. He currently suckles on the enormous government teat of biomedical research funds as a Postdoctoral Fellow at the Salk Institute for Biological Studies in La Jolla. He would like to take this opportunity to formally thank President Obama for mentioning "nonbelievers" in his inaugural address, thus bringing us one step closer to the day when America can be truly god-blind.

STEVE GIMBEL is an Associate Professor of Philosophy at Gettysburg College. His research focuses on the history and philosophy of science. Regularly teaching logic at 8:00 A.M., he adores Formidable Opponent because he likes watching someone else talk to himself for a change. He is an amateur stand-up comedian who accepts the advice to keep his day job since being a tenured philosopher sure beats working for a living.

JOHN E. JACOBSON is a PhD Candidate at the University of California, San Diego and a Graduate Student Researcher in the Computational Neurobiology Lab at the Salk Institute for Biological Studies in La Jolla. He's an experimental neurophilosopher, which means that he studies the brain, not the gut—conducts EEG recordings, not hunch surveys. He recommends that we call the branches of "Experimental Philosophy" which study intuitions to learn which ones provide reliable metaphysical insight "Colbertian Experimental Philosophy," and call those branches of philosophy which do not trade in experiments at all "Colbertian Philosophy," to honor Colbert's aprioristic, truthy, gut centrism. His hobby is conversation.

DAVID KYLE JOHNSON is currently an assistant professor of philosophy at King's College in Wilkes-Barre. His philosophical specializations include philosophy of religion, logic, and metaphysics. He has also written chapters on *South Park, Family Guy, The Office, Battlestar Galactica, Quentin Tarantino, Johnny Cash*, and *Batman*, and is currently editing a forthcoming book on *Heroes*. He has taught many classes that focus on the relevance of philosophy to pop culture, including a course devoted to *South Park*. Kyle has two pieces of advice. "First, when car dealers tell you 'We'll accept your trade in no matter how much you owe' that does not mean that they are going to pay off what you still owe; it's just added to your new loan. Listen to the fast talking guy at the end, people. Second, the best career advice I can give you is this: 'Write a chapter in a pop culture and philosophy book.' It pays squat, it takes up tons of time, and you'll be just as un-famous as you were before you began. And eventually, a nice editor will let you add your own jokes to your profile."

Until recently **NICOLAS MICHAUD** taught philosophy at the University of North Florida, Jacksonville University, and the Art Institute of Jacksonville. Now, having discovered that Mr. Colbert is the man of the future, Nick has given up a life of philosophy in the hopes that he might find a job serving the *Übermensch* himself. Nick's talents could be best put to use on the Colbert Report as an official pencil sharpener or perhaps as a lookout for bears. Nick has one true hope left for his life—that he might meet Mr. Colbert, shake his Herculean hand, and hear these ringing words: "Pick up my dry cleaning; don't expect a tip."

ETHAN MILLS is a PhD student in the Department of Philosophy at the University of New Mexico in Albuquerque, where he lives with his wife, Beth, and cat, Elsie. His interests include epistemology (especially skepticism), Indian philosophy, cross-cultural philosophy, feminist philosophy, philosophy of science, ethics, metaphilosophy and translating *The Colbert Report* into Sanskrit ("truthiness" = "satyavattvam"). He will soon begin the next segment of his academic career entitled, "Better Know a Dissertation: A Seemingly-Infinite Part Series."

MICHAEL F. PATTON, JR. is proud to have his co-author Samantha Webb as his official Canadian friend. He had to do a lot of work to keep her parts from being too thinky and snooty, but in the end, his gut tells him that the finished product is both grippy and full of truthiness. Michael teaches Philosophy at the University of Montevallo in Alabama, where he lives and loves with his wife Cheryl and their cats.

MATTHEW PIERLOTT is Assistant Professor of Philosophy at West Chester University of Pennsylvania, located in Pennsylvania's Sixteenth Congressional District (the fighting Rams!). He received his PhD in Philosophy from Marquette University. His area of specialization is in the philosophy of freedom, because he's an American. . . . 'nuff said. Matt is starting a campaign to remove the polar bears from the Philadelphia Zoo, not just because they are a monstrous danger to our community, but also because their kind has been complicit with liberals in perpetuating the hoax of global warming. For the children's sake, we must fight to keep our zoos politically neutral! He enjoys listening to NPR, because you have to know what the enemy is thinking.

MARK RALKOWSKI has published in ancient philosophy and twentieth-century Continental philosophy. He currently teaches at the University of New Mexico, where he has his students discuss one question all semester, every semester: who would win if Jesus were to fight America? "Stephen Colbert could answer it," he tells his class, "or could he?" Can you, Stephen? You can tell Ralkowski when (not if) you have him on your show to discuss his forthcoming book, *Heidegger's Platonism*. In fact, Ralkowski is so touched by the invitation *you will* offer him to be on your show, he would like you to write the foreword for his book. No need to thank him. You are welcome in advance.

KORY SCHAFF is Assistant Professor of Philosophy at Occidental College in Los Angeles (whose noteworthy alumni include Terry Gilliam and Barack Obama). He received his BA at North Central College, his MA at Loyola University Chicago, and his PhD at the University of California, San Diego. He has edited a volume titled *Philosophy and the Problems of Work: A*

Reader (2001), and has published essays on various topics in social, political, and legal philosophy. Most of the time while watching *The Colbert Report* he's of two minds about whether to laugh or cry.

AARON ALLEN SCHILLER is currently a Visiting Assistant Professor of Philosophy at the University of Wisconsin at Milwaukee, where he lives with his wife, Denise, and their two cats, Taco and Pickle. He received his BA in Philosophy from the University of California, Berkeley, and his PhD in Philosophy from the University of California, San Diego. He researches what he calls (with all *gravitas*) the Philosophy of Content, and has published in the Philosophy of Mind. He considers himself an it-getter.

KURT SMITH earned his BA in Philosophy at UC Irvine, and MA and PhD in Philosophy at Claremont Graduate University. As if this isn't awesome enough, among those who contributed to this volume Smith is the one who looks most like Stephen. In fact, he went as Stephen last Halloween, hooking up with Marilyn Monroe at the annual party. Stephen should learn to look more carefully at the size of hands (and for the presence of Adam's Apples). Stephen should also stop painting a clown-face on his face and entering homes late at night, taking polaroids of himself posed with unsuspecting sleepers. And, he should probably get his story straight about sending that turd to Jon Stewart. Seriously, Stephen, what is your problem? Oh yeah, Smith teaches philosophy at Bloomsburg University of Pennsylvania (which, for those "looking" for Smith, is not located in Bloomsburg, Pennsylvania).

SOPHIA STONE is a PhD hopeful in the Philosophy and Literature program at Purdue University. Her specialty is the study of ethics and humor, as you need one to do the other. She received her MA in Philosophy from those funny Catholics at the Dominican School of Philosophy and Theology. Her thesis, "The Good, The True, and The Funny: Plato and His Philosophy of Humor," passed with honors and was the first of several attempts of her writing about the philosophy of humor which was finally taken seriously. She earned her BA in Philosophy at the University of California, Berkeley, where she received the Finkeldink Tiddlywink award for Erotic Origami Sculpture.

RACHAEL SOTOS is an adjunct professor at New York City College of Technology in Brooklyn. As an undergraduate she studied political theory at the University of California, Santa Cruz and later received her PhD in philosophy from the New School for Social Research. She is presently the parent/guardian of a sixteen-year-old and pursuing a second doctorate in classics at Fordham University. Her dissertation in philosophy, *Arendtian Freedom in Greek Antiquity*, is a sympathetic critique of the political theorist Hannah Arendt, and will be published as a book. Her interests range from environmental philosophy and feminist theory to pre-Socratic philosophy and ancient Greek Comedy. As soon as her ward helps her to figure out this "internets" thing, she is going to put an order in for some of Stephen Colbert's "manseed."

JASON SOUTHWORTH is an ABD graduate student at the University of Oklahoma in Norman, Oklahoma, and is also an adjunct instructor of philosophy at Fort Hays State University, Hays, Kansas. He has contributed articles to several pop culture and philosophy volumes, including *Batman and Philosophy, Heroes and Philosophy,* and *X-Men and Philosophy.* While Jason likes the *Colbert Report* enough to write an article for this volume, he would still like to see Stephen find the time to give us more *Strangers with Candy.*

MICHAEL TIBORIS is a PhD candidate in philosophy at the University of California, San Diego. He wonders whether he will be put "on notice" for his dissertation: "Anarchy, State, and Bear-topia."

ROBEN TOROSYAN is associate director of the Center for Academic Excellence at Fairfield University, Connecticut, where he teaches philosophy (undergrad) and curriculum and instruction (graduate). A facilitator of faculty development, he has been invited presenter at thirty teaching conferences, where many participants were not paid to attend. His scholarship on transformation and communication has appeared in scholarly and lay publications—including on Critical Thinking and the War on Bullshit in *The Daily Show and Philosophy.* Roben managed to finagle a PhD in Cultural Studies, Philosophy, and Education from Teachers College, Columbia University. He's moved by not only himself but also by his latest and most glorious student, new daughter Catherine Anne, who should teach him a thing or two for the rest of his life.

As a Canadian, **SAMANTHA WEBB** grew up at a serious disadvantage. She was suspicious of maple syrup, feared bears, disliked hockey, and always had a vague feeling that she was living in Greenland's Mexico. Luckily, she was able to escape over the border fence into the U.S., where she learned how to speak American and love freedom. She now teaches English (or rather American) at the University of Montevallo in Alabama. She is Michael F. Patton Jr.'s Canadian friend.

Factinista's Choice